American Culture in the 1980s

Twentieth-Century American Culture
Series editor: Martin Halliwell, University of Leicester.

This series provides accessible but challenging studies of American culture in the twentieth century. Each title covers a specific decade and offers a clear overview of its dominant cultural forms and influential texts, discussing their historical impact and cultural legacy. Collectively the series reframes the notion of 'decade studies' through the prism of cultural production and rethinks the ways in which decades are usually periodized. Broad contextual approaches to the particular decade are combined with focused case studies, dealing with themes of modernity, commerce, freedom, power, resistance, community, race, class, gender, sexuality, internationalism, technology, war and popular culture.

American Culture in the 1910s
Mark Whalan

American Culture in the 1920s
Susan Currell

American Culture in the 1930s
David Eldridge

American Culture in the 1940s
Jacqueline Foertsch

American Culture in the 1950s
Martin Halliwell

American Culture in the 1960s
Sharon Monteith

American Culture in the 1970s
Will Kaufman

American Culture in the 1980s
Graham Thompson

American Culture in the 1990s
Colin Harrison

American Culture in the 1980s

Graham Thompson

Edinburgh University Press

city centre, always

© Graham Thompson, 2007

Edinburgh University Press Ltd
22 George Square, Edinburgh

Reprinted 2011

Typeset in 11/13 pt Stempel Garamond by
Servis Filmsetting Ltd, Manchester, and
printed and bound in Great Britain by
CPI Antony Rowe, Chippenham, Wiltshire

A CIP record for this book is available from the British Library

ISBN 978 0 7486 1909 2 (hardback)
ISBN 978 0 7486 1910 8 (paperback)

The right of Graham Thompson to be identified as author of this work
has been asserted in accordance with the Copyright, Designs and Patents Act 1988.

Published with the support of the Edinburgh University Scholarly Publishing Initiatives Fund.

Contents

List of Figures   vi
List of Case Studies   vii
Acknowledgements   viii
Chronology of 1980s American Culture   ix

Introduction: The Intellectual Context   1

1. Fiction and Poetry   37

2. Art and Photography   63

3. Film and Television   89

4. Music and Performance   123

5. American Culture and Globalization   153

Conclusion: The Cultural Legacy of the 1980s   179

Notes   185
Bibliography   197
Index   221

Figures

1.1   *In Country* (1989)   54
2.1   *Basquiat* (1996)   69
3.1   *Top Gun* (1986)   95
3.2   *Back to the Future* (1985)   105
3.3   *Blue Velvet* (1984)   107
3.4   *Wall Street* (1987)   109
3.5   J. R. Ewing of *Dallas*   116
3.6   The cast of *Hill Street Blues* (1981–7)   120
4.1   *Do the Right Thing* (1989)   126
4.2   Michael Jackson in the 'Thriller' video (1983)   128
4.3   *Desperately Seeking Susan* (1985)   132
5.1   The Vietnam Veterans Memorial   174

Case Studies

Introduction
Televangelism   16
Silicon Valley   27
The Closing of the American Mind (1987)   34

1. Fiction and Poetry
White Noise (1985)   46
In Country (1985)   52
Borderlands/La Frontera: The New Mestiza (1987)   59

2. Art and Photography
Jean-Michel Basquiat   67
Jeff Koons   71
Cindy Sherman   81

3. Film and Television
Top Gun (1986)   93
Wall Street (1987)   107
Hill Street Blues (1981–7)   117

4. Music and Performance
Madonna   129
Public Enemy   144
Split Britches Company   150

5. American Culture and Globalization
CNN   158
Disneyland Resort Paris   165
The National Vietnam Veterans Memorial, Washington   171

Acknowledgements

I am grateful to several people who have helped in the writing of this book. Martin Halliwell has been a patient and supportive Series Editor, while all the staff at Edinburgh University Press – Nicola Ramsey, James Dale, Esmé Watson and Stuart Midgley – have been impeccably efficient and helpful. Thanks to Sarah MacLachlan for prompting me to re-read *In Country*, to Paul Grainge and Julian Stringer for their help with film matters, and to Celeste-Marie Bernier for her advice on art. I am grateful to Paul Giles for his initial comments on the book proposal and to Sharon Monteith for sharing conversations about decades. Thanks also to the University of Nottingham for providing the study leave that enabled the completion of the book.

Chronology of
1980s American Culture

Date	Events	Criticism	Literature	Performance
1980	Jimmy Carter signs Banking Deregulation Act and Motor Carrier Act deregulating interstate trucking. Mount St Helens erupts. Military mission to rescue fifty-two hostages held at the US Embassy in Teheran fails. US boycotts summer Olympics in Moscow in protest at Soviet invasion of Afghanistan. Ronald Reagan elected President. Republicans control the US Senate for the first time since 1956. John Lennon shot and killed by Mark Chapman in New York. Rubik's Cube goes on sale and Pac-Man released.	Milton and Rose Friedman, *Free to Choose* Stephen Greenblatt, *Renaissance Self-Fashioning* Victor Navasky, *Naming Names* Alvin Toffler, *The Third Wave* Immanuel Wallerstein, *The Modern World-System, Vol. II*	John Kennedy Toole, *A Confederacy of Dunces* E. L. Doctorow, *In Loon Lake* Marilynne Robinson, *Housekeeping* Maxine Hong Kingston, *China Men* James Schuyler, *The Morning of the Poem*	Philip Glass, *Satyagraha* Kirke Mechem, *Tartuffe* *Barnum* *42nd Street* *Fame* (Alan Parker)
1981	John Hinckley attempts to assassinate Ronald Reagan. The first space shuttle, Columbia, is launched. US hostages released in Tehran. First cases of AIDS identified. The first American test-tube baby is born The IBM Personal Computer goes on sale.	Stephen Jay Gould, *The Mismeasure of Man* bell hooks, *Ain't I a Woman?* Fredric Jameson, *The Political Unconscious* Tracy Kidder, *The Soul of a New Machine* Tom Wolfe, *From Bauhaus to Our House*	Toni Morrison, *Tar Baby* John Updike, *Rabbit is Rich* David Bradley, *The Chaneysville Incident* Leslie Marmon Silko, *Storyteller* Raymond Carver, *What We Talk About When We Talk About Love*	Split Britches lesbian theatre company formed *Dreamgirls* (1,522 performances) Steve Reich, *Tehillim* Tennessee Williams, *Something Cloudy, Something Clear* *The Jazz Singer* (Richard Fleischer/Sidney J. Furie)

Film	Television	Music	Art
Ordinary People (Robert Redford) *The Empire Strikes Back* (George Lucas) *Raging Bull* (Martin Scorcese) *Coal Miner's Daughter* (Michael Apted) *Heaven's Gate* (Michael Cimino)	*Dallas* (CBS, 1978–91) *The Dukes of Hazzard* (1979–85) *Knots Landing* (1979–1993) *Magnum, P.I.* (CBS, 1980–8) Cable News Network (CNN) begins broadcasting	Blondie, 'Call Me' Lipps, Inc., 'Funkytown' Christopher Cross, *Christopher Cross* Kurtis Blow, *Kurtis Blow* Bruce Springsteen, *The River*	Various, 'Times Square Show' Julian Schnabel, *Exile* Fab 5 Freddy, *Campbell's Soup Cans*, South Bronx, New York Robert Mapplethorpe, *Man in Polyester Suit* Jasper Johns's *Three Flags* (1958) bought for $1 million
Raiders of the Lost Ark (Steven Spielberg) *Nine to Five* (Colin Higgins) *On Golden Pond* (Mark Rydell) *Wolfen* (Michael Wadleigh) *Reds* (Warren Beatty)	*Hill Street Blues* (NBC, 1981–7) *Dynasty* (ABC, 1981–9) *Falcon Crest* (1981–90) *The Fall Guy* (1981–6) MTV is launched	Kim Carnes, 'Bette Davis Eyes' Blondie, 'Rapture' Talking Heads, 'Once in a Lifetime' Mötley Crüe, *Too Fast For Love* Van Halen, *Fair Warning*	Sherrie Levine, 'After Walker Evans' Mark Morrisoe, *Untitled (Self-Portrait Standing in the Shower)* Jean-Michel Basquiat, *Untitled (Skull)* Cindy Sherman, *Centerfolds* Richard Serra, *Tilted Arc* sculpture

Date	Events	Criticism	Literature	Performance
1982	De Lorean car factory in Belfast goes into receivership. The first successful artificial heart transplant, at the University of Utah Medical Center. Graceland, Elvis Presley's Memphis home, opened to the public. Vietnam Veterans Memorial opens in Washington. Ronald Reagan becomes first US president to address British parliament. *Time* magazine's Man of the Year is a computer.	Dennis Altman, *The Homosexualisation of America* Jonathan Culler, *On Deconstruction* Jane Gallop, *The Daughter's Seduction* Tom Peters and Robert H. Waterman Jr, *In Search of Excellence* Cornel West, *Prophesy Deliverance! An Afro-American Revolutionary Christianity*	Anne Tyler, *Dinner at the Homesick Restaurant* Alice Walker, *The Color Purple* Don DeLillo, *The Names* Saul Bellow, *The Dean's December* Sylvia Plath, *Journals*	August Wilson, *Ma Rainey's Black Bottom* *Cats* (7,485 performances) Charles Fuller, *A Soldier's Play* *Little Shop of Horrors* (2,209 performances) *Victor/Victoria* (Blake Edwards)
1983	Ronald Reagan announces Star Wars missile defence initiative. 241 US Navy and Marines personnel killed in a suicide bombing attack in Beirut. US invaded Grenada to guard evacuations of US citizens after a Marxist takeover. Sally Ride first American woman in space. Final episode of *M*A*S*H*. US cruise missiles arrive at Greenham Common airbase in Britain.	Jonathan Arac, *The Yale Critics* Benedict Anderson, *Imagined Communities* Manning Marable, *How Capitalism Underdeveloped Black America* Edward Said, *The World, the Text, and the Critic* Susan Sheehan, *Is There No Place on Earth for Me?*	Kathy Acker, *Great Expectations* William Kennedy, *Ironweed* Gary Snyder, *Passage Through India* Ruth Prawer Jhabvala, *In Search of Love and Beauty* Joan Didion, *Salvador*	Leonard Bernstein, *A Quiet Place Baby* (241 performances) Neil Simon, *Brighton Beach Memoirs* Edward Albee, *Finding the Sun* Tina Howe, *Painting Churches*

Film	Television	Music	Art
E.T. the Extra-Terrestrial (Steven Spielberg) *On Golden Pond* (Mark Rydell) *Blade Runner* (Ridley Scott) *Tron* (Steven Lisberger) *The Thing* (John Carpenter)	*St. Elsewhere* (NBC, 1982–8) *Knight Rider* (NBC, 1982–6) *Family Ties* (NBC, 1982–9) *Cagney and Lacey* (CBS, 1982–8) *Cheers* (NBC, 1982–3)	Human League, 'Don't You Want Me' Survivor, 'Eye of the Tiger' Grandmaster Flash and the Furious Five, 'The Message' Michael Jackson, *Thriller* Bruce Springsteen, *Nebraska*	Jenny Holzer, *Truisms* (1982) Jean-Michel Basquiat, *Two Heads on Gold* (1982) David Salle exhibition at Leo Castelli's gallery, New York Nan Goldin, *Greer and Robert on the Bed* Roni Horn, *Gold Field*
Trading Places (John Landis) *Flashdance* (Adrian Lyne) *Star Wars Episode VI: Return of the Jedi* (George Lucas) *The King of Comedy* (Martin Scorsese) *Silkwood* (Mike Nichols)	*The A-Team* (NBC, 1983–7) *V* (NBC mini-series) *The Thorn Birds* (ABC mini-series) The Disney Channel is launched Country Music Television is launched	Irene Cara, 'Flashdance . . . What a Feeling' The Police, 'Every Breath You Take' REM, *Murmur* Madonna, *Madonna* Metallica, *Kill 'Em All*	Richard Prince, *Spiritual America* Christo and Jeanne-Claude, *Surrounded Islands*, Biscayne Bay, Miami, Florida David Salle, *Pitcher* *International Directory of Corporate Art Collections* first published Shopping-mall developer Alfred Taubman takes over Sotheby's

Date	Events	Criticism	Literature	Performance
1984	The US re-established full diplomatic relations with the Vatican for the first time since 1867. Marvin Gaye shot and killed by his father. Ronald Reagan re-elected in biggest Republican landslide in US voting history. Agent Orange Fund for Vietnam veterans started by chemical companies. Soviet Union boycotts Olympic Games in Los Angeles. Velma Barfield becomes first woman to be executed in the US since 1962	Christopher Lasch, *The Minimal Self* Mark McCormack, *What They Don't Teach You at Harvard Business School* Fredric Jameson, 'Postmodernism, or, The Cultural Logic of Late Capitalism' Charles Murray, *Losing Ground* Studs Terkel, *The Good War*	William Gibson, *Neuromancer* Sonia Sanchez, *Homegirls and Handgrenades* Gore Vidal, *Lincoln* Thomas Pynchon, *Slow Learner* (collection of early short stories) Robert Creeley, *The Collected Prose of Robert Creeley*	David Mamet, *Glengarry Glen Ross* *Sunday in the Park with George* (604 performances) Philip Glass, *Akhnaten* August Wilson, *Joe Turner's Come and Gone* *The Cotton Club* (Francis Ford Coppola)
1985	Mikhail Gorbachev becomes leader of Soviet Union. Reagan and Gorbachev meet later in the year. Rock Hudson dies from AIDS-related illnesses. First commercial (.com) domain names registered on the Internet Domain Name System. Live Aid concerts in London and Philadelphia. Coca-Cola unsuccessfully tries to change its recipe. Microsoft releases first version of Windows.	T. J. Jackson Lears, 'The Concept of Cultural Hegemony' J. Anthony Lukas, *Common Ground* Richard Slotkin, *The Fatal Environment* Eve Kosofsky Sedgwick, *Between Men* Walter Benn Michaels and Donald Pease, *The American Renaissance Reconsidered*	Paul Auster, *City of Glass* Don DeLillo, *White Noise* Bharati Mukherjee, *Darkness* Cormac McCarthy, *Blood Meridian* Bret Easton Ellis, *Less Than Zero*	Sam Shepard, *A Lie of the Mind* August Wilson, *Fences* Larry Kramer, *The Normal Heart* Dorothy Rudd Moore, *Frederick Douglass* Terence McNally, *The Lisbon Traviata*

Film	Television	Music	Art
Ghostbusters (Ivan Reitman) *Indiana Jones and the Temple of Doom* (Steven Spielberg) *The Terminator* (James Cameron) *Paris, Texas* (Wim Wenders) *A Nightmare on Elm Street* (Wes Craven)	*Miami Vice* (NBC, 1984–9) *The Cosby Show* (NBC, 1984–92) *Murder, She Wrote* (CBS, 1984–96) *Kate and Allie* (CBS, 1984–9) *Santa Barbara* (NBC, 1984–93)	Van Halen, 'Jump' Prince, 'When Doves Cry' Hüsker Dü, *Zen Arcade* Madonna, *Like a Virgin* Bruce Springsteen, *Born in the U.S.A.*	Louise Lawler, *Pollock and Tureen, Arranged by Mr. and Mrs. Burton Tremaine, Connecticut* (1984) Robert Longo, *Tongue to the Heart* Jean-Michel Basquiat, *Flexible* The Border Art Workshop established Chase Manhattan Bank acquired 1,300 pieces of art for its collection
Back To The Future (Robert Zemeckis) *Out Of Africa* (Sydney Pollack) *The Breakfast Club* (John Hughes) *Desperately Seeking Susan* (Susan Seidelman) *Rambo: First Blood Part II* (George P. Cosmatos)	*The Golden Girls* (NBC, 1985–92) *Moonlighting* (ABC, 1985–9) *North and South* (ABC, mini-series) *The Equalizer* (1985–9) Discovery Channel is launched	USA for Africa, 'We Are the World' Dire Straits, 'Money for Nothing' Megadeth, *Killing Is My Business . . . And Business Is Good!* Phil Collins, *No Jacket Required* LL Cool J, *Radio*	Jeff Koons, *One Ball Total Equilibrium Tank* Keith Haring, 'The Ten Commandments' Robert Mapplethorpe, *Lindsay Key* PC Paintbrush software first released Fractal art emerges after publication of *Scientific American* article on Mandelbrot Set

Date	Events	Criticism	Literature	Performance
1986	Space shuttle *Challenger* explodes shortly after take-off. Iran–Contra scandal. Clint Eastwood elected Republican mayor of Carmel, California. First personal-computer virus discovered. Chernobyl nuclear disaster. Failure of nuclear arms reduction talks in Reykjavík, Iceland, between US and Soviet Union. Mike Tyson become world heavyweight boxing champion.	Cathy Davidson, *Revolution and the Word* Barry Lopez, *Arctic Dreams* Janice Radway, 'Identifying Ideological Seams' Russell Reising, *The Unusable Past.* Richard Rhodes, *Making of the Atomic Bomb*	Ann Beattie, *Where You'll Find Me* Art Spiegelman, *Maus* Philip Roth, *The Counterlife* Richard Ford, *The Sportswriter* Kathy Acker, *Don Quixote*	*Me and My Girl* (1,420 performances) August Wilson, *The Piano Lesson* *Sweet Charity* (369 performances) George Furth, *Precious Sons* A. R. Gurney, *The Perfect Party*
1987	Ronald Reagan undergoes prostate surgery. Tower Commission Report published on Iran–Contra scandal. Single European Act passed by the European Union. Black Monday stock market crash. Death of Andy Warhol. Prozac released in the US.	Allan Bloom, *The Closing of the American Mind* Michael Denning, *Mechanic Accents* James Gleick, *Chaos* Randy Shilts, *And the Band Played On* Gayatri Chakravorty Spivak, *In Other Worlds*	Stephen King, *Misery* Toni Morrison, *Beloved* Tom Wolfe, *Bonfire of the Vanities* Scott Turow, *Presumed Innocent* James Ellroy, *Black Dahlia*	*Les Misérables* (6,680 performances) *Starlight Express* (761 performances) *Into the Woods* (765 performances) John Adams, *Nixon in China* *Cabaret* (revival, 261 performances)

Film	Television	Music	Art
Top Gun (Tony Scott) *Ferris Bueller's Day Off* (John Hughes) *Aliens* (James Cameron) *Blue Velvet* (David Lynch) *Manhunter* (Michael Mann)	*The Oprah Winfrey Show* (syndicated, 1986–present) *L.A. Law* (NBC, 1986–94) Space Shuttle Challenger explodes on live television Fox Broadcasting Company is launched Boy George appears in *The A-Team*	Whitney Houston, 'Greatest Love of All' Prince and the Revolution, 'Kiss' Run-DMC, *Raising Hell* Slayer, *Reign in Blood* Janet Jackson, *Control*	Jeff Koons, *Rabbit* Gran Fury, *Silence = Death* Judy Pfaff, *Wasco* Julian Schnabel, *Self-Portrait in Andy's Shadow* Mark Tansey, *Forward Retreat*
Fatal Attraction (Adrian Lyne) *Wall Street* (Oliver Stone) *Dirty Dancing* (Emile Ardolino) *The Fly* (David Cronenberg) *Full Metal Jacket* (Stanley Kubrick)	*thirtysomething* (ABC, 1987–91) *Teenage Mutant Ninja Turtles* (syndicated, 1987–96) *Star Trek: The Next Generation* (syndicated, 1987–94) *Amerika* (ABC, mini-series) *The Simpsons* first appears as a series of short animations on *The Tracey Ullman Show*	Bon Jovi, 'Livin' on a Prayer' Bill Medley and Jennifer Warnes, '(I've Had) The Time of My Life' Public Enemy, *Yo! Bum Rush the Show* Joe Satriani, *Surfing with the Alien* Jane's Addiction, *Jane's Addiction*	David Wojnarowicz, *Seven Miles a Second* Andreas Serrano, *Piss Christ* Julian Schnabel, *Grace High Tower* Andy Warhol dies while undergoing gallbladder surgery Roman Verostko pioneers algorithmic art using a plotter connected to a paintbrush

Date	Events	Criticism	Literature	Performance
1988	Soviet Union begins withdrawal from Afghanistan. House of Representatives refuses Ronald Reagan request for financial support of Contras in Nicaragua. Iran–Iraq war ends after eight years. Space shuttle flights resume after *Challenger* disaster. George H. W. Bush defeats Michael Dukakis to become US president. Pan Am flight 103 from London to New York explodes over Scottish town of Lockerbie.	Jean Baudrillard, *America* Sacvan Bercovitch and Myra Jehlen, *Ideology and Classic American Literature* Stanley Cavell, *In Quest of the Ordinary* Catherine McKinnon and Andrea Dworkin, *Pornography and Civil Rights* Neil Sheehan, *A Bright Shining Lie*	Kathy Acker, *Empire of the Senseless* Nicholson Baker, *The Mezzanine* Don DeLillo, *Libra* Raymond Carver, *Where I'm Calling From* Annie Proulx, *Heartsongs and Other Stories*	*The Phantom of the Opera* (7,709 performances at 23 July 2006) Wendy Wasserstein, *The Heidi Chronicles* David Mamet, *Speed-the-Plow* *Madame Butterfly* (777 performances) *Sarafina* (597 performances)
1989	Serial killer Ted Bundy executed in Florida. Exxon Valdez oil tanker runs aground in Alaska spilling 240,000 gallons of oil. Tiananmen Square protests in Beijing, China. Revolutions across Central and Eastern Europe see communist governments overthrown. Dilbert comic strip published for the first time. First sales of Nintendo Game Boy.	Richard Rorty, *Contingency, Irony, Solidarity* Henry Louis Gates Jr, *The Signifying Monkey* Donna Haraway, *Primate Visions* Francis Fukuyama, 'The End of History?' Immanuel Wallerstein, *The Modern World-System, Vol. III*	Maxine Hong Kingston, *Tripmaster Monkey* Bharati Mukherjee, *Jasmine* Amy Tan, *The Joy Luck Club* New Revised Standard Version of *The Bible* Paul Auster, *Moon Palace*	*City of Angels* (878 performances) Conrad Cummings, *Photo-Op* Anthony Davis, *Under the Double Moon* Mandy Patinkin in Concert: 'Dress Casual' *Meet Me in St. Louis* (revival, 252 performances)

Film	Television	Music	Art
Rain Man (Barry Levinson)	*Roseanne* (ABC, 1988–97)	Guns N' Roses, 'Sweet Child O' Mine'	Julian Schnabel, *Joe Glassco*
Who Framed Roger Rabbit (Robert Zemeckis/Richard Williams)	*The Wonder Years* (ABC, 1988–93)	Rick Astley, 'Never Gonna Give You Up'	Jeff Koons, *Michael Jackson and Bubbles*
Die Hard (John McTiernan)	*Murphy Brown* (CBS, 1988–98)	Public Enemy, *It Takes a Nation of Millions to Hold Us Back*	John Baldessari, *Seashells/Tridents/Frames*
Working Girl (Mike Nichols)	*America's Most Wanted* (Fox, 1988–present)	R.E.M., *Green*	Roman Verostko, *Pathway 1*
The Accused (Jonathan Kaplan)	Turner Network Television is launched	Tracy Chapman, *Tracy Chapman*	Jean-Michel Basquiat dies of a heroin overdose
Batman (Tim Burton)	*Seinfeld* (NBC, 1989–98)	Madonna, 'Like a Prayer'	Richard Prince, *Untitled (Cowboy)*
Do the Right Thing (Spike Lee)	*The Simpsons* (Fox, 1989–present)	The Bangles, 'Eternal Flame'	Group Material, *AIDS Timeline* (1989–91)
Honey, I Shrunk the Kids (Joe Johnston)	*Baywatch* (NBC, 1989–2001)	De La Soul, *3 Feet High and Rising*	Gran Fury, *Kissing Doesn't Kill: Greed and Indifference Do*
Glory (Edward Zwick)	*America's Funniest Home Videos* (ABC, 1989–present)	Fugazi, *13 Songs*	Robert Mapplethorpe, 'The Perfect Moment'
Heathers (Michael Lehmann)	1956 Christmas special episode of *I Love Lucy* shown on CBS	N.W.A., *Straight Outta Compton*	Cindy Sherman, *History Portraits*

The Intellectual Context

Decade Culture

If there are several expressions that can help to try and distil the values of a particular historical moment – Zeitgeist, 'spirit of the age,' 'sign of the times' – none automatically coincides with the ten-year period known as the decade. Although potentially tempting as an object of study, the tendency to make decade-length periods in American cultural history cohere under catchy epithets now seems clumsy and inadequate. Plenty of the culture produced during the 1920s, for instance, cannot be sufficiently understood by relying on terms like the Jazz Age or the Roaring Twenties; much is lost by substituting the Great Depression for the 1930s; while using the 'sixties' as a signifier for a whole array of positive or negative changes – depending on one's point of view – may satisfy the desire for cultural nostalgia, the demands of conservatism, or a belief in the possibility of liberal progress, but does little to provide critical leverage on the decade's complex social and cultural changes.

This situation is even more obviously a problem for those looking in on the US from the outside. Distance, and an attitude towards area studies that emphasizes national and cultural homogeneity, have tended to result in US culture being looked at through the telescope rather than the microscope. Paul Giles has noted how British and European treatments of American culture, from Henry Salt in the nineteenth century and D. H. Lawrence in the 1920s onwards, have been dominated by the 'illusion of synchronicity,'[1] whereby cultural texts are subsumed within thematic generalizations, the purpose of which is to try to sum up a national cultural condition. Developments in the study of American culture from the 1970s onwards, particularly in the US, increasingly tested the viability of this kind of methodology as the recovery of marginalized histories and texts redefined the very notion of what constituted a national culture. The experiences of African, Asian and native Americans, of women and sexual subcultures, of religious, regional and ethnic communities and of globalization, have become woven into the study of American culture to such an extent that the usefulness of the 'national' as a delimiter of culture is now laid open to question, with such a questioning potentially preparing the way for a different approach to American culture. Narratives of consensus have been usurped by narratives of confrontation; culture is now multicultural; and the nation now postnational.

In trying to approach the 1980s as a decade of cultural production, then, there are two major obstacles – one temporal, one spatial – to overcome. It is with the qualification that the decade is neither an obvious nor a necessarily coherent object of study that I imagine the decade temporally, since one reasonable question to ask of a narrative that deals with American culture in the 1980s is 'why this particular time span'? And it is with the qualification that the 'American' dimension to this study refers to an arena of cultural production that does not coincide with what might be described as a national culture that I also begin. A decade in American culture is too long a period of time, and the national space to which it refers too diverse, to allow a definition of the decade that can sustain narratives of uniformity and commonality.

Some of the potential pitfalls inherent in trying to pin down and characterize a particular decade are evident in one of the most recent of decade studies, Stephen Paul Miller's *The Seventies Now: Culture as Surveillance* (1999). In attempting to give a pattern to what is a relatively neglected and undefined decade, Miller stresses the importance of surveillance and self-surveillance to such an extent that he ends up overstating and undermining his case at the same time. He turns history back to front to claim that 'Richard Nixon's overt surveillance and self-surveillance were ingested by the nation as a whole during Watergate and shortly thereafter internalized.'[2] Fixated with the project of establishing the terms of reference that will define the decade, Miller neglects the historical importance of surveillance and self-surveillance in American culture. It was there, after all, that Calvinism and Puritanism instituted a scrupulous culture of religious surveillance through the discourses of nomination, election, and predestination. It was there too that Bentham's panopticon was taken up more readily in prison design than in Britain or Europe. And it would be difficult to imagine a more overt system of political surveillance than that instituted by the House Un-American Activities Commission in the 1940s and 50s. All of these manifestations of surveillance, one could argue, produced a correspondingly acute self-surveillance. Miller only hints that there may have been an intensification and reorganization of surveillance in the seventies – through technological innovations like computerization – since to make the case for linkage more boldly would be to draw attention to the long-standing importance of surveillance and self-surveillance and consequently undermine the project in which he is engaged. Yet the fact that he is forced to reiterate the special importance of surveillance and self-surveillance in the 1970s serves exactly the same purpose and makes his argument too unwieldy and all-embracing to sustain. Which is not to say that Miller does not have interesting and important reflections to add to our understanding of the 1970s. But it is to say that producing a narrative of a decade that seeks to establish overarching definitions and to analyse specific cultural products and cultural production itself in the light of these definitions is to mistake American narratives for totalizing narratives about America.

With this in mind, one of the central problems confronting anyone looking at the 1980s is a narrative that very quickly established itself as a means for understanding the period: the narrative of 'Ronald Reagan's America'. As early as 1987, with Reagan still in presidential office, Gary Wills was advocating the nature of the special relationship between Reagan and America when he wrote of Reagan as 'the great American synecdoche.'[3] According to Wills, 'Reagan does not argue for American values, he embodies them'[4] and can be seen to represent not just a decade in American cultural history, but also an entire era:

> Reagan gives our history the continuity of a celluloid Mobius strip. We ride its curves backward and forward at the same time, and he is always there. There is an endlessness of surface that becomes a kind of depth, a self-reflecting omnipresence in the cultural processing of Americans over the second half of the twentieth century.[5]

Wills reads Reagan, then, as a character who stands in for America during a whole decade, but also then reads that decade as standing in for the entire postwar period of American history. Reagan becomes, literally, the embodiment of postwar America in the way that he is 'just as simple, and just as mysterious, as our collective dreams and memories.'[6] In Wills' writing, and in many other critical treatments of American culture and society in the 1980s, there is an assumption that

Reagan's accession to power was, if not inevitable, then somehow consonant with broader social, economic and cultural transformations. This can in part be accounted for by a proximity to the events being narrated: in seeking to understand and to provide a rationale for a historical moment, it is often difficult to imagine things being otherwise. But the span of his time in office – elected in 1980 and sworn out in 1989 – means that there is also a temporal neatness to the idea of the eighties as 'Ronald Reagan's America'. Likewise, the collapse of communism in eastern Europe after 1989 seems intimately linked to Reagan's hard-line anti-communism, his rhetorical dismissal of the Soviet Union as an 'evil empire' and, in retrospect, as the affirmation of neo-liberal economic values that were at the heart of the Reaganite project. Richard King appears to be right when he suggests that 'illusory though such assumptions often are, some decades *do* seem to possess a unity of tenor and tone, a common ethos.'[7]

As Wills suggests above, there is also something in Reagan's 'celluloid' past which make him particularly well suited to be US President during the 1980s. Michael Rogin emphasizes this idea of Reagan in his essay '*Ronald Reagan*, the Movie', where he argues that Reagan came to consciousness as a young man during the 1940s as a result of the film roles he played and subsequently 'merged his on- and off-screen identities'. For Rogin this 'confusion between life and film produced *Ronald Reagan*, the image that has fixed our gaze.'[8] Rogin persuasively illustrates how, while in office, Reagan not only quoted from movies – his own and others – but more subtly established himself as an 'idol of consumption'[9] and as a celebrity for whom 'oppositions that traditionally organized both social life and social critique – oppositions between surface and depth, the authentic and the inauthentic, the imaginary and the real, signifier and signified – seem to have broken down.'[10] The result, according to Rogin, is not only a culture where 'sacred value [has] shifted from the church . . . to Hollywood',[11] but also one where the distinctions between history and fiction are increasingly tenuous.

As a national leader, then, Reagan assumes his synecdochic power because he appears to be in tune with the changing cultural landscape. Other events, like the attempted assassination of Reagan by *Taxi Driver*-fanatic John Hinckley and Reagan's video-link appearance at the Oscar ceremony a day later, a resurgent Hollywood film industry increasingly integrated with other important media forms, and the proliferation of visual imagery and iconography during the 1980s, all help cement Reagan's presidency as the natural political counterpart to an eighties culture driven, and dominated, by the production and circulation of the image. With Reagan it is almost as if biography can stand in for history. And yet there are clearly problems with this process of cultural condensation. Why should 'Ronald Reagan's America' be any more an appropriate epithet for the 1980s than the Jazz Age is for the 1920s? The same problems of what exactly one is focusing upon arise. While it would be hard to contest the importance and proliferation of new image economies in the 1980s, people's lives were affected by change in all sorts of other ways. The impact of new cable and media technologies went hand in hand with declining industrial prosperity in rustbelt cities like Detroit, Cleveland or Pittsburgh. How people experienced the relative impact of these changes is difficult to assess. And it becomes even harder when one has to take into account regional variations between East Coast and West, Midwest and South West, North and South. It is an imperative to coalesce experience that undergirds the 'illusion of synchronicity' about which Giles writes. But while decades gain a sense of consistency only retrospectively, they are experienced without the benefit of hindsight. If Wills and Rogin help in that process whereby American culture in the 1980s coalesces around the figure of Reagan, they neglect to mention one important fact: Reagan was clearly the exception to the rule. If a movie background made Reagan the perfect President for a decade when the boundaries between fact and fiction, image and identity, blurred to the point of collapse, why was it that American politics in the 1980s was not replete with former movie actors eager for office? Reagan's background in the movies was, and is, entirely untypical. When Wills suggests that Reagan was synecdochic in his embodiment of American values, he is creating a narrative of synchronicity and using Reagan as his own synecdoche for the 1980s. Like Stephen Paul Miller, Wills, notwithstanding his creative and convincing account of Reagan's rise to power, is overstating his case.

For the purposes of this book a more workable starting point is needed. Richard King provides this with his depiction of the 1980s as a decade that sees a continued tension in the US between 'homogenization and dispersal, between uniformity and diversity.'[12] Less striking in the sense that it does not readily provide a way of pinning down the 1980s, it is nevertheless also more alert to the ways in which national cultures move in several different directions at the same time and are not easily embodied in a single figure, let alone a political president. What follows in this chapter is a discussion of some of the intellectual contexts within which these contrary movements are taking place during the 1980s. These are the intellectual contexts which not only enable the election and re-election of Reagan and mark a shift to the right in politics and religion, but also lead to the Culture wars towards the end of the decade and drive the imperative to view the US as a multicultural nation. They are the contexts within which culture is both produced and consumed, in all its various modes, and which – strikingly in the case of AIDS – allow the possibilities in which people's lives can be lived out. I make claim neither to completeness nor impartiality. Selectivity should be the very nature of decade study. I don't downplay the importance of the Reagan administrations and their economic radicalism, although neither do I see them as emerging from a fiscal void nor as being uniform or predictable in their impact.

Reaganomics

One of the key ways in which decades or periods are defined is by economic context. The Gilded Age in the US, for instance, spanning the last quarter of the nineteenth century, was a period of rapid industrialization that saw fundamental structural changes in the way business was carried out and in the ownership of wealth. The rise of the large corporation, urbanization, the opening up of a continental market thanks to new transport networks, and new supplies of immigrant labour, all combined to fashion a different world in which Americans lived. Hand in hand with these economic changes, often as a result of them but sometimes helping to drive them, was a new intellectual and cultural climate. Social Darwinist ideas about progress, feminist demands for equality and emancipation and new forms of cultural production and circulation – advertising, fashion, leisure, sport and exhibitions – coexisted with an increasingly active populist reform movement. Similarly, the 1930s was a decade dominated by the fall-out from the economic crash of 1929. The subsequent depression was so severe that it demanded new forms of political intervention – in the shape of the New Deal – to help ameliorate the worst effects. As far as the 1980s is concerned, its economic context is one that can be approached by way of an epithet that quickly achieved widespread usage: Reaganomics. One of the aims of this book is to demonstrate how the policies and practices bound up in Reaganomics spin off in directions that have substantive impacts for culture, not just in terms of how economic conditions are represented but also in terms of how culture is produced and consumed.

In terms of periodization, I don't intend Reaganomics to be equivalent with Ronald Reagan or the Reagan term of office. If anything, Reaganomics is shorthand for a repackaging of longstanding economic ideas in the US for a new situation and a new audience. Elsewhere, particularly in the UK during the 1980s, but also in Canada and West Germany, the theoretical models and principles that lay behind Reaganomics were working in other geographical locations as well. Reagan's achievement in the US was to popularize and make easily digestible the economic ideas that George H. W. Bush, ultimately Reagan's Vice President but initially his adversary for Republican nomination, once disparagingly called 'voodoo economics'. These ideas consisted of two main strands – lower taxes and smaller government – and emerged as a vote-winning combination during the economically pessimistic late 1970s.

As in many other Western economies, the 1970s was a decade of economic uncertainty in the US. Competition from industrializing Asian economies, the oil crisis of 1973 and the war in Vietnam all contributed towards a new phenomenon that became known as stagflation: for the first time in the postwar period, the US was hit by a combination of rising inflation and economic stagnation that saw unemployment shoot up, particularly in traditional manufacturing regions of the Midwest. A spiral of high government spending, high interest rates, increasing wages and increasing prices threatened to undermine the prosperity of the 1950s and 60s. Reagan emerged during this period as a politician with radical economic answers to these problems. He had cut his political teeth as a supporter of Barry Goldwater in the 1964 presidential election campaign. Goldwater campaigned on the kinds of lower tax and smaller government issues that would become emblematic of Reaganite conservatism both during Reagan's governorship of California between 1966 and 1975 and his presidency of the 1980s, but in 1964 Goldwater was considered too extreme by many. During the 1970s, however, stagflation prompted Republicans and conservatives to re-evaluate the kinds of economic strategies governments should pursue. The consensus during the 1960s and 70s was that government efforts should stimulate demand in order to ward off economic stagnation; the experience of the 1970s was that not only did this not work, but also that it exacerbated economic uncertainty by driving up inflation.

The emphasis on demand now switched to an emphasis on supply among an influential group of economists who included Robert Mundell, Jude Wanniski, Arthur Laffer and Milton Friedman, of whom the latter two were appointed to Reagan's Economic Policy

Advisory Board in 1981, while Friedman won the Nobel prize for
Economics in 1976. Wanniski had coined the phrase 'supply-side economics' in 1975 and they all believed that economic policy should be
focused not on stimulating demand but on stimulating investment and
consumption. This was to be achieved, it was argued, by controlling
the money supply and interest rates; by decreasing public spending,
since it was taken for granted that individuals and businesses were
better than governments at producing and investing efficiently and
should therefore have more money at their disposal; and, in order to
provide them with more money, by lowering marginal rates of personal and corporate taxation to create incentives for wealth creation.
Whatever the rights or wrongs of these ideas, and despite their less than
strict implementation during the 1980s, these supply-side ideas of
lower taxation and less government spending became embedded in a
political and ideological rhetoric whose purpose was to reinvent
American myths for a contemporary audience. If the Gilded Age at the
end of the nineteenth century had been succeeded by an era of reform
when business monopolies were reined in by anti-trust legislation, by
social welfare programmes of the kind that would be seen to be essential during the 1930s and by a culture of social critique led by muck-
raking journalists eager to highlight corruption, exploitation and
exclusion, 1980s conservatism in the guise of Reaganomics heralded a
period – which the US is, arguably, still experiencing – in which the
political and social fabric of intervention, restraint and critique had
worn thin. One of the crucial elements of Reaganomics was that it was
not simply an economic solution to economic problems. As Haynes
Johnson points out, 'supply-side economics would also work a political miracle. By stimulating economic growth, it would permit both
Republicans and Democrats to enjoy the best of political worlds – a
prosperous, productive, recession and inflation proof America.'[13]
Reaganomics had about it a crusading zeal that emphasized regenera-
tion and reinvention; it spoke to a perceived sense of decline and
responded with a vision of a 'miracle.' Reaganomics, then, was not just
an economic vision but a moral vision too.

   This moral vision was a conservative one with its roots in myths
about family values, individuality, national strength and the importance of technological progress. Reagan managed to conjoin these
issues into an effective political and cultural rhetoric that answered
back to a sense of malaise and decline which followed Vietnam, the
political scandal of Watergate and waning economic prowess. In doing
so, Reagan and conservative voices for whom he stood as leader and

spokesperson rewrote a narrative about the passage of the US from the 1960s to the 1980s. For many on the left in the US, the post-sixties period was one of decline and fall. If the sixties were a liberal high point – with Kennedy and Johnson in the White House, civil rights reform and a burgeoning counterculture – the Vietnam War and Nixon's election in 1968 were when liberal hopes were dashed and put on hold. The 1970s bore witness to this, especially Jimmy Carter's inability to effect change, and Reagan's election in 1980 consolidated the impression of a damaging drift to the right. For those happily on the right, the election of Reagan was evidence not that the next stage of decline had been reached but the point at which the liberal sixties might finally be expunged from national memory. One of the features of moral conservatism in the 1980s was the frequency with which the sixties served as a spectre of damaging moral, social and cultural promiscuity. The increasing visibility during that decade of new lifestyles and family formations and of new political configurations – the second wave of feminism, black power and gay and lesbian rights movements – seemed to augur a breakdown in what were perceived to be national social values. For many conservatives the sixties became a decade from which the US had to rescue itself; the journey from the sixties to the 1980s was one of a reaction against liberalism. As Richard King puts it, 'A kind of counter-revolution promised to usher in a new political and cultural order. With Reaganism the conservative *kulturkampf* had been successful.'[14]

The use of the word *Kulturkampf* is interesting here. Literally meaning 'cultural fight', it was a term originally used at the end of the nineteenth century to describe German leader Otto von Bismarck's battle with the Roman Catholic church for control not just of economic and political power, but for control over intellectual and cultural power too. The word has been applied to the US by social conservatives like Pat Buchanan, but has more readily been translated as 'culture war' to describe the battle over social and cultural power between those on the left and the right. From the mid-1980s these battles become particularly marked and form one of the most distinctive of the lenses through which one can explore American culture in the 1980s. While I will deal with this battle in more detail later, what is worth stressing at this point is that the social conservative backlash against the 1960s was every bit as important an element in Reaganomics as was the supply-side economics aimed at turning round the American economy. Reaganomics was the ideological coincidence of supply-side economic policy with political and moral conservatism; an ideological coincidence that succeeded because it cut through class politics and traditional party allegiances and recruited blue-collar support – the so-called 'Reagan Democrats' – even if the major beneficiaries of lower taxation were the already affluent. It was the moral and social conservatism of voters – around issues such as abortion, crime and patriotism – that enabled Reaganomics to shape the decade.

Wall Street Mania

Some of the most visible manifestations of the shifting nature of the US economy during the 1980s were played out on Wall Street and in what Wall Street came to represent during this period. Home to the New York Stock Exchange, whose low-tech origins were under a button-wood tree close to the barricade built by Peter Stuyvesant in 1653 to protect early Manhattan settlers from local Indian tribes, Wall Street has long held a place in the American imagination. Cycles of specula-tive boom and bust, common enough in the history of US stock trading – as the crash of 1929 illustrates – can be dramatic events with devastating effects. The years of bull markets, when speculation is intense and profits high, also make for a dramatic spectacle as urban locations like New York are transformed by the sums of money being generated in financial markets. The 1980s had all of these things.

Leading up to the 1980s, US stock trading was in a state of depres-sion. Like the rest of the US economy there was little optimism and, in an economy where inflation was at historically high levels, the incentives for investment were limited. Several key developments led to a turnaround in this situation and the implementation of supply-side economic principles was at the heart of this change. As if to emphasize how Reaganomics was not owned by Ronald Reagan, the first of these developments was directed by Jimmy Carter in 1979 when he appointed Paul Volcker as Chairman of the Federal Reserve, a position he held until 1987.[14] Volcker was charged with the task of reducing inflation and set about it by following the supply-side prin-ciple of decreasing the Federal Reserve's money supply, increasing interests rates and reducing lending. At the same time, the new Reagan administration was bringing supply-side economics to its initial legis-lation. The Economic Recovery Tax Act of 1981 decreased business and individual income taxes and lowered the tax rates on long-term capital gains. The Depository Institutions Deregulation and Monetary Control Act of 1980 brought all banks under the control of the Federal

Reserve but also enabled bank mergers and greater competition in the banking sector. Other legislation was enacted to deregulate the transport industries. While associated with Reagan, deregulation actually began under Carter when he deregulated the airline and gas industries. The objective of all these pieces of legislation was to increase market competition. The implicit and explicit justification was that competition would stimulate economic growth. The immediate impact, however, was economic recession. Squeezing the economy through high interest rates with an emphasis on controlling inflation at all costs was devastating for already depressed industries, particularly in the Midwest. The US entered an economic recession which lasted until 1982.

While economic recovery out of this recession was slow, for Wall Street the raft of deregulation legislation, together with a steady stock price recovery as high interest rates boosted the dollar on the foreign exchanges, had a profound impact. Not only did the level of trading increase, but also a whole wave of mergers and acquisitions buoyed the banking and underwriting sectors. After the depressed years of the late 1970s and early 1980s there were many companies in the US that were struggling to survive. But although their stock prices remained low they had valuable assets that were attractive to other companies. Buying these assets was a much cheaper and easier way of expanding than building a business from scratch. Such was the activity in this field that by 1987 merger activity was worth $300 billion. Between 1980 and 1988, 25,000 merger and acquisition deals were completed, worth a total of $2 trillion.[15] Big investment banks, which facilitated the mergers and acquisitions, were involved in up to 200 deals each year.[16] The reluctance of the Reagan administrations to enforce antitrust laws only added to the sense that the buying and selling of companies was a free for all. Investors looking for returns bought companies, often financed by debt, which they thought were likely to be subject of a takeover bid.

To bankroll this activity, notorious forms of financing emerged. 'Junk bonds' played a central role in the mergers and acquisitions frenzy of the 1980s. Basically high-risk bonds sold at a low price, junk bonds have the potential for producing high yields. The most famous investment banker to utilize the junk-bond market in the 1980s was Michael Milken who worked for Drexel Burnham Lambert. Milken's use of junk bonds was certainly not illegal and he transformed the traditionally sober world of investment banking with his glitzy promotional events, like the Annual Predator's Ball, that attracted show business celebrities and forged a market of investors willing to buy junk bonds. Milken himself became a celebrity as his banking activities raked in huge commissions. He turned Drexel into a company with a multi-billion-dollar turnover, accumulated a personal fortune of $3 billion and in 1991 alone secured a bonus of $550 million. Milken was not the only business celebrity either. Donald Trump mixed bold real-estate projects with vanity as he put up buildings which he then named after himself: Trump Tower, Trump World Tower, Trump Place, Trump Taj Mahal.

While Milken and Trump represent the dizzying heights of financial success, they were joined by a cohort of professional workers in Wall Street, the financial services sector and the white-collar world more generally, who were also enjoying the fruits of the stock market boom and economic recovery after 1982. This cohort became known as 'yuppies.' Although the term was an invention of the advertising industry looking to codify a new generation of consumers, yuppies – young upwardly mobile professionals – became synonymous with wealth, their allegiance to expensive, branded products (cars, the new cell phones emerging in the mid-1980s, and consumer technology in general) and urban lifestyles revolving around drinking, eating, shopping, fashion and body-sculpting. 'Not in decades,' Haynes Johnson suggests, 'perhaps not in the century, had acquisition and flaunting of wealth been celebrated so publicly by so many.'[17] Career-oriented, yuppies became one of the most important and visible social groups of the 1980s. Although they stood in stark contrast to the hippies of the 1960s, yuppies were sometimes ex-hippies who had entered the world of business, and were often members of the baby-boom generation born between the end of the Second World War and the mid-1960s. Beginning or forging a career in the early and mid-1980s, they were able to take advantage of Reagan's tax breaks and indulge their tastes in a consumer market buoyed by the economic goods pouring into the US from Asia and Europe and creating record US trade deficits.

Almost from its inception the word 'yuppie' was used in a derogatory sense. Although television shows like *thirtysomething* (1987–91) and *L.A. Law* (1986–94) portrayed the details of yuppie life in a more sympathetic way, and Lawrence Kasdan's film *The Big Chill* (1983) offered a sensitive account of the passage from hippie to yuppie amongst a group of college friends, the yuppie was most often the object of satire and criticism. Even among writers like Jay McInerney, Bret Easton Ellis, Tama Janowitz and Jill Eisenstadt, who both wrote about the yuppie experience and were themselves turned into fashionable commodities by the increasing corporatization of publishing in the 1980s, there was a desire to expose what was seen to be a moral vacuum at the heart of the yuppie moneymaking enterprise. From a different generation, Louis Auchincloss's *Diary of a Yuppie* (1986) and, more famously, Tom Wolfe's *The Bonfire of the Vanities* (1987) were equally as disparaging of New York yuppie culture. Through the figure of the aptly-named Gordon Gekko, Oliver Stone's film *Wall Street* (1987) depicted the quick-moving and predatory nature of financial capital in the 1980s and tried to show the damaging impact on the jobs and lives of the people who worked for companies at the heart of the mergers and acquisitions frenzy.

This cultural critique became all the more apposite following the stock market crash of October 1987 and a series of high-profile scandals that undermined public confidence in the opaque world of financial dealing. Ivan Boesky's arrest and prosecution for insider trading – the practice of buying stocks and shares based on information not available to the public – was the most famous of these scandals. Public knowledge of a company's impending takeover usually increased the price of shares in the targeted company. What Boesky did was to take tip-offs about impending takeovers, buy shares in the company and then realise the profit once the share price increased. This was illegal, and had been for many years. The vast increase in the number of takeovers during the 1980s meant that not only was there more opportunity for insider trading to take place, but also that it was increasingly difficult for the Securities and Exchange Commission to enforce the law. They did, however, investigate Boesky and once caught he gave evidence against his fellow traders who were also profiting illegally from insider trading. Most prominent amongst these was Milken. While Boesky received a $100 million fine and a three-and-a-half-year prison sentence, Milken was charged on ninety-eight counts of racketeering and fraud. In a plea bargain he admitted to half a dozen lesser charges, paid a $200 million fine, another $400 million in civil lawsuit settlements and he served just under two years in prison. At his sentencing, the judge referred to a series of letters she had received from members of the public which reflected, she said:

a perception that we as a society must find those responsible for the alleged abuses of the 1980s, economic harm caused by savings and loan associations, takeover targets and those allegedly injured by the issuance of junk bonds as well as by insider trading and other alleged abuses, and punish these criminals in proportion to the losses believed to have been suffered. These writers ask for a verdict on a decade of greed.[18]

Unable to offer such a verdict through Milken because he was not charged with these offences, there is, nevertheless, a sense in which the prosecution of Boesky, Milken and other insider traders, along with the cultural backlash against yuppies and an uninhibited Wall Street, marks a point at which the deregulated market was checked by the rule of law. It was Boesky who gave a speech at the University of California which would inspire Gordon Gekko's 'Greed is good' speech in *Wall Street*. According to Boesky, 'greed is all right . . . I want you to know that. I think greed is healthy. You can be greedy and still feel good about yourself.' Yet, by the end of the 1980s, the fraudulent acquisition of what many considered to be obscene amounts of money helped temper the decade of greed.

In some ways, while yuppies and huge sums of money were the most visible manifestations of a changing economic sphere in the 1980s, other changes were taking place that would have longer-lasting structural effects on US society and culture. The way stocks were bought and sold on a day-to-day basis was transformed from the early 1980s by the advent of computerized trading. Most importantly, digital technology increased the speed at which trading took place and, as a consequence, the number of transactions that could be performed within a given amount of time. Allied with the connection of information networks across different continents, what this wave of technological transformation facilitated was a truly globalized trading environment. In 1985 Americans bought foreign shares worth $12.8 billion, pushing total overseas stock ownership up to $41 billion. In the same year, non-Americans bought $30.2 billion worth of US stocks, taking their total holdings to $126 billion.[19] In January 1987 the US investment houses Merrill Lynch, Morgan Stanley and Goldman Sachs were invited to become members of the Japanese stock exchange, while direct Japanese investment in the US was marked by the notable acquisition of symbolic sites like the Rockefeller Center in New York and the Pebble Beach Golf Course in California. Perhaps most notable of all was Sony's entry into the US entertainment industry with its acquisition of CBS Records in 1988 and Columbia Pictures in 1989.

These twin changes – new technology and the integration of increasingly global trading markets – were characteristic of realignment in the American economy during the 1980s. In the context of Reaganomics, digital technology represented the next stage of capitalist development and was a means of forging new markets away from the traditional sectors of manufacturing industry which had been so damaged by competition from Europe and Asia during the late 1970s.

The consequences of such changes were not just economic, however. The shakeout in the American economy created new forms for the delivery and consumption of culture and new forms of ownership of culture industries. It was hardly surprising, then, that culture itself became a subject of intense debate and attention during the 1980s. At the same time that the economic market was deregulated, so the cultural sphere and the sphere of everyday life were increasingly a battleground for control by opposing factions. Attacks on the state of the US in the 1980s were spurred on by a resurgent conservative Right.

New Conservatism

I have already emphasized how Reaganomics was both an economic and moral ideology in the 1970s and 1980s and how a gradual disillusionment with Democratic liberalism in the face of stagflation and a backlash against the social movements of the sixties stimulated what William Berman has called 'America's Right Turn.'[20] This New Right politics, or neo-conservatism, was new in several important ways that would help reshape the political landscape of American Republicanism and American society and culture more generally. Rising from the grass roots movement that supported Barry Goldwater's campaign in 1964, the New Right existed rather nebulously through the early years of the 1970s and established itself in two main areas: economic and social policy think tanks like the Heritage Foundation, established in 1973 and the Cato Institute (1977); and pro-life, religious and family orientated organizations like the Eagle Forum (1972), Feminists for the Life of America (1972), Focus of the Family (1977), American Life League (1979), Concerned Women for America (1979) and the Family Research Council (1983). These are only some of many such organizations that proliferated during this period, often at a state and local level, and that would gradually coalesce under the leadership of people like Paul Weyrich, Richard Viguerie, Howard Phillips, Jesse Helms, Phyllis Schlafly and Pat Buchanan to form a potent political force that not only rejuvenated the Republican party and helped ensure the election and re-election of Reagan but also made itself increasingly visible through lobbying campaigns and strategic uses of the media.

At the forefront of this new social movement were a variety of often diverse Protestant and Catholic religious groups. As Michael Lienesch has shown, the revival of religious organizations in the late 1970s and 1980s was the next peak in a cycle of rise and fall for the Christian Right in the US.[21] While there are differing opinions about the popularity of New Right Christianity – with estimates about national participation ranging from the tens of millions to the hundreds of thousands – what was perhaps more important was the level of commitment of those who were involved and their capacity for setting political agendas and focusing debate. Lienesch draws out the continuities between earlier twentieth century and the 1970s and 80s variants. Chief amongst these was the role of the popular preacher and the willingness to utilize mass media in the service of spreading the word.

Televangelism

With its history in public address and preaching before audiences, it is hardly surprising that religion in the US had long made use of the media to spread its message. Radio was popular as a method of communication in the 1920s and 30s. The Catholic priest Charles Coughlin, an early supporter and then harsh critic of Franklin Roosevelt's New Deal policies, used his weekly radio show to try and turn opinion against Roosevelt and became increasingly extreme in his diagnosis of the nation's problems, denouncing both capitalism and communism for their internationalist preoccupations which victimized US citizens. Nativist, anti-Semitic and sympathetic towards the rise of fascism in Europe, Coughlin was hugely popular, capturing an audience in the millions and receiving tens of thousand of letters each week, and influential enough to have Roosevelt send prominent Catholic figures like Joseph Kennedy to try and get Coughlin to temper his broadcasts. During the 1950s and 60s, Ronald Reagan had himself narrated films with titles like *Communism on the Map* and *The Truth about Communism* produced by Billy James Hargis, a Protestant evangelical, radio preacher and head of Christian Crusade.

It is in this tradition of right-wing extremism that the televangelists followed in the 1980s, as television evangelists like Jimmy Swaggart, Jim Bakker, Pat Robertson, Jerry Falwell and Oral Roberts revived the role of the preacher as a media phenomenon and used their own media organizations not only to raise huge sums of money but also to preach about moral issues around which the New Right coalesced: abortion, homosexuality and AIDS, sex education and pornography. Religious groups had easily made the transition to television. The evangelist Pat Robertson founded the Christian Broadcasting Network (CBN) in 1961 and many of the religious leaders who became infamous for their television performances during the 1980s had been involved in broadcasting during the 1960s and 70s. Jim Bakker and his wife Tammy Faye, for instance, hosted a children's show and then a talk-show on CBN from 1964 to 1972 before moving over to Trinity Broadcasting Network and then forming PTL – The Inspirational Network in 1978. Cable and satellite technology during the 1980s helped religious networks syndicate their programmes to a nationwide audience and to make religious leaders into national celebrities. Their dramatic performances – both as preachers and as money-raisers – combined the conviction of the neo-conservative New Right with the entrepreneurial skills of the new business strategies that were coming to dominate the American economy. Religion and television were well suited in the 1980s because television could package and commodify religion for an increasingly image-oriented audience. New cable and satellite networks facilitated the transition of religion to the media age.

The money these Christian groups and media networks raised meant that they needed sophisticated organizational structures and they were quick to diversify into other areas. Jim Bakker and his wife, Tammy Faye, opened a Christian theme park in 1978 called Heritage USA and by the mid-1980s this had become the third most popular theme park in America, attracting six million people a year and employing two thousand staff. It was behind only Florida's Disney World and California's Disneyland in popularity. Together with economic and media success came interest from politicians on the Right and in the Republican Party who were looking to form alliances with, and make best use of the lobbying power of, the televangelists and their grass roots followers. Paul Weyrich, head of the Committee for the Survival of a Free Congress, and Howard Phillips of the Conservative Caucus were active in this process, making links with Robertson and Falwell. For Christian groups this allowed freer access to conservative organizations and right-wing politicians, most notably Jesse Helms. In return they offered access to mailing lists of religious followers and huge television audiences.[22]

But just like Billy James Hargis before them, the televangelists of the 1980s became as famous for the scandals which beset them while some even served penance on their own television shows. Hargis was disgraced by accusations that he had slept with students at his American Christian College. In 1987, Jim Bakker was forced to resign from Heritage USA and PTL when he was accused of drugging and raping the then twenty-one year old Jessica Hahn along with another man seven years earlier. It was also revealed that he tried to pay her $265,000 to keep the story quiet. In 1989 Bakker was also subsequently charged with fraud and tax evasion and served five years in prison. The person to benefit from Bakker's fall from grace was Jerry Falwell, who took control of PTL and Heritage USA, although under his leadership Heritage USA filed for bankruptcy. One of the fiercest critics of Bakker's crimes and misdemeanours was Jimmy Swaggart, who described the Bakker affair as 'a cancer on the body of Christ'. But after exposing the affair of a rival evangelist, Swaggart became the victim as he was himself photographed leaving a hotel room with a prostitute. In February 1988 Swaggart went on air to tearfully confess his sin.

The huge sums of money raised by corporate televangelists, the correspondingly opulent lifestyles they led and their pious moral statements all meant they were often subject to accusations of financial irregularity and hypocrisy. Over the course of the 1980s the reputation of the visible religious Right foundered, even if it continued to be potent at grass roots level.

At certain moments during the early to mid-1980s the coalition between the Christian New Right and Republican and right-wing conservative politicians was powerful enough to carry through a conservative social and moral agenda. With its geographical heartlands stretching from Virginia and North Carolina in the east, through the Bible Belt of the southern states and across to the South West and to southern California, this coalition ensured that the Republican Party dropped its support for the Equal Rights Amendment (ERA), an amendment to the US constitution that would guarantee in law equal rights for men and women irrespective of gender. The tortuous constitutional history of the ERA stretched back to the 1920s, but a push by Congress in the early 1970s and a series of ratifications by individual states raised the prospect of the ERA being adopted. Under the fierce leadership of Phyllis Schlafly, who campaigned forcefully against the amendment on the grounds that it would open the floodgates to societal changes – the drafting of women into the armed services, same-sex marriage, state-funded abortions and an overall extension of government power – the deadline by which ERA needed to be ratified expired.

Religious and conservative groups also made numerous forays into the field of culture. In 1986, Jimmy Swaggart accused rock music of breeding 'adultery, alcoholism, drug abuse, necrophilia, bestiality and you name it' and in response Wal-Mart, temporarily at least, removed potentially offensive albums and magazines such as *Rolling Stone* from its displays. Popular music, because it was directly marketed so explicitly to young consumers, became the subject of several campaigns. Chief amongst these was the Parents Music Resource Center (PMRC). Formed in 1985 by several wives of congressmen, the group published a list of songs dubbed the 'Filthy Fifteen' because of the subject matter of their lyrics which focused on sex, violence, drugs or the occult. Surprisingly, the list included Cyndi Lauper's 'She Bop' (1983), Sheena Easton's 'Sugar Walls' (1984) and Madonna's 'Dress You Up' (1985) along with a group of more predictable material from heavy-metal bands such as the British group Def Leppard and American bands Venom, W.A.S.P and Twisted Sister. The PMRC formed coalitions with the National Parents and Teachers Association and the National Education Association. Drawing on this national network of sympathizers it asked people to monitor the output of local radio stations and to write letters of complaint if material to which they objected – what Reagan called 'the glorification of drugs and violence and perversity' – was broadcast. Local groups were persistent lobbyists and later in

1985, after a Senate enquiry, the Recording Industry Association of America voluntarily introduced the 'Parental Advisory' sticker which was to be put on music CDs with explicit content.

In the field of cinema, the religious Right forged an unlikely coalition with anti-pornography feminists (led by Andrea Dworkin and Catherine MacKinnon) during the 1980s at a time when pornography was entering mainstream popular culture thanks to the video technology which extended audience reach and produced new revenue streams. The lobbying of politicians by these groups helped create a solid and organized network of support and the religious Right was able to draw on this after the release of Martin Scorsese's *The Last Temptation of Christ* (1988), a film which created a fictional Christ character given to philosophical doubt and sexual desire. The film's distributor, Universal/MCA, was bombarded with protests and threatened boycotts. Many of the leaders of religious Right groups, including Jerry Falwell, were at the forefront of these protests. Bill Bright, head of the Campus Crusade for Christ, even offered to give Universal $10 million for the film prints so he could destroy them.[23] Despite such adverse publicity, the film still went on general release, although several exhibition chains – General Cinema, Carmike Cinemas and Wometco Theaters amongst them – were not prepared to face potential localized demonstrations and did not show it.

Many of these interventions in the cultural field were played out in the context of the culture wars which I discuss below, but it is also worth making the point at this stage that while there was a general concern across religious and neo-conservative groups about moral corruption in the US – as witnessed by the touchstone issues of pornography, abortion, liberal education, and homosexuality – these groups could quite easily also be at odds in other ways. The Christian Right in the 1980s was a multi-dimensional alliance of fundamentalist, charismatic and evangelical faiths, each with different objectives. Where fundamentalists emphasized adherence to biblical doctrine, evangelicals were more concerned with spreading the word and moral reform while for charismatics religious belief was a much more personal experience. While these religious differences could be suspended for the purpose of fighting a common cause, they were reactivated at other moments to prevent the religious Right from forming a more effective ideological force.

For Michael Lienesch, the religious Right coalition ultimately fell apart during Pat Robertson's presidential election campaign of 1988.[24] After starting strongly, Robertson was damaged by the Jimmy

Swaggart revelations and his own political incompetence. Not only did he lie about his military career, claiming to have seen active combat as a marine in Korea when in fact he had been a 'liquor officer' supplying officers' clubs with alcohol, but his policies of getting rid of the Department of Education, the Department of Energy and Amtrak attracted scorn. More importantly, Robertson – a charismatic – alienated fundamentalists, like Falwell, who supported George Bush Sr, and evangelicals who supported alternative candidates. Robertson's candidacy foundered and the religious Right coalition evaporated as a formal political force. Ultimately, Lienesch argues, the 'ardency of their activism notwithstanding, religious conservatives are at best ambivalent about politics. In fact, the members of this movement tend toward an apolitical stance. For most of them, a quietistic approach to politics is ingrained in their religious views.'[25]

AIDS

Neo-conservative religious and political leaders were constantly fascinated by sex and sexuality during the 1980s. While this was nothing new in American history, their reflections on promiscuity, pornography and the sexualization of culture in general were given a more sinister and immediate edge by the emergence of Acquired Immune Deficiency Syndrome, or AIDS as it quickly became known, in the early 1980s. AIDS is a disease of the human immune system that most scientists believe to be a result of infection by the Human Immunodeficiency Virus (HIV). HIV is a type of lentivirus – viruses notable for having long latency periods, up to fifteen or twenty years in the case of HIV – and both strains of the virus (HIV-1 and HIV-2) are thought to have originated in West-Central Africa and to have jumped across species from primates to humans. Once HIV begins to attack the immune system, those infected with the virus present symptoms which have come to be seen as AIDS-defining illnesses – Kaposi's Sarcoma, toxoplasmosis of the brain, and various liver, bronchial and lymph node diseases. Although there is some dispute today about the link between HIV and AIDS, it is understood that HIV is transmitted through blood and other bodily fluids and that common forms of transmission are unprotected penetrative and oral sex, blood transfusion, the sharing of contaminated needles, pregnancy, childbirth and breastfeeding.

While the biology of AIDS and HIV may now seem straightforward, from the moment of its emergence as an identifiable illness,

AIDS operated in the broader cultural and social domain less as a biological fact than as an opportunity to pass moral judgement. From the moment the Atlanta-based Centers for Disease Control and Prevention (CDC) reported on a cluster of pneumocystis pneumonia in five gay male drug users in the Los Angeles area on June 5 1981, and clusters of Kaposi's sarcoma and pneumocystis pneumonia among gay men in California and New York City on July 4 1981, AIDS became intimately connected with homosexual men. Indeed, what was called AIDS from 1982 was initially labelled GRID (Gay Related Immune Deficiency) and only lost its specificity once the CDC realized that it was not only gay men who were presenting symptoms but also blood transfusion patients, heroin users, heterosexual women and newborn babies. Despite these findings, the early years of AIDS in the US – and elsewhere – were marked by a mixture of ignorance, hysteria and homophobia, which later gave way, in some circles at least, to compassion, fund-raising initiatives for further research, a renewed politicization of gay men, and a whole host of conspiracy theories about the origins of AIDS and HIV.

In part the ignorance was caused by the medical community's inability to confirm what caused AIDS. The variety of symptoms presented meant that it was difficult to isolate the disease's trajectory and not until 1986 did most scientists accept the link between HIV and AIDS. But the vacuum left by the scientists was often filled in the first half of the decade by speculation and prejudice. Since the 1960s and the Stonewall riots at the end of that decade, homosexual men and women in the US had become increasingly visible and, especially in large cities like San Francisco and New York, their lifestyles were a feature of the urban scene where they developed their own social, cultural and economic networks. For gay men in these cities, Dennis Altman argues, there was a recognizable shift in their behaviour. The growing prevalence of bath-houses and sex clubs along with the use of recreational drugs were part of this shift. Sexually transmitted diseases became a major homosexual health issue.[26] For many on the conservative and religious Right in the US the emergence of AIDS was seen as evidence of the inherently dangerous (and potentially fatal) nature of male homosexuality and provided the Right with the ammunition it needed to project AIDS as a gay plague and, once it was clear AIDS was a heterosexual health issue too, to fulminate against sexual promiscuity in general. In 1983 Pat Buchanan, in a clear attempt to situate AIDS as a legacy of the 1960s, declared: 'The sexual revolution has begun to devour its children. And among the vanguard, the Gay Rights activists,

the mortality rate is highest and climbing . . . The poor homosexuals,'
he continued, 'they have declared war upon nature, and now nature is
exacting an awful retribution.'[27] The apocalyptic tenor of this rhetoric
fitted with the plague scenario, and one of the consequences of this
kind of approach was that soon AIDS was seen to be a threat to everyone in the US, with the origin of this threat to be located in promiscu-
ous gay male behaviour. Late in 1983 Jerry Falwell, during a live
television debate with a gay San Francisco psychotherapist, claimed
not to hate homosexuals themselves only their 'perverted life-style'
and their 'sub-animal behaviour'.[28] Calling on bath-houses to be
closed down and for blood donors to complete questionnaires about
their sexual activity, Falwell suggested that 'If the Reagan administration does not put its full weight against this . . . what is now a gay
plague in this country, I feel that a year from now, President Ronald
Reagan, personally, will be blamed for allowing this awful disease to
break out among the innocent American public.'[29] Reagan, famously,
did not speak publicly about AIDS until 1987, by which time more
than 20,000 had died from the condition.

For Dennis Altman, such a combination of factors and 'the way in
which AIDS has been perceived, conceptualized, imagined, researched
and financed makes this the most political of diseases.'[30] In the context
of a shift to the Right in the US during the 1980s, the politicization of
AIDS did not bode well for health education, medical research or
public understanding. And yet while a politics of demonization per-
sisted through the decade and a series of conspiracy theories – many
involving fanciful notions about the CIA and military bio-warfare
research – muddied the waters of medical evidence, a quite different
response was also emerging. Two factors were important here: the
organization of gay men themselves, and the altered perception of
AIDS following the death of several cultural icons, most notably
Rock Hudson.

If homosexual men were targeted by discourse about a 'gay
plague', then they also helped cement the link between AIDS and gay
male life because 'no other affected group has comparable political
will and resources to deal with the issue.'[31] This political will was in
part a result of the network of support groups and national organizations which had sprung up in the 1960s and 70s. The National Gay
Task Force, founded in New York in 1973, had a solid record of lobbying to overturn anti-gay and homophobic legislation. It backed the
successful ruling of the US Civil Service Commission allowing gay
people to serve in government employment; worked on the first gay

rights bill in Congress in 1975; overturned an IRS policy denying tax-exempt status to organizations promoting homosexuality; and its executive director Jean O'Leary was appointed to President Carter's International Women's Year commission. When attempts were made to overturn gay rights ordinances it helped organize counter-campaigns. Organizations such as this were well placed to react to the emergence of AIDS in the early 1980s, offering support and lobbying for research funding. While Gil Troy may be right in suggesting that some gay men 'reacted slowly' to AIDS and 'resisted the public health measures and private precautions required',[32] the efforts of other gay men to mobilize was much more notable. Within weeks of the publication of the first CDC findings, eighty men gathered in the apartment of New York writer Larry Kramer to discuss the new disease and to raise money for research. This group would become Gay Men's Health Crisis (GMHC) and Kramer and his colleagues the most vociferous of AIDS activists and fund raisers. In its first year the GMHC raised $150,000 and used this for research as well as to produce and distribute health brochures and newsletters. When the stakes were so high and the public authorities so reluctant to offer this kind of support, Kramer's GMHC was an invaluable organization for many gay men.

The work of New York activists also included the Silence = Death campaign which linked the plight of homosexual men and women in the US to a history of marginalization, death and indifference. Using the same pink triangle for their logo that homosexuals had been forced to wear in Nazi concentration camps, the Silence = Death Project was forthright and controversial in approach. Its founder members later joined another influential campaigning organization, AIDS Coalition to Unleash Power (ACT UP). Formed in 1987, ACT UP saw itself as an organization which should take responsibility for people living with AIDS rather than leaving them to health officials, government researchers, medical bureaucrats, doctors and pharmaceutical company executives who believed themselves to be 'AIDS experts'. One of the problems for gay activists as the 1980s wore on was that although the public authorities did belatedly get involved with safe-sex health education, much of the information was directed at an uneasy heterosexual population. Not only were gay activist groups important for educating gay men and women in the early stages of the disease's spread, then, when the public authorities did finally enter the fray, activist groups like ACT UP remained important for a gay community largely neglected by public bodies.

Caught between the homophobic rhetoric of neo-conservative political and religious leaders and the dedicated activism of gay rights groups was a confused heterosexual population for whom AIDS was, at one and the same time, something which happened to other people – haemophiliacs, intravenous drug users and homosexuals – but also threatened their own well being and made them reassess their sexual behaviour. This reassessment was helped, and prompted, by the public reassessment of the sexuality of celebrity figures. Rock Hudson died from AIDS on October 2 1985. Rumours that he was suffering from the disease had circulated since earlier that year. Following his death, Hudson's homosexuality became common knowledge to the nation rather than just common knowledge inside Hollywood. Morgan Fairchild, one of Hudson's co-stars in the hit television show *Dynasty*, remarked that 'Hudson's death gave AIDS a face.' The fact that that face was gay did not seem to register as much as Hudson's celebrity status as a heterosexual hero of 1960s romantic comedies where he starred alongside that paragon of American Christian femininity, Doris Day. Hudson, then, became the acceptable 'face' of homosexuality – a lifelong Republican and friend of Ronald and Nancy Reagan – and helped break AIDS to heterosexual culture and provided the opportunity for newspapers and magazines to discuss AIDS. According to Gil Troy, the number of AIDS stories in the print media in the US increased threefold in the six months following Hudson's death.[33]

Show business now got involved with AIDS fund raising, using celebrities to grab the public's attention. The Oscar-winning actress, and friend of Hudson, Elizabeth Taylor became Founding National Chairman of the American Foundation for AIDS Research (amfAR) in 1985. She appeared before Congress and in several public-service television advertisements to heighten public awareness of AIDS and to encourage compassion for its victims. It was at an amfAR benefit function that Reagan first discussed AIDS publicly. Madonna raised funds for amfAR at one of her concerts in 1987. Critics like Douglas Crimp have suggested that, while important, the emphasis on fund raising also goes hand in hand with a form of cultural production that does not deal directly with AIDS:

> Raising money is the most passive response of cultural practitioners to social crisis, a response that perpetuates the idea that art itself has no social function (aside from being a commodity), that there is no such thing as an engaged, activist aesthetic practice.[34]

But the aesthetic response was coming from within those groups most directly affected by AIDS. Larry Kramer, the Silence = Death Project and the artist David Wojnarowicz, amongst others, all produced work which went beyond the culture of loss and suffering which marked many mainstream attempts to confront AIDS in the 1980s and 1990s, the most successful of which was probably Tom Hanks' Oscar-winning performance in *Philadelphia* (1993).

AIDS became an important dimension of life during the 1980s because it tested the capacity of American society to cope with the unknown. AIDS emerged when Western medicine had eradicated other epidemics and the specificity of the groups in which it first became noticeable elicited the worst and best of responses. The worst came from neo-conservative religious and political leaders whose homophobic rhetoric and unwillingness to react swiftly to the epidemic created animosity and contributed to confusion. Ultimately, these reactions were superseded by the intervention of committed activists, by celebrities who began to see their own friends and colleagues falling victim to the disease, and by global organizations like the World Health Organization and the United Nations. All this, together with the institution of World AIDS day and the red ribbon as symbol of AIDS awareness, made AIDS a startlingly contemporary disease.

Technoculture

If the medical profession and its pharmaceutical offshoots were struggling during the 1980s to come to terms with the viral threat presented by HIV and AIDS and was unable to reassure a Western public for whom antibiotics and vaccinations had eradicated major health threats, it was not for want of sophisticated technological resources. The 1980s was a decade that saw crucial developments in the field of biotechnology that would raise important moral and philosophical issues for later generations to deal with. Genetics was a key field. In 1980 the US Supreme Court agreed the principle of patenting genetically engineered life forms. Micro-organisms were now economic products owned by organizations. Patents for gene cloning were granted, genes were successfully transferred from one animal species to another, DNA fingerprinting was developed and the first genetically engineered vaccine was produced. By the end of the decade plans and funds were in place for the Human Genome Project, an international project involving countries across the world but coordinated by the US Department of Energy and National Institutes of Health, whose goal was to identify all human genes and to make them accessible for further biological study. The Project was completed in 2003. The 1980s, then, was a time when the human body – its genetic structure and the possibility of altering this – was at the forefront of scientific developments. The radical nature of this scientific enquiry was often driven by pharmaceutical corporations for whom breakthroughs and discoveries could be turned into profit. And yet for scientists to interfere with the human body provoked criticism and anxiety from both liberals and conservatives: for liberals the motivations of corporations were suspect and human bodies the potential victims of corporate greed; for conservatives, scientists were in danger of tampering with the natural world and 'playing God'.

These anxieties about the human body and its place in a society increasingly dominated by science and technology spill out into American culture during the 1980s and become even more pervasive in the 1990s. Ailing and mutilated bodies were a staple of slasher horror films, a particularly gruesome development of the horror genre in the 1980s; David Cronenberg remade *The Fly* (1986) for a contemporary market with a narrative about genetic splicing; while the figure of the cyborg, a genetically engineered mix of organic and mechanical parts, became an increasingly familiar component of American culture, not only in films like *Blade Runner* (1982) and *Terminator* (1984), but also in William Gibson's short story 'Burning Chrome', where he coined the term cyberspace, his influential novel *Neuromancer* (1984) and in the cultural theory of Donna Haraway whose essay 'Manifesto for Cyborgs: Science, Technology, and Socialist Feminism in the 1980s' (1985) was one of the key documents in the study of what is now known as cyberculture.

The coming together of technology and culture was most noticeable in the cyber domain. Although the full impact would not be felt until the second half of the 1990s with the exponential growth of internet use and the dotcom boom, and although computer technology has been a feature of American society since the Second World War, the 1980s witnessed a digital revolution which would lay the groundwork for what followed. Although 'cyber' is taken primarily from the word cybernetics – a theory of the communication and control – the prefix cyber more generally refers to experiences or actions achieved through the use of a computer. Hence its current usage in cyberculture, cybersex or cyberspace. What marks the late 1970s and the 1980s is the movement of powerful computers from the back office to the individual desktop. Ever cheaper microprocessors, Michael Cerruzzi suggests, meant that businesses soon discovered that 'having a computer at each worker's desk, networked to other machines, was more efficient than having a centralized time-shared computer accessed through "dumb" terminals.'[35] Apple, Commodore and IBM soon began producing powerful machines for this office environment, but the real surge in computer use only really occurred once calculation and word-processing software became available. The 'killer app' for the personal computer was the VisiCalc spreadsheet program. Once copies of the IBM PC appeared, Microsoft was able to offer an operating system capable of running on them all and so began the company's rise to its current status and the almost universal use of Windows.

Silicon Valley

The introduction of computers to Wall Street trading was one of the most visible daily manifestations of 1980s new technology in the economic landscape of the United States. But while the imagery of Wall Street circulated freely in American culture, the research and development that produced the technological innovations that would touch so many American lives in the 1980s went on in a much more sedate environment: the low-rise, high-tech area of California that Don C. Hoefler, in 1971, called Silicon Valley and which Po Bronson has described as 'an endless suburb, hushed and nonchalant, in terrain too flat to deserve the term "valley".'[36] Originally named because of the prevalence of silicon chip manufacturers in the northern part of the Santa Clara Valley in the San Francisco Bay area, this geographical region also came to encompass the more general concentration of high-tech businesses in the San Francisco Peninsula and East Bay areas, including the cities of Palo Alto, Menlo Park and Los Altos.

High-tech aerospace industries began to spring up in the region, primarily an agricultural region before the Second World War and the largest canning and dried-fruit packing centre in the world, after the US military established US Naval Air Station Moffett Field. The proximity of Stanford University, with its ready supply of graduates and close links with businesses, helped establish other engineering industries in the region. Bill Hewlett and Dave Packard graduated from Stanford in 1934 and set up what would become the dominant electronics company in the area. The silicon transistor was first developed by Fairchild Semiconductor in Mountain View in 1957, while in 1971, Intel, formed as an offshoot of Fairchild, created the first microprocessor and paved the way for the development of the personal computer which would receive a further boost with the Apple I, created by Steve Jobs and Steve Wozniak in Cupertino in 1976.

One other notable element in the rise of Silicon Valley as the pre-eminent centre for high-tech development was the Xerox Palo Alto Research Center (PARC). A blue skies institution, many of the most fundamental aspects of personal computer design that transformed the use of computers in the 1980s – graphical user interfaces, use of the mouse, what-you-see-is-what-you-get (WYSIWYG) software programs, and Ethernet network connections – were first developed at PARC.

There is little doubt that the concentration of silicon chip and microprocessor manufacturers stimulated the clustering of high-tech industries in the Valley, but new technology often requires significant capital investment in order for new companies to enter the market. As the home to so many bright ideas, then, it is not surprising that Silicon Valley relied for its growth on the presence of venture capitalists – an alternative source of private equity to that provided by Wall Street – eager, especially in the 1980s, to fund new projects. Sand Hill Road in Menlo Park became the centre of the venture capital world in the 1980s. By the end of the decade it was home to more than twenty-five venture capital firms. There were numerous others through the valley and the successful public launches of Apple Computers and Genetech, backed by venture capital money, heralded a successful decade for the industry.

The success of Silicon Valley, however, is based not so much on what it is – a manufacturing and production area – but on the way in which the computing and high-tech ideas produced there have so successfully replaced the traditional manufacturing industries that entered decline in the 1970s. Silicon Valley regenerated the American economy through the microchip and at the digital level. This change was central to the way the US changed in the 1980s. And as well as being an economic shift, the digital era also ushered in a cultural sea change: it changed the cultural products people consumed – compact discs and videos, for instance; it changed the way culture was produced – in film studios, television stations and music studios; and it changed the people who were able to produce culture – no longer just large organizations, but also individuals or small groups of collaborators. Many of the effects would reach fruition only in the 1990s, particularly in the field of personal computing and use of the internet, and, while Silicon Valley was not the only motor in this transition, looking at the companies based there is like reading a who's who of the digital and multimedia world: Adobe, Apple, Cisco Systems, eBay, Electronic Arts, Hewlett-Packard, Intel, Oracle, Sun Microsystems, Symantec, Yahoo!, Google, McAfee, Netscape (AOL), NVIDIA, Palm, Inc., PayPal and Verisign.

What is surprising about the development of the personal computer, and the importance of the personal computer both at work and at home, is that few people predicted it.

Robert Cringely's book *Accidental Empires* (1992) gives something of the flavour of the *ad hoc* nature of the personal-computer story and the grass roots entrepreneurism which outsmarted big corporations.

In broader terms, however, it is possible to see the rise of high-tech industries as a part of a structural adjustment at the end of the 1970s and into the 1980s. Losing competitive advantage to Asia and Europe in traditional industrial sectors, the US economy carved out new markets in areas in which it would become a world leader. Not only did these industries start to provide investment, jobs and profits, but they also started to alter the culture people consumed. Together with Japan, the US was at the forefront of new computer game technology. *Space Invaders* was released in 1978 and, although the program itself was written for the Japanese Taito Corporation, its publisher was the American Midway Games, the company also responsible for licensing and distributing *Pac-Man* (1980). Originally arcade games running on Intel processors, *Space Invaders*, *Pac-Man* and a whole series of other games soon found their way onto home computers and were often responsible for the purchase of the computer itself. This model of software driving the purchase of hardware is one that has dominated the computing industry since the early 1980s. After a slump in popularity between 1983 and 1985, the next generation of video games arrived in 1987 with the launch of Nintendo's Entertainment System and Sega's Master System.

Another new cultural product that arrived in the late 1970s and early 1980s and invented a whole new form of cultural consumption was the video cassette. A piece of technology developed in Europe by Philips and in Japan by Sony, the video cassette and the video cassette recorder (VCR) initially prompted opposition from US film corporations which was soon tested in court. Universal Studios sued Sony for manufacturing a device that could be used for copyright infringement. The Supreme Court ruled for Sony in 1984 and by the time this decision was reached the VCR had found a mass market. The home video was born and, as it turned out, the major beneficiaries of this new cultural product were the Hollywood film companies who now had a whole new market in which to sell their films. Phillips and Sony were also at the forefront of the revolution in digital audio. The launch of the compact disc in 1982 and 1983 offered music companies a new format to go alongside vinyl and tape, not to mention the opportunity to re-release a whole back catalogue of music in the new format.

The 1980s, then, was not only an era of new cultural products, it was also a decade of new cultural forms. No longer was one restricted to watching the films put on in a movie theatre or a television schedule. Watching television could mean watching last night's programmes the following day. No longer was one tied to a fixed music system, following the release – and colossal success in the US – of Sony's Walkman and its clones. Culture was suddenly portable and more easily reproducible. The digital world which had for several years only been projected was now becoming a new order of reality and a new space in which culture would be produced and consumed. While the years after the 1980s have seen the more startling possibilities of this new digital domain, the 1980s is a decade of genuine innovation on a mass scale at the point where technology meets culture. New economic sectors began to establish themselves and the ways in which people interacted with culture, as I will show in the later chapters, began to change. One further factor to consider at this stage is the way in which the reach of more cultural products was becoming global. *Space Invaders* was not just a Japanese or American phenomenon. The anxieties about the influence of video games – to what extent they were addictive or fostered violence – were also just as likely to be aired in one country as another. American culture was becoming part of an increasingly global culture. Not only did American cultural products become more pervasive around the world, but so too did American culture import technologies and cultural products.

The Culture Wars

One of the problems with defining the 1980s as Reagan's America is that it projects a sense of unity that does not stand up to analysis. If one looks at exactly who elected Reagan to office it soon becomes apparent that his presidential campaigns relied on a core of white male support. In 1980 Reagan took 59 per cent of white male votes; in 1984 that figure rose to 67 per cent.[37] Support among this constituency was incredibly strong. Correspondingly, however, Reagan's support among women and among African and ethnic Americans was much weaker. For Todd Gitlin, this Republican bias amongst white men 'is the most potent form of identity politics in our time: a huddling of men who resent (and exaggerate) their relative decline not only in parts of the labor market but at home, in the bedroom and the kitchen, and in the culture.'[38] This decline was imagined to be at the expense of women and feminism; of immigrants and ethnic minorities and the legacy of affirmative-action policies that had sought to redress inequalities in employment and education; of sub-cultural groups like gays and lesbians whose lifestyles were increasingly visible; of multiculturalism in general and the push to recognize cultural production and activity that was not white or European in origin. These groups were not homogenous and neither did they necessarily support one another's aims. In fact, the other feature of the culture wars in the 1980s and 1990s was precisely a lack of consensus amongst these groups. The idea of difference underlay their sense of a politics of identity so that difference, rather than commonality, became what was considered to be universal.

This situation made for ideological conflagration at the level of culture. James Davison Hunter argues that the culture wars – the battles over gay rights, abortion, education and the arts – can be seen as part of an American tradition of cultural conflict that has pitted minority cultures against white protestant populism. The contemporary version of this conflict, like previous ones, is not based on doctrine or religion, but is about how Americans define who they are and about who holds moral authority: 'It is the commitment to different and opposing bases of moral authority and the world views that derive from them that creates the deep cleavages between antagonists in the contemporary culture war.'[39] With a battle between orthodoxy and progressivism, and the public culture that is 'the repository of the symbols of national life and purpose',[40] Hunter argues that the culture wars are 'largely a discourse of elites'[41] in a culture increasingly replete with knowledge workers – lobbyists, journalists, academics, religious and political leaders, lawyers and so on. The shift from an industrial to an information economy, which quickened during the 1980s, saw a huge increase in the number of people for whom control of knowledge and information was a key part of the way they made a living.

One of the most contentious battles over information took place around the issue of abortion. After the Supreme Court decision in *Roe* v. *Wade* (1973), abortion in the US became legal but never ceased to be a battleground between 'pro-life' and 'pro-choice' advocates. During the 1980s new organizations were formed whose tactics were more confrontational and aimed at targeting medical staff and closing down clinics that performed abortions. Operation Rescue was at the forefront of this movement, organizing prayer vigils, demonstrations and civil disobedience across the country while its publicity materials – with graphic pictures of aborted foetuses – aimed to persuade as much by shock as argument. But while much of the rhetoric of the anti-abortion movement is about the killing of innocent human lives and the morality of doing so, abortion has always been an issue about gender and the right of women to control their own bodies. Operation Rescue was founded, as its website declares, 'by a cadre of men'[42] including Randall Terry who, in 1992, would be sentenced to five months in prison for having a dead foetus delivered to President Clinton. Inextricably bound up with conservative ideas about the role of women as mothers and child-carers, the anti-abortion rhetoric of the 1980s was part of a broader backlash against women who put career ahead of family and motherhood.

Susan Faludi coined the term backlash to describe a cultural climate in which women were the subject of two conflicting narratives: one which told them they had won the equal rights battle and were now successful; another which told them that the consequences of this success were unhappiness in the form of 'burn-out', an 'infertility epidemic' and a 'man shortage'.[43] What was driving the second of these narratives, according to Faludi, was a backlash not just against women, but also against the feminism that had fostered the demands for equality and freedom. The end result of feminism was pain: 'Women are unhappy precisely *because* they are free. Women are enslaved by their own liberation . . . The women's movement, we are told time and again, has proved women's own worst enemy.'[44] Faludi sees evidence of this backlash not only in the rhetoric of New Right religion and politics, but also in its practical policies. Judicial appointments of women fell after 1980, the number of women appointed to the White House staff dropped from 123 in 1980 to 62 in 1981, while both the Coalition on Women's Appointments and the Working Group on Women were scrapped after Reagan's re-election.[45] Noted feminists from the 1960s, Faludi argues, also turned into revisionists 'yanking out the stitches in [their] own handiwork'.[46] Betty Friedan followed up her 1963 classic *The Feminine Mystique* with *The Second Stage*, published in 1981, which called for a less political and more maternal, feminine attitude from women. It was welcomed by Phyllis Schlafly as 'another nail in the coffin of feminism'.[47]

As both neo-conservatives and notable feminists questioned the usefulness of feminism and the state of contemporary womanhood, so the representations of women in popular culture displayed a similar anxiety about women's roles, according to Faludi. Popular psychology and self-help books picked up on journalistic coverage that often claimed to be spotting emerging trends when it in fact was driving debates about women's lives; debates that circulated by being quickly and effortlessly repeated 'as the "independent" press fell into a very few corporate hands'.[48] On television, Faludi notes the declining number of independent female leads, while in film the apotheosis of the cultural backlash against women was achieved in *Fatal Attraction*, Adrian Lyne's 1987 movie starring Michael Douglas as a family man whose weekend affair with a single, childless, early-thirties business-woman, played by Glenn Close, threatens to destroy his entire life. Close's character, the original and literal 'bunny boiler', condensed many of the backlash stereotypes. A successful and hardworking career woman, Close is anxious about her ticking body clock and the emotional gaps in her life. This anxiety is played out in the film as cunning, neurosis and violence as Close becomes increasingly demonic and witchlike in her appearance.

One factor constantly complicating the issue of cultural authority in America was the nation's racial and ethnic make-up. Simply put, from the 1960s onwards the US was becoming an increasingly non-white nation as black, Latin American and Asian sections of the population grew. Between 1970 and 1990 the white percentage of the population shrank from 87.6 per cent to 83.9 per cent, although this latter figure also included Hispanics classified as white.[49] Mixed-race marriages were also increasing dramatically. At the same time, growing wealth inequality during the 1980s disproportionately affected non-white groups. What emerged in the 1980s was a situation whereby in an increasingly multicultural society, different interest groups found it necessary to defend their cultural positions. Straight white men perceived themselves to be under threat from discourses that attacked the preponderance of WASP (White Anglo-Saxon Protestant) and DWEM (Dead White European Male) culture in this increasingly multicultural climate. The relevance of this culture – or canon of culture – to African American, Hispanic American and Asian American peoples living in the US was questioned by a number of vocal and politically active African American public intellectuals – Cornell West, Henry Louis Gates Jr, bell hooks, Michael Dyson – and left the straight white male 'scrambling for cultural space'[50] while perceiving himself to be a victim.

University and school curricula were the subject of particular conflict. Departments of African American and Black Studies first appeared at US universities and colleges during the 1960s and 1970s following demands from students and staff, and often alongside programmes in women's studies, gay and lesbian studies and Hispanic studies. These programmes politicized the curriculum and tried to make it more representative of the diversity of student experience. Universities instituted regulations to prevent and punish behaviour that victimised on the basis of race, ethnicity, disability or sexuality, while much was made in the marketing of higher education of difference and diversity. While institutions were often in conflict with student demands – as at Stanford in late 1980s when proposals to replace the Western Culture programme with one entitled Culture, Ideas and Values were only implemented after two years of debate and protest – the emphasis in higher education on multicultural curricula attracted criticism from neo-conservatives who claimed that traditional educational values were suffering as a result of a curriculum dominated by a left or liberal political agenda that was trying to be 'politically correct'.

Allan Bloom, *The Closing of the American Mind* (1987)

Bloom's book was one of the unlikeliest bestsellers of the 1980s. A philosopher and academic by trade, Bloom was little known outside academic circles before the publication of *The Closing of the American Mind*. His foremost academic achievement was his translation of *The Republic of Plato*, published in 1968. From this unpromising background Bloom became a fixture on the bestseller lists in 1987 and 1988 with a book that mixed philosophy and history with a jeremiad about America's contemporary higher education system and the nation's general cultural decline. The book's subtitle – 'How Higher Education Has Failed Democracy and Impoverished the Souls of Today's Students' – gives a flavour of what follows. The target of Bloom's attack is liberal and multicultural university education that no longer has any concern for the 'permanent concerns of mankind' and is instead obsessed with the 'spirit of the times'.[51] He is damning of an education system in which students are 'indoctrinated'[52] to the extent that they are 'unified only in their relativism and in their allegiance to equality.'[53] These are not positive values for Bloom. Relativism, for instance, 'has extinguished the real motive of education, the search for a good life',[54] while a belief in equality and an 'openness' towards other cultures and societies 'results in American conformism'.[55] No longer ethnocentric, US culture and education, Bloom believed, had replaced hard thinking about good and evil with what he calls 'value relativism'.[56] This was anathema to Bloom: 'History and the study of cultures do not teach or prove that values or cultures are relative . . . that is a philosophical premise that we now bring to our study of them. This premise is unproven and dogmatically asserted for what are largely political reasons.'[57] The origins of this sea change in American education Bloom locates squarely in the 1960s. A veteran of the Cornell University demonstrations of 1969 when armed black students took over University buildings and demanded changes to what was seen to be a Eurocentric curriculum, Bloom resigned his post in 1970 and, looking back from the mid-1980s, sees the submission to the student demands as that point when American universities gave up their belief in 'rational enquiry' and capitulated 'to a highly ideologized student populace'.[58]

The beginning and the end of the book are where Bloom is at his most vociferous and provocative. What comes in between is a philosophical justification for his argument and one which pits his beloved Greek philosophers against Enlightenment thinkers like Jean-Jacques Rousseau and German philosophy, particularly Nietzsche and Heidegger. Bloom is damning of the influence of German and French philosophy in the US. Their historicist traditions stand in opposition to the universalism Bloom admired in the Greeks. Bloom even goes so far as to compare the German university system of the 1930s after the rise to power of Hitler to what was happening in the 1960s in the US. Both 'abandoned all claim to study or inform about value – undermining the sense of the value of what it taught, while turning over the *decision* about values to the folk, the *Zeitgeist*, the relevant. Whether it be Nuremburg or Woodstock, the principle is the same.'[59] To compare a hippie festival with anti-Jewish legislation is obviously controversial, but arises out of Bloom's sense that his own beliefs are now minority ones in US higher education. This narrative of endangerment was a familiar one during the culture wars which gathered in the mid- to late 1980s and continued into the 1990s.

By ignoring the ways in which his own intellectual responses were themselves political or ideological, what Bloom provided in his book was the substantive philosophical rhetoric and knowledge to make the case against multicultural education all the more compelling. Bloom was not merely a critical voice: he was a believer in Great Books and himself a practitioner of the old way of doing things. This was undoubtedly part of the appeal of *The Closing of the American Mind*. For a neo-conservative audience increasingly confident and ready to listen after Reagan's re-election in 1984, Bloom took up the fight against multicultural and liberal education in terms which made it a matter of cultural survival: 'the crisis of liberal education is a reflection of a crisis at the peaks of learning, an incoherence and incompatibility among the first principles with which we interpret the world, an intellectual crisis of the greatest magnitude, which constitutes the crisis of our civilization.'[60] One of the paradoxes of the 1980s, of course, was that this rhetoric of crisis coincided not with liberal Democratic but with conservative Republican governance. As such, Bloom's stinging assault can be seen as the intellectual and conceptual branch of the effort to realign the US on conservative principles during this period and it gave rise to a series of books which carried on the process into the late 1980s and early 1990s, for example: E. D. Hirsch's, *Cultural Literacy* (1987); Roger Kimball, *Tenured Radicals* (1990); Dinesh D'Souza, *Illiberal Education: The Politics of Race and Sex On Campus* (1991); Arthur Schlesinger, *The Disuniting of America* (1991).

Like the narratives about successful but unhappy women, the debates about political correctness circulated extensively in the popular press and media and have led some, like James Davison Hunter and Todd Gitlin, to suggest that the culture wars of the 1980s and early 1990s were more a media phenomenon than a popular experience. Hunter may be right that the culture wars often operated as an exchange between knowledge workers. But the 1980s was a decade in which knowledge and information began to circulate more quickly and to penetrate further than ever before. And anybody who had access to a cinema or a video recorder could witness the destruction of Glenn Close's character in *Fatal Attraction*. One did not need to be a Harvard professor to see the connections the film was making between a woman of a certain age and the havoc she wreaks on family life.

In the chapters that follow, the intersection of this and the other contexts outlined here will be mapped out across a range of cultural forms and instances of cultural production. Fitting forms, texts and contexts, however, should not necessarily be a scientific process and the way in which ideas and discourses emerge within and around culture can often be complex and surprising. Different cultural forms will also have different relationships to particular contexts. What this book tries to avoid is establishing a rigid template within which American culture in the 1980s can be contained. The emphasis is upon suggesting certain approaches towards American culture. But as the 1980s is a period of study that still lacks the kind of critical heritage decades like the 1950s and 1960s have established, hopefully these approaches might provide a constructive starting point.

Chapter 1

Fiction and Poetry

The New Postmodernists

Writing a cultural history of a decade ultimately requires that a large amount of that decade's cultural production be neglected. This is as true of accounts which try to deconstruct overarching narratives of decades as it is of the narratives which helped to consolidate such definitions in the first place. One of the critical commonplaces institutionalized in the 1980s – in theoretical approaches such as poststructuralism, new historicism and cultural materialism – was that cultures tend to produce not only sufficient feedback to upset the possibility of a settled vision of a period, but also that the range of voices and positions represented within that culture fractures the possibility of unity. In the field of literature, many of these critical debates were played out in the study of Shakespeare and Elizabethan and Jacobean drama, the former treatment of which had long been dominated by a critical discourse emphasising what E. M. W. Tillyard famously described as the 'Elizabethan world picture'. In the literature of the US, although no such explicit 'world picture' existed, by the 1980s it became apparent that the category 'post-war American literature' was insufficient as anything but a nominal descriptor of work published since 1945. Not only was the phrase being stretched temporally, but also the coherent project towards which it gestured, and the hegemony of an influential group of writers – many of whom were still publishing during the 1980s – was losing explanatory value.

This chapter, then, does not consider the work of some of these writers. Saul Bellow, winner of the Nobel prize for Literature in 1976, was productive during the 1980s, publishing two novels (*The Dean's December*, 1982, and *More Die of Heartbreak*, 1987), two novellas (*A Theft* and *The Bellarosa Connection*, both 1989), along with a

collection of short stories – *Him with his Foot in his Mouth* (1984).
All were codas to a distinguished career that had peaked from
its beginning in *Dangling Man* (1944) all the way through to
Humboldt's Gift (1975). John Updike continued to be as productive
as ever, publishing novels, short stories and poetry, but revisited
familiar characters and themes. Norman Mailer, who had pioneered
the non-fiction novel with *Armies of the Night* (1968) and *The
Executioner's Song* (1979) after a series of novels in the 1940s and 50s,
produced little of note in the 1980s. *Ancient Evenings* (1983) was a
distended novel which tried to do for ancient Egypt what Melville did
for whales and whaling, while Mailer became best known during the
decade for championing convicted killer Jack Abbott's parole
request. Mailer helped him publish *In the Belly of the Beast*, the
letters he had written to Mailer while in prison. Six weeks after being
released from prison, and just after the publication of his book in
1981, Abbott murdered a restaurant waiter. Philip Roth published
several of his Zuckerman novels during the 1980s – *Zuckerman
Unbound* (1981), *The Anatomy Lesson* (1983), *The Prague Orgy*
(1985) and *The Counterlife* (1986) – but would produce far more
influential work in the 1990s and into the twenty-first century.
Thomas Pynchon produced nothing between *Gravity's Rainbow* in
1973 and *Vineland* in 1990, while John Barth and William Gaddis,
Pynchon's postmodernist fellow travellers, published work which
seemed not to take any further the work they had produced with
greater energy and effect in the 1950s, 60s and 70s.

From this perspective, the 1980s can be seen as a period when a
hugely influential generation of writers was in decline or, in the case of
Roth and, arguably, Pynchon, entering a fallow period from which they
would emerge rejuvenated in the 1990s. While these writers were still
residually important, different voices were emerging, some whose
writing careers began in the 1970s and earlier, others whose publishing
careers would begin – and peak – in the 1980s. A rainbow coalition of
interests and preoccupations, writers such as Don DeLillo, Toni
Morrison, Cormac McCarthy, Kathy Acker, David Mamet, Gloria
Anzaldúa, August Wilson, William Gibson, Bobbie Ann Mason,
Raymond Carver, Ron Silliman and Lyn Hejinian, have little in
common. Yet all their work, in one way or another, provides a fascinating mediation both of the 1980s itself and the way that longstanding discourses – about technology, history, race, gender and identity – are
reconfigured in the 1980s. They belong to a new literary generation
whose ties are loose but whose work is probing, difficult and powerful.

To group these writers together under the heading 'New Postmodernism' is not to suggest a new movement but to gesture towards the way in which the dominant modes of postmodernist writing were changing from the late 1970s. Postmodernist writing was certainly nothing new in American literature in the 1980s. If the formal experimentation of modernism was interrupted by the Second World War and its aftermath, it returned in the 1960s as male writers like Thomas Pynchon, John Barth, Kurt Vonnegut and Donald Barthelme fashioned fictional worlds firmly at odds with the more formally and thematically realist work of Jewish writers like Updike, Bellow and Mailer. Postmodern fictional worlds were often impossible places – physically and spatially – but constructed in a self-conscious manner that stopped them being classified as genre fiction like science fiction or fantasy. By turns absurd, playful and prodigiously knowledgeable, these fictions assembled information the quantity or contradictory nature of which was too much for any system to contain and often self-consciously defied resolution and interpretation. Size and virtuosity were central to the projects with which these fictions engaged. But by the mid-1970s, what John Barth, in 1967, called 'The Literature of Exhaustion' – the postmodernist response, inspired by Jorge Luis Borges and Samuel Beckett, to the used-upness of traditional literary forms – had exhausted itself. Pynchon's *Gravity's Rainbow* (1973) and William Gaddis' *JR: A Novel* (1975) represent the high-water mark of this postmodernist enterprise.

One of the features of the new postmodernism during the 1980s was a return to history. Never entirely absent from earlier American postmodernism – the history of Maryland had provided the opportunity for pastiche and satire in John Barth's *The Sot-Weed Factor* (1960) and the settings for Pynchon's *Gravity's Rainbow* were Second World War London and Germany – the engagement with history in the emerging works of fiction in the 1980s was less comic, more concerned with tracing the historical roots of the contemporary and with recovering marginal voices not always considered part of the historical record. The Canadian critic Linda Hutcheon, identifying a resurgence of historical fiction in the late 1970s and 1980s in both Europe and America, described much of this work as 'historiographic metafiction.'[1] It is metafiction in the sense that it self-reflexively contemplates the process of fictional representation – it is fiction that is about the writing of fiction – and it is historiographic in the sense that it asks the reader to consider how knowledge about the past is produced and circulated. For Hutcheon, 'Historiographic metafiction shows fiction to be historically conditioned and history to be discursively structured.'[2] Fictions in this mode retain the self-consciousness associated with postmodernism, but 'also both re-introduce historical context into metafiction and problematize the entire question of historical knowledge.'[3] They do this by using a variety of techniques: multiple narrators; overly controlling narrators whose perspective thus becomes suspect; mixing real-life characters with fictional characters; combining known incidents with invented incidents; and rewriting historical narratives.

In his 1987 novel *Libra*, Don DeLillo ventured into this terrain of historical fiction after the success of his previous novel *White Noise* (1985). Publishing novels since the early 1970s, DeLillo had until this point been a novelist steadfastly concerned with the contemporary American scene in all its vivid manifestations. His gestures towards history had circled around Hitler – *Running Dog* (1978) is about the rumoured existence of a pornographic film of Hitler; Jack Gladney in *White Noise* is Professor of Hitler Studies – but before *Libra* DeLillo had not dealt with historical settings or characters in his work. In *Libra*, DeLillo takes on one of the shaping historical moments of postwar US history, the assassination of John F. Kennedy in 1963. DeLillo's attraction to this story is founded not just on the historical significance of the event at a time when, as I pointed out in the Introduction, the 1960s is interpreted variously in the 1980s as a lost opportunity or a wrong turning, but also on the controversy surrounding the interpretation of the event itself. While the official investigation into Kennedy's shooting – the Warren Commission – concluded that Lee Harvey Oswald was solely responsible, popular suspicion of this verdict resulted in countless conspiracy theories that question the Commission's verdict. In many ways, then, the shooting of Kennedy – while historical fact – is clouded by interpretative uncertainty. The final report of the Commission is itself a narrative that tries to order events, testimonies and facts into a coherent form. It literally tries to construct the historical record.

DeLillo's novel revisits this historical record, and while the conclusions it reaches are similar – Oswald was acting alone, although he was a character easily manipulated – it arrives at them by entirely different narrative means. *Libra* is partly a fictionalized biography of Oswald, partly a fictionalized account of real-life characters – Win Everett, Lawrence Parmenter, Guy Banister and Jack Ruby amongst others – and also, crucially, the story of fictional CIA archivist Nicholas Branch, who spends his time in a 'book-filled room, the room of documents, the room of theories and dreams'[4] and whose task it is to 'write the secret history of the assassination of President Kennedy.'[5] As the novel opens, he has already been at work on the project for fifteen years. While Branch has little substantive presence in the narrative, his thoughts frame the novel's content and instigate a constant blurring of the boundaries between fiction and history. In one way *Libra* uses fiction to infuse witness testimony and historical characters like Oswald with a human quality, but it never does the job of settling the nature of these observations. When Branch returns at the end of the novel, the reader finds him still receiving new information that might modify the narrative he is trying to construct. And if 'the stuff keeps coming',[6] it is stuff in all kinds of forms: surveillance logs; television footage; FBI reports on the dreams of eyewitnesses after the assassination; novels about the assassination; radio debates. Branch feels compelled to study this material and believes 'it is essential to master the data',[7] but the overwhelming emphasis of DeLillo's novel, and what causes Branch to feel 'disheartened, almost immobilized',[8] is the inescapable sense that more information only modifies his secret history and means that it can never be completed, only continually revised.

Another major piece of fiction published in the 1980s that illustrated the return to history is Cormac McCarthy's fifth novel *Blood Meridian, or the Evening Redness in the West* (1985). Although McCarthy had already utilized historical settings in his earlier work (*The Orchard Keeper* (1965) is set in interwar Tennessee, *Outer Dark* (1968) in Appalachia at the turn of the twentieth century, and *Sutree* (1979) in 1951 Tennessee), *Blood Meridian* returns to a formative scene in the public imagination of US history: the mid-nineteenth-century West. McCarthy's West, however, is not the place of heroism or the story of survival against the elements. It is the story of a young man known only as 'the kid' who joins a scalp-hunting gang led by John Joel Glanton and which murders Indians on the US–Mexico border in order to claim the bounty offered by Governor Trias of Chihuahua. Unlike McCarthy's other novels, *Blood Meridian* is based on known historical sources, some of which are more reliable than others. Glanton was a US Army Ranger, a veteran of the Mexican War and a known Indian fighter and scalp hunter who appears in several historical documents. Alongside Glanton, however, stands the figure of Judge Holden who appears only in General Samuel Chamberlain's memoir, *My Confession*, which recounts Chamberlain's time with the Glanton gang after the end of the US–Mexico War. Various critics have noted the similarities between the Holden of Chamberlain's memoir and McCarthy's depiction of Holden,[9] but in bringing together a known historical figure like Glanton and a barely substantiated figure like Holden and treating them as partners with the same status in his narrative, McCarthy clearly seems to be fascinated by the gaps in the historical records and with offering the fictionalized means whereby those gaps might be imaginatively rather than objectively filled.

In recovering such marginalized figures of the West, McCarthy's novel also attempts to lift the veil on the history often forgotten or purposely ignored in the myth of Manifest Destiny that was used ideologically to justify the US settlement of the continent. McCarthy's novel is unremittingly violent, both in its representation of the scalping and killing committed by whites, Indians and Mexicans alike, and in its depiction of the landscape in which the many brutal events of the novel take place. Battle scenes are not redemptive in McCarthy's West but squalid and visceral. One ends as follows:

> Dust stanched the wet and naked heads of the scalped who with the fringe of hair below their wounds and tonsured to the bone now lay like maimed and naked monks in the bloodslaked dust and everywhere the dying groaned and gibbered and horses lay screaming.[10]

The unending repetition of these violent encounters reveals a Western history which has violence and murder at its very core and it means that *Blood Meridian* works both as a piece of imaginative fiction and a revisionist account of the West. Stylistically, McCarthy blurs the boundary between the contemporary 1980s novel and nineteenth-century sensational adventure story by carving out epic sentences with little punctuation and peppered with archaic vocabulary that heightens the intensity and pitch of his prose. Even the layout of the novel suggests a book from another time. The antique motif under each chapter number and the subheadings which presage the events of the chapter – 'Adrift on the Bolson de Mapimi – Sproule – Tree of dead babies – Scenes from a massacre' – are reminiscent of nineteenth-century novels.

Although they cover very different subject matter, then, both *Libra* and *Blood Meridian* intervene in the process by which history is known and understood. By doing so, they question the objectivity that history traditionally claimed to provide in its separation from fiction and as a result, and however unintentionally, DeLillo and McCarthy can be seen to be writing in the context of those 1980s culture-wars debates driven by an increasingly multicultural agenda in the US that itself sought to recover different narrative histories from those provided by mythic accounts of the nation's foundation and formation. The return to history in 1980s fiction affected not just writers of race and ethnicity, then, and whose work in this vein I consider later, but also the fiction of white male writers who would emerge during this decade as key successors to, and assume ascendancy over, Bellow, Mailer, Updike and Pynchon.

At the same time as history began to loom large in American fiction, a different cohort of white male writers was paying attention to the changing technological and consumer contexts of contemporary culture. The digital revolution that was beginning to alter the cultural forms circulating in the US – video recorders, CDs, computers – prompted early attempts by imaginative writers to assess the impact of this change on human bodies and lives. William Gibson's *Neuromancer* (1984) was one of the most influential examples of this and helped coin and circulate the terminology of cyberspace and the style of cyberpunk that would become a new literary genre in the hands of writers like Bruce Sterling, John Shirley, Pat Cadigan and Rudy Rucker. As well as regenerating science-fiction literature, the figure of the cyborg in much of this work also keyed into changes in the nature of capitalist production made evident in the Reaganomic restructuring of US capitalism. What the man in the gray flannel suit was to the 1950s, so the cyborg was to the 1980s. Whereas the suited white-collar worker of the 1950s engaged with capitalism in the office, the cyborg in Gibson's *Neuromancer* 'jacked into a custom cyberspace deck that projected his disembodied consciousness into the consensual hallucination that was the matrix.'[11] In many ways, Gibson's 'cyberspace' imagines a whole new territory which capitalism will need to dominate in order to solve the crisis point it reached in the 1970s. According to David Brande, 'Gibson's construction of cyberspace responds to the tendency toward crises of overaccumulation with a fantastic – although not entirely incredible – vision of limitless virtual space for market expansion.'[12]

Neuromancer also makes an interesting point of contrast with *Blood Meridian*, since while McCarthy revises our understanding of the nineteenth-century frontier, Gibson creates cyberspace as a new frontier on which works the novel's anti-hero Case, who is repeatedly imagined as a cowboy: 'Case was twenty-four. At twenty-two, he'd been a cowboy, a rustler, one of the best in the Sprawl.'[13] Similarly, Case embodies the attributes of the traditional cowboy – independence, anti-authoritarianism, risk-taking, virility – while his name, and particularly the narrative style, also suggest he follows in the footsteps of the cowboy's early twentieth-century urban successor, the hard-boiled detective epitomized in the work of Raymond Chandler and Dashiell Hammett:

> Case picked at a shred of bacon that lodged between his front teeth. He'd given up asking her where they were going and why; jabs in the ribs and the sign for silence were all he'd gotten in reply. She talked about the season's fashions, about sports, about a political scandal in California he'd never heard of.[14]

While Gibson was fashioning his genre fiction and attempting to push the boundaries of the science-fiction genre, other writers, working in a more realist mode, were producing fiction which tried to articulate thematically and stylistically the experience of commodification as it changed the face of American culture in the 1980s. The subject for much of this fiction was the lives of the wealthy and upwardly mobile urban elites best placed to take advantage of the economic upturns provided by Reaganomics and the redistribution of wealth from poor to rich that marked the 1980s. Collectively, this cluster of writers became known as the Brat Pack. Bret Easton Ellis, Jay McInerney, Tama Janowitz and Mark Lindquist produced a series of novels which, in the spirit of F. Scott Fitzgerald, testified to the decadence, excess and shallowness that marked the lifestyles of the contemporary rich. In *Less Than Zero* (1985), Ellis's narrator, Clay, returns from college to his Los Angeles home for the Christmas vacation and the novel follows him and his similarly affluent friends through a sequence of parties, bars and drug-fuelled casual relationships. Popular culture constantly punctuates the narrative as songs play on televisions and radios and characters play computer games and discuss films. Jay McInerney's *Bright Light, Big City* (1984), set in the world of New York style magazines, portrays a similar reliance on alcohol and drugs in the life of his nameless narrator. Tonally, both novels use a bleak and resigned register that testifies to the 'seen everything' lifestyles of their central characters. Mystery and desire in the novels are replaced by an ability to buy anything and low-level addiction. In one way, then, these novels are nihilistically pessimistic and might too easily be read as simple critiques of what commodified culture does to those who know life only through a credit card.

And yet, as James Annesley point outs, to read this kind of 'blank fiction' as merely a reflection of a social context is to miss the ways in which Ellis' and McInerney's writing 'concerns itself with the processes through which a text thematises contemporary conditions on structural, stylistic, linguistic and metaphorical levels.'[15] Commodified culture seeps into the very language of these fictions. While Ellis exemplified this in his 1990 novel *American Psycho*, where the listing of brand names replaces traditional methods of character description, he began the process in *Less Than Zero*. While Clay's mother shops at 'Neiman-Marcus' and his sisters at 'Jerry Magnin', he sits 'at the bar at La Scala Boutique for most of this time, bored out of my mind, smoking, drinking red wine.'[16] His psychiatrist drives 'a 450 SL'[17] and Clay drinks Perrier rather than mineral water. The brand names of consumer culture become integral to the language of the novel rather than just objects on which Ellis is commenting; they are the very texture of the contemporary world. Rather than equating blankness, or the stylistic reliance on the language of commodification, with fiction's bankruptcy in the face of consumerism, then, the fiction of Ellis and McInerney offers new and important literary responses to this process.

While Ellis and McInerney's response to consumer culture and commodification may have been the dominant one, it was not shared by all writers. Nicholson Baker's *The Mezzanine* (1988) is a coruscating narrative about the interdependence of personal identity and the products of consumer culture. A minimalist work in the sense that the entire narrative spins out from the length of time it takes Howie, the narrator, to travel from the bottom to the top of an escalator, stylistically the novel owes more to Marcel Proust than it does to a disaffected blank realism. Howie builds his personal and private life during the novel in the context of his relation to the public, very often mass-produced, corporate, multinational objects such as shoelaces, drinking straws, staplers and doorknobs, which endlessly circulate around him. In doing so, Baker rescues the ephemera of everyday life from the texturelessness and familiarity of brand names and imbues them, through a stylistic homage to the long sentence, with a weight and significance they have rarely been given elsewhere. For Howie, life is nothing without the 'things' that Peter Stallybrass has argued are often subordinated to the life of the mind, 'As if consciousness and memory were about minds rather than things, or the real could only reside in the permeated impurity of the material.'[18] For Howie 'things' are the starting points for the representation of his life. The exploration of how consumer products signify is also one element of the novel that introduced Don DeLillo to a wider audience in the 1980s.

Don DeLillo, *White Noise* (1985)

With the publication of *White Noise* in 1985, Jayne Anne Phillips remarked in her review of the novel, 'the fiction of Don DeLillo is no longer the well-kept secret of a dedicated following.'[19] The success of *White Noise* as a novel is dependent on two factors. First of all it possesses a tonal ambiguity which illustrates the quirky, comic and often disturbing nature of life in high-tech, mass culture, contemporary America without ever imposing a moral or ethical framework in order to pass judgement on that world. In this way, and through a process of defamiliarization, the novel genuinely illuminates the context of its production. Neither does *White Noise* parody the cultural moment it is representing, despite the many opportunities where parody might seem appropriate: in the department of Hitler Studies, of which the narrator Jack Gladney is founder and chair; in Jack's visit, with his Elvis-obsessed colleague Murray Siskind to THE MOST PHO-TOGRAPHED BARN IN AMERICA; or in Jack's trips with his wife, Babette, and their children to the supermarket. Instead, the novel's mode is ironic: the trappings of a culture which might too easily be dismissed as superficial are invested with weight, importance and often awe. While Jack's position is often one of scepticism, his friendship with Murray constantly keeps him in the orbit of a different, and more embracing, centre of consciousness. So while Jack hears the sound of feet in the supermarket aisles as 'a sad numb shuffle',[20] when he meets Murray there, he also recognizes its 'dense environmental texture'[21] and is jealous of his son Wilder's ability to experience the world as 'a series of fleeting gratifications' where he 'took what he could, then immediately forgot it in the rush of the subsequent pleasure. It was this forgetfulness I envied and admired.'[22]

Allied to Jack Gladney's fearful but inquisitive narration, *White Noise* also interweaves a series of themes which together provide access to a post-modernist landscape replete with transformations in the nature of every-day life that lead to new challenges and dilemmas. Most notably, *White Noise* dramatizes the move into a culture of simulation where reality is constantly mediated. THE MOST PHOTGRAPHED BARN IN AMERICA is important not because of any qualities it possesses as a barn, but because of what Murray calls 'a collective perception'.[23] The signs that lead Jack and Murray to the barn's location and proclaim it as the most photographed barn make it 'impossible to see the barn', only the 'aura' that surrounds it now: 'we've read the signs, seen the people snapping the pictures. We can't get outside the aura.'[24] Picking up Jean Baudrillard's understanding of the simulacrum in advanced capitalist economies where objects and images are copies of copies without originals, meaning accrues for many of the characters in *White Noise* only through the exchange values of the signs associated with objects and events. And it is television which becomes the medium for the exchange of signs.

Almost another character in the novel, the voice of television constantly interferes with the flow of information in the Gladney household while advertising brand names litter the narrative. Jack walks past a woman on the street whose language sounds like an advertisement – 'a decongestant, an antihistamine, a cough suppressant, a pain reliever'[25] – while Steffie, Jack's daughter, mutters 'Toyota Celica' in her sleep.[26] At the heart of the novel is a simulated evacuation of the town which is actually a response to a real emergency – the airborne toxic event. So far have the boundaries between reality and simulation blurred, that SIMUVAC views the real evacuation as a practice for a simulated evacuation.

As well as the world of simulation, *White Noise* illustrates the knowledge economy of higher education in a period when the kind of knowledge considered important shifts away from traditional disciplines into specialized fields, and also considers the state of family life as it enters a non-nuclear stage and intergenerational relationships where the world is often a more comfortable place for children than parents. But the novel completes its thematic cycle by introducing into this postmodernist scene a more philosophical issue which contrasts sharply with the exchange culture of contemporary capitalism: the fear of death. Babette embarks on a duplicitous affair with the shadowy figure of Dr Gray in order that he will give her Dylar, a drug that is meant to counteract her fear of death, while Jack's fear of dying begins to dominate his life after he is infected by the airborne toxic event. But if the juxtaposition of the superficial and the immutable in *White Noise* suggests a close relationship between the two, then the novel does not offer ready answers as to what this relationship might be. The tonal ambiguity and irony which dominate the narration suggest possible answers are pragmatic and rooted in the everyday rather than principled positions of faith.

Dirty Realism

While Ellis and McInerney were writing from and about the metropolitan centres which house and service US social elites, other writers were emerging whose focus was on the often unseen blue-collar worlds far away from New York and Los Angeles. These writers were grouped together under the label 'Dirty Realism'. While it attempted to connect many different writers, this label is perhaps just as interesting because it marked a moment of literary classification in 1980s transatlantic culture. Dirty Realism first appeared as a category in the eighth issue of the new *Granta*, a literary journal that had been published out of Cambridge University since the 1880s, but which was revamped in 1979 as a magazine for new writing. The first issue of the new series was titled *New American Writing* and reflected the interests of its editor and publisher Bill Buford, an expatriate American. What is notable about this first issue, however, is that while it claims to represent 'new' American writing, with the

exception of Paul Auster's 'The Red Notebook' the issue really looks
back at the kind of postmodernist writing – included work by John
Hawkes, William Gass, Donald Barthelme and Ronald Sukenick –
that would lose relevance during the 1980s. In 1983, after its June
issue selected what it considered the best twenty young British
writers, issue eight was titled *Dirty Realism: New Writing from
America*. Distancing himself for the kind of work which had dominated the first issue, in his editorial Buford makes both exceptionalist and periodizing claims about Dirty Realism. Not only is it 'unlike
anything currently written in Britain', he notes, but it is 'also remark-
ably unlike what American fiction is usually understood to be': it is
not heroic in the tradition of Bellow or Mailer; nor is it playfully
postmodern like Barth, Gaddis or Pynchon.[27] Instead, Buford identifies criteria he thinks mark out this work from anything that has
preceded it. Dirty Realism, for Buford, is 'devoted to the local details,
the nuances, the little disturbances in language and gesture',[28] while
the stories it narrates are

> unadorned, unfurnished, low-rent tragedies about people who watch
> day-time television, read cheap romances or listen to country and
> western music. They are waitresses in roadside cafés, cashiers in super-
> markets, construction workers, secretaries and unemployed cowboys
> . . . They are from Kentucky or Alabama or Oregon, but, mainly, they
> could just about be from anywhere: drifters in a world cluttered with
> junk food and the oppressive details of modern consumerism.[29]

It is not just content that marks out this writing. Buford identifies a 'flat,
"unsurprised" language, pared down to the plainest of plain styles . . . it
is what's not being said – the silences, the elisions, the omissions – that
seems to speak most.'[30]

  While these are interesting enough comments that I will return to
below, it is also worth noting that Buford concludes his introduction
to the collection that follows with a thanks to Penguin Books for
their new co-publication deal with Granta that started with the previous issue. Taken over in 1970 by Pearson, an international media
group, during the 1970s and 1980s Penguin embarked on an expansion programme that saw it buy out the UK publishers Michael
Joseph and Hamish Hamilton and gain a substantial foothold in the
US through a merger with Viking Press in 1975 and the acquisitions
of New American Library and Dutton Books in 1986 and The
Putnam Berkley Group to form Penguin Putnam Inc. in 1996. In

the spirit of this entrepreneurial expansion, Buford's coining of the phrase Dirty Realism was clearly designed to attract literary and publishing attention. As the previous issue had made clear, *Granta* was in the business of talent-spotting and trend-setting. The question it raises is whether Raymond Carver, Jayne Anne Phillips, Bobbie Ann Mason, Richard Ford and Tobias Wolff represent an exercise in branding more than they represent a new literary school, movement, or style.

The answer is probably somewhere between the two. I have already suggested that postmodernism in its more expansive mode ran out of steam at the end of the 1970s, although writers like T. Coraghessan Boyle, William Vollman and David Foster Wallace would emerge in the 1980s as inheritors of this tradition. The so-called Dirty Realists identified by Buford are in many ways literary minimalists reacting against extravagant and disjointed postmodernist narratives and drawing on an American storytelling tradition that incorporated a diverse range of stylists, from Ernest Hemingway and John Steinbeck and southern writers like Flannery O'Connor to the hard-boiled prose fiction of Chandler and Jim Thompson. But neither was publishing any longer an industry that could escape the cult of celebrity or the cycles of fashion as publishing houses were increasingly incorporated under the wings of large, often multinational, multimedia enterprises. *Granta* may only have been one small element in that market but its link-up with Penguin helped foster this classificatory impulse. It certainly helped to circulate the Dirty Realist tag both in the UK and the US.

Raymond Carver is the writer most closely associated with Dirty Realism. By the time his first collection of stories was published in 1976, Carver had already published two volumes of poetry. Carver would never publish a novel, but instead found the shorter literary forms well suited to the minimalist aesthetic he crafted over the years. His fiction published during the 1980s – *What We Talk About When We Talk About Love* (1981), *Cathedral* (1983) and *Elephant* (1988) – amounts to the most consistent illustration of the principles laid out by Buford. 'Preservation', from *Cathedral*, tells the story of Sandy and her unnamed husband who is laid off from his job as a roofer one Valentine's Day. Their reaction to this news is typical of the 'unsurprised' language about which Buford writes. They drink the whiskey and chocolates he has bought Sandy as a Valentine's gift and 'They talked about what he might be able to do instead of putting roofs on new houses. But they couldn't think of anything. "Something will turn up," Sandy said.'[31] Nothing does turn up and Sandy's husband spends his days on the sofa, reading the print off the newspaper and watching the television. A broken refrigerator becomes the central focus of the story. Replacing it with a new one is more than they can afford. Sandy finds an advertisement in the paper for a new and used appliance barn auction. She determines she will go and that all the food in the freezer compartment of the refrigerator needs to be cooked to save it from spoiling. The story ends with Sandy looking at her husband's feet in a pool of water which has dripped on to the floor from the food packing on the table above: 'She knew she'd never again in her life see anything so unusual. But she didn't know what to make of it yet.'[32]

Carver's minimalist style relies upon a refusal to explore the psychological thoughts and motivations of his characters. Simple description and dialogue forbid this. What Buford is gesturing towards when he suggests that the silences are the most important aspect of Dirty Realist writing is precisely this wilful failure to articulate thoughts and feelings – which is not to say that these thoughts and feelings do not exist. Endings such as that in 'Preservation' do not deny depth, but instead they question the distinction between surface and depth and in many ways force the two to coexist at the same level. As indeed does the whole story. The incidents and details Carver recounts are not trivial but the place in which the lives of his characters are shaped and performed. Surface is depth in Carver's fiction. The 'Preservation' of the title may well refer to Sandy's attempts to salvage what she can from the broken refrigerator, but it also clearly refers to the problems with her marriage and how her relationship with her husband might possibly be saved. Broken and breaking relationships form the cornerstone of Carver's work; his fiction is acutely aware of how relationships work, not at the level of grand passion and romantic love, but at the level of the ordinary, the everyday and the familiar. The prospect that her husband might spend the next thirty years on the sofa strikes Sandy not with a determination to do something about it, but with shame. By accepting that she can say no more about it to her friend for fear of rebuke, Sandy accommodates her husband's acceptance of his joblessness as the foreseeable future of her day-to-day life. The fact that this irritates her is never made plain by Carver. Instead, one is left to sense it through Sandy's reactions to the sound of the TV around the house, the sign that her husband is on the sofa, not working, and ultimately not looking for work. The memory of her parents that the barn auction inspires is likewise undetermined by the narrative. All the reader is given is small details. After Sandy tells her husband she used to go to auctions with her father, 'She suddenly wanted to go to this auction very much.'[33] The reader also learns that her parents divorced and Sandy lived with her mother. But how these details link together and impact on how Sandy understands her own marriage is left untouched by Carver.

All of the potential thematic concerns in Carver's fiction are promoted to the level of literary style. If the 'unsurprised' nature of this style has affinities with the blank fiction of writers like Bret Easton Ellis, then the connections between them might lead to the consideration of Dirty Realism as another arm of postmodernist writing in the US. The French critic Jean-François Lyotard argued in *The Postmodern Condition: A Report on Knowledge* (originally published in 1979 but not translated into English until 1984) that one of the features of the condition of postmodernity is an increasing distrust of large explanatory ideas – or metanarratives – like religion, science, historical progress, freedom as ways of understanding the world. In their place, Lyotard argues, there is a turn to smaller, more localized narratives – or *petit récits*.[34] Just as writers like DeLillo and McCarthy undermine the possibility of objectively knowing the past, so writers like Carver write about the commonplace and everyday in the face of this distrust. In a similar vein, Philip E. Simmons has suggested that in American postmodernist fiction, 'gestures toward "depth" of historical understanding are continually returned to the "surface" of postmodern image culture with its rejection of epistemological foundations and master narratives.'[35]

In some ways, so closely do the tenets of Dirty Realism fit the work of Raymond Carver that once one begins to look at other writers the category is not so easily applicable. Richard Ford's early fiction, the novels *A Piece of My Heart* (1976) and *The Ultimate Good Luck* (1981), are necessarily more expansive and owe more to the legacy of southern fiction and hard-boiled detective fiction than can be seen in Carver. *The Sportswriter* (1986) develops the existential elements noticeable in Ford's earlier writing. The story of a sports journalist grieving the death of his son, the novel's central character, Frank Bascombe, would reappear in Ford's Pulitzer prize-winning novel *Independence Day* (1995). It is only in his short-story collection, *Rock Springs* (1987), that Ford approaches the pared-down style and attenuated detail of Carver. Jayne Anne Phillips published her first novel, *Machine Dreams*, in 1984 and a collection of short stories,

Fast Lanes, in 1987. *Machine Dreams* is a historical family chronicle stretching over seventy years and explicitly embedded in the kinds of historical contexts, most particularly the Vietnam War, eschewed by Carver. Although Phillips mines the same small-town, blue-collar seams as Carver for her characters, the writing style in much of her work is also more lyrical and poetic than Buford's definition of Dirty Realism allows. A narrow understanding of Dirty Realism, then, might misunderstand a commonality of theme, character type and setting for a commonality of style. Carver, Ford and Phillips write very differently about similar issues and character types. What connects them is a much broader return to realist modes of literary representation and a concern with class that often gets blurred by narratives about the 1980s that highlight the winners in the economic shakeout and a culture of urban excess rather than those who experienced the downside of economic change away from the urban centres.

Bobbie Ann Mason, *In Country* (1985)

The daughter of Kentucky dairy farmers, Bobbie Ann Mason began publishing fiction only after she had established a career as a literary academic, writing books on Vladimir Nabokov and the detective heroines of children's fiction during the 1970s. In her own fiction, Mason returned to her native Kentucky and a series of working-class characters for whom the struggles of everyday life are accompanied by the soundtrack of consumer culture. In 'Still Life With a Watermelon', the story which appeared in *Granta*'s Dirty Realist issue, the protagonist, Louise Milsap, has lost her job at a supermarket, while her husband has left her to live in Texas. She spends her time painting while her housemate 'reads Harlequin romances and watches TV simultaneously'[36] with Dixieland music playing in the background.

The gendered experience of estrangement and the mediation of one's personal life through consumer culture are key themes in Mason's first novel, *In Country*. Set during the summer of 1984, 'the summer of the Michael Jackson *Victory* tour and the Bruce Springsteen *Born in the U.S.A* tour',[37] the novel revolves around seventeen-year-old Sam Hughes who lives with her uncle Emmett. Sam's mother has moved to Lexington to remarry, while her father was killed in the Vietnam War before she was born. Sam spends her time during the summer obsessively watching the TV series *M*A*S*H*, worrying about the health of her unemployed uncle and coming to terms with her fading affection for her boyfriend, Lonnie. But this is also the summer that Sam 'started thinking about war'.[38] Although set during the Korean War, *M*A*S*H* brought home vividly to a domestic audience between 1972 and 1983 the human cost of the most recent US war in Asia. It is also one of the shows Sam used to watch with her mother as a child.[39] Springsteen's *Born in the U.S.A* is, as Sam tells her best friend Dawn, a song about a working-class Vietnam veteran: ' "Yeah. In the song, his brother gets killed over there, and then the guy gets in a lot of trouble when he gets back home. He can't get a job, and he ends up in jail. It's a great song." '[40] Emmet is a veteran himself and is plagued by fears, which then pass to Sam, that he may have been contaminated by Agent Orange on the battlefield. Vietnam, then, haunts Mason's narrative and marks that point where history and context, particularly the 1960s, intervene in contemporary life during the early 1980s.

The novel is book-ended by two short sections which relate the journey of Sam, Emmet and Sam's grandmother to Washington to visit the Vietnam Veterans Memorial. While the cheap motels they stay in and Sam's ailing car are the familiar territory of Dirty Realism, the evocation of Sam's desire to forge an understanding of her dead father and Emmett's attempts to come to terms with his time in Vietnam, that provide the impetus for this journey, take the novel beyond such easy categorization. After reading her father's diary, in which he reports in a matter-of-fact manner killing a Vietnamese soldier, Sam – confused and angry and disappointed with her father – retreats to Cawoods Pond to try and simulate the experience of being 'in country', the phrase given to being in Vietnam during the war. Cawoods Pond 'was the last place in western Kentucky where a person could really face the wild'[41] and it is where Sam contemplates the gendered nature of war: 'Women didn't kill . . . To hell with all of them – Lonnie, her dad, her uncle, her grandfathers.'[42] If the US could be accused of exporting the myth of Manifest Destiny in its ideological justification of war in South East Asia, then Mason intriguingly reverses this process and imports the frontier back to Kentucky for Sam to experience. Although it is a pale imitation of the real thing it is sufficient for Sam to come to terms with the forces driving the attitudes and actions of her father and enough for her to accept the complex, rather than idealistic, life that her missing father led before his death.

As Kenneth Millard has pointed out, the trip to Washington brings 'the margins of culture to the nation's capital as a way of showing that small-town life is of national significance', but it is also true to say that books like *In Country* and the literature of Dirty Realism can show how national and international events impact at a regional and local level and manifest themselves in the seemingly ordinary and everyday.[43] The centrality of consumer culture both to *In Country* and to the work of a writer like Bret Easton Ellis witnesses the reach and penetration of contemporary capitalism. What remains fascinating is the way that this material is shaped into such differing literary responses.

Race, Ethnicity and Gender

In a recent edition of the *New York Times*, over one hundred 'prominent writers, critics, editors and other literary sages' nominated Toni

Figure 1.1 Emily Lloyd in the film adaptation of *In Country*, set in the year of 'the Bruce Springsteen *Born in the U.S.A* tour' (Norman Jewison, Warner Bros, 1989). © Warner Bros/The Kobal Collection.

Morrison's *Beloved* (1987) as 'the single best work of American fiction published in the last 25 years', ahead of Don DeLillo's *Underworld* (1997) and Cormac McCarthy's *Blood Meridian* (1985).[44] If the recovery and reassessment of an African American writing tradition – from Olaudah Equiano and Phillis Wheatley in the eighteenth century, through Fredrick Douglass and Harriet Jacobs and the slave narrative genre of the nineteenth century, the Harlem Renaissance poets and novelists of the early twentieth century and the civil rights-era work of Gwendolyn Brooks, Richard Wright, Ralph Ellison and James Baldwin – was an important feature of US cultural activity from the 1960s onwards, the popular and critical success of Morrison's *Beloved* meant that it achieved that rarest of accolades: becoming, almost instantaneously and at most within the space of a few years, a 'classic' text in the sense that it was quickly taken up in higher-education teaching as well as achieving a wider audience through its success in winning the Pulitzer prize for Fiction in 1988 and propelling Morrison towards the Nobel prize for Literature in 1993.

The author of four novels before *Beloved* (*The Bluest Eye*, 1970; *Sula*, 1973; *Song of Solomon*, 1977; *Tar Baby*, 1981), Morrison is another writer whose career began before the 1980s, but reached its crescendo during that decade. Morrison had also worked in university education, teaching English at Texas Southern University and Howard University in the 1950s and early 1960s, before entering the publishing industry and becoming an editor at Random House in New York where she helped publish the work of African American writers like Toni Cade Bambara and Gayl Jones. Morrison's background, then, is both intellectual and intertwined with the process of promoting African American voices in US culture. Her fiction is similarly steeped in an American literary tradition that embraces canonical nineteenth-century writers like Melville and Hawthorne but whose primary purpose is the recovery of black experience. In this, Morrison can be considered alongside other important African American intellectual voices of the 1980s, the most prominent of which was Henry Louis Gates Jr, who taught at Yale and Cornell during the 1980s and reshaped the study of African American literature with his books *Figures in Black: Words, Signs, and the Racial Self* (1987) and especially *The Signifying Monkey: Towards A Theory of Afro-American Literary Criticism* (1988). Gates' theoretical reassessments of African American literature went hand in hand with vigorous attempts to recover and create archives of historical African American literature. Gates helped found the Black Periodical Literature Project in 1980 and in 1983 he republished Harriet E. Wilson's *Our Nig*, the first novel to be published in the US by an African American but ignored and lost since its original publication in 1859. At the end of the 1980s, Gates became embroiled in the trial of rap group 2 Live Crew who were charged with obscenity for some of their songs' lyrics. Gates defended the group on the basis that they were following in an African American tradition of parody and hyperbole.

While Morrison's earlier novels are set in the past, *Beloved* was the first to go back to the nineteenth century. In many ways, it is a novel of recovery and returns attention, just like Gates had done with *Our Nig* and his Black Periodical Literature Project, to a time just before and just after the Civil War and the abolition of slavery. It is also a novel which engages with the historical record, since it is based on the story of Margaret Garner (Sethe in the novel), an escaped slave who murdered her daughter rather than see her returned to slavery and who attempted to kill herself and her other children in order to avoid the same fate but was stopped before she could do so. Also the subject of Thomas Satterwhite Noble's painting *The Modern Medea* (1867), Garner was tried not for murder but for the destruction of property and returned to slavery. Morrison changes the known details of Garner's life in several ways but, rather than just investigating the events of Garner's escape and

return, projects Garner's life into the future to imagine the undocu-
mented legacy of these events and, most hauntingly, the return of the
murdered child, Beloved, to Sethe's house at 124 Bluestone Road,
Cincinnati. The imaginative creation of this after-story serves several
purposes. Not only does it allow Morrison to engage the historical consequences of the trauma of slavery in the post-Civil War nation, but as
a contemporary novel it also demands to be read at a broader cultural
and allegorical level: not only is Sethe haunted by the trauma of the
actions forced upon her by slavery, but so the legacy of slavery haunts
the story of African American and US national culture right up to the
present day. Just as DeLillo and McCarthy complicate the process by
which the historical record is written and knowledge of it circulates, so
Morrison utilises similar postmodernist literary techniques to politicise
US history and race relations to write into the record the complex ways
in which slavery does not cease to be felt even after abolition, reconstruction and the Civil Rights crusades.

   Beloved also revolves around certain themes that have become associated with slavery's legacy, notably trauma – the violence, rape and
murder on which slavery relied – and the separation of families caused
by the buying and selling of people as property. At the opening of the
novel, Sethe's two young sons have already run away: 'as soon as merely
looking in a mirror shattered it (that was the signal for Buglar); as soon
as two tiny hand prints appeared in the cake (that was it for Howard).
Neither boy waited to see more.'[45] The ghost of Beloved is the manifes-
tation of slavery in its post-abolition state: as spectre, as haunting and as
ideological terror. The book's dedication – 'Sixty Million and more' – is
a reminder of the scale of the trauma of slavery and invests Morrison's
imaginative recovery of history with a social awareness that is made
abstract in DeLillo and McCarthy. Morrison also brings to her fiction a
Faulknerian sense of the rootedness of experience in family, history and
place. The centrality of 124 Bluestone Road to the return of Beloved
signals the way in which domestic space, a place most closely associated
with women in the ideology of gender, is itself riven with conflicts of
history. Allied to all of this is Morrison's ability to resist a centre of consciousness in her fiction. There are many voices in her work, but, rather
than ordering them in a hierarchy of reliability and truthfulness,
Morrison passes their stories to the reader seemingly unmediated. In
Beloved, Paul D.'s memories are not a corrective to Sethe's, but an alternative which offers potential for moving forward.

   Morrison's fiction stands as perhaps the most influential of a series of
writings by African American women in the 1980s. Although less inter-

esting in terms of form and style, Alice Walker's *The Color Purple* (1982), which tells the story of the sexual and physical abuse of women by African American men, was an incredibly successful novel, winning the Pulitzer prize for Fiction in 1983 and attracting the attention of Steven Spielberg and Oprah Winfrey who made and starred in the 1985 film version. Gloria Naylor began her publishing career in the 1980s with three important novels – *The Women of Brewster Place* (1982), *Linden Hills* (1985) and *Mama Day* (1988) – which emphasize the diversity of female black experience and the impact of class divisions not only between white and black but within the black community itself.

Alongside these African American voices during the 1980s emerged fictions from ethnic groups with an even less well-established literary inheritance in the US. Fear of Chinese immigration in the nineteenth century, which led to a series of Chinese Exclusion Acts, and the twentieth-century wars with Japan, Korea and Vietnam, meant that the place of Asian Americans within the US was a vexed one. Denied full rights of citizenship and naturalization until 1965, it was only after this point, and as part of the multiculturalization of US higher education in the 1960s and 1970s, that Asian Studies programmes sprang up together with African and African American Studies programmes, particularly on the West Coast of the US at the University of California, and at San Francisco and California State universities. These programmes helped vitalize the presence of Asian American literature in the US and in 1975, the publication of Maxine Hong Kingston's *The Woman Warrior* marked a breakthrough in the wider visibility of Asian American literature. A mixture of autobiography and fiction, *The Woman Warrior* fuses memories of Kingston's Chinese ancestry with her experiences of growing up in the US as the child of first-generation immigrants. It incorporates elements of Chinese folklore and storytelling to investigate the issues of gender, ethnicity and assimilation. In *China Men* (1980), Kingston worked in a similar mode, mixing historical details of early California and Hawaii with accounts of the influential men in her life. Kingston's first novel, *Tripmaster Monkey: His Fake Book* (1989), is a complex novel set in California in the 1960s. It has metafictional qualities and follows the attempts of Wittman Ah Sing to write an epic novel based on Chinese legends and tales. Wittman's name is, of course, suggestive of the American poet who, in the nineteenth century, was writing about the connections between the US and Asia in poems like 'Passage to India' and urging Americans to voice their new selves in 'One's-Self I Sing'. Wittman Ah Sing is clearly, then, meant to be an ethnic hero in an American tradition at the same time as he illustrates, through his journeys round California, all the obstacles preventing him being considered 'American'.

Amy Tan, like Kingston the child of Chinese immigrants, published one of the bestselling Asian American novels, *The Joy Luck Club*, in 1989. A collection of stories told by the mothers and daughters from four immigrant families while eating and playing Mahjong, Tan's novel addresses the importance of generational change in the immigrant experience. The daughters are US-born and face very different experiences from their mothers who have gone through the process of moving and having to adapt to a new culture. For Jing-mei, an unfamiliarity with her Chinese ancestry often confuses her and leaves her alienated from other members of her Chinese family, while for Waverly Jong, her mother's interference in her life is a source of tension. These generational issues surrounding assimilation would become an important feature in the Asian American literature of the 1990s written by the likes of Chang-rae Lee and Gish Jen. Tan's emphasis on the female experience of ethnicity in the US also draws on a Western feminism that intersects uncomfortably with traditional Chinese understandings of gender roles and helps to emphasize the different traditions in which second- and later-generation Asian Americans are growing up.

The work of Kingston and Tan has not, however, escaped criticism from within the Asian American community. Frank Chin, in the introduction to *The Big Aiiieeeee!*, an anthology of Chinese and Japanese American writing published in 1991, distinguished between what he called 'real' and 'fake' Asian American writers. He attacked Kingston and Tan for fabricating the supposedly Chinese folklore they draw on in their work and argues that it is not true that Chinese immigrants lose touch with their Chinese literary and folk traditions that Kingston and Tan then take it upon themselves to recover. More seriously, Chin's charge is that Kingston and Tan are successful because their faking of Asian American history appeals to and reinforces white stereotypes of Asian Americans.[46] Chin's anthology, co-edited with Jeffrey Paul Chan, Lawson Fusao Inada and Shawn Wong, marked an important intervention in the visibility of Asian American literature and part of its remit was to provide access to more authentic and undiscovered writing. While the criticisms of Kingston and Tan may have an element of truth, Chin's reaction can be seen as part of that process whereby the early acceptance and popularity of Asian American writing is dismissed by a subsequent generation eager to stake their own claim to understand more fully the range of Asian American voices. It signals, then, the point at which Asian American culture is entrenched enough to begin disagreeing with itself.

Gloria Anzaldúa, *Borderlands/La Frontera: The New Mestiza* (1987)

One of the problems with discussing Asian American literature is the imprecision of the word 'Asian', which is used to cover a broad geographical area and many different traditions and experiences that make questionable the extent to which a common experience might be shared. Hispanic culture in the US shares this problem. Immigration from counties in southern and central America had long been a feature of US demographic change but in 1980, the US Bureau of the Census attracted attention to Hispanic immigration when it highlighted the fact that Hispanics were the fastest-growing section of the US population. By far the largest source of this immigration was Mexico. The history of the relations between Mexico and the US and the place of Mexico in American culture is a complex one. Texas split off from Mexico in 1836 to become an independent republic, only joining the US in 1845. After the Mexican–American war of 1846–48 (the aftermath of which is the setting for McCarthy's *Blood Meridian*), Mexico lost not only claims to Texas, but also land that is now California, Nevada and New Mexico, as well as parts of what are now Utah, Arizona and Colorado. Many of the Mexicans living in these areas stayed and became part of the US and found themselves living in a strange space that has given rise to a popular motif of the border as a scar in the history of Mexican American identity.[47]

In *Borderlands/La Frontera*, Gloria Anzaldúa describes this scar as a

> 1,950 mile-long open wound
> dividing a pueblo, a culture
> running down the length of my body
> staking fence rods in my flesh [48]

As someone who has grown up on the Mexican–American border, Anzaldúa sees it as a place where 'the Third world grates against the first and bleeds. And before a scab forms it hemorrhages again, the lifeblood of two worlds merging to form a third country – a border culture.'[49] What this culture produces is 'tension', which 'grips the inhabitants of the borderlands like a virus' and where 'death is no stranger.'[50] What it makes impossible, however, because of the constant migrations across the border, is a sense of fixed or stable identities. Anzaldúa creates herself as the new *mestiza*: a woman of mixed racial ancestry. And rather than seeing her identity as a victim of border tensions, Anzaldúa fashions the notion of the new *mestiza* as a figure who draws on the history of Mexican women's resistance and for whom 'Living on border and in margins, keeping intact one's shifting and multiple identity and integrity, is like trying to swim in a new element . . . There is an exhilaration in being a participant in the further evolution of humankind, in being "worked" on.'[51] Anzaldúa uses spatial metaphors to suggest fluidity, transformation and multiple identities in the 'New West' in which old binary oppositions such as North/South, Anglo/Hispanic, Anglo/Indian, male/female no longer apply.

The generic hybridity of *Borderlands/La Frontera* makes Anzaldúa's work in some ways similar to Kingston's *The Woman Warrior*. Mixing memoir, history, poetry and polemic – Anzaldúa's lesbian feminism is a key part of her *mestza* identities – the book not only excavates a historical but also a personal past and places the individual in history. It combines this with a commitment to the importance of the imaginative realm of identity. The border for Anzaldúa is not just a physical space but the point at which geography intersects with the psychological and the spiritual and the linguistic. 'If you want to really hurt me, talk badly about my language', she writes, stating that 'Ethnic identity is twin skin to linguistic identity – I am my language. Until I take pride in my language, I cannot take pride in myself.'[52] *Borderland/La Frontera* can also be read, therefore, as an attempt to fashion a kind of language which will bestow pride both on her and other *mestiza* in similar situations.

Both a recovery narrative and a blueprint for future development, *Borderland/La Frontera* appeared at a key moment in the history of Hispanics in the US. It was published in the same year as the Tower Commission Report, the investigation into the sales of weapons to Iran and the transfer of the proceeds of these sales to the Contra guerrillas in Nicaragua who were plotting the downfall of the democratically elected government. The vigour with which the Reagan administration policed the borders of central America, under the fear that communism would spread quickly across these borders, was often at odds with the feelings of Hispanic groups within the US and sat uneasily with those corporations beginning to rely on the cheap immigrant labour that Hispanics often provided and would increasingly provide in the 1990s and into the twenty-first century. Anzaldúa's truly multicultural voice emerges from this complex situation with clarity and insight. While twenty years later it seems at times to exaggerate the positive possibilities of hybridity, it stands as a key text in the debates about the status and aspirations of Mexican Americans and the nature of their identities.

Poetry

During the 1980s, while US fiction continued to manage the crossover between poetics and storytelling and engage a significant audience whilst doing so, poetry fractured along lines which were not always distinct but which did little to halt its slide in cultural influence. Just as race, gender and ethnicity were key markers in the kinds of fiction being produced, so poetry produced writers who dealt with similar issues of assimilation and racial identity. Sandra Cisneros' first collection of poems, *My Wicked, Wicked Ways* (1987), followed the success of her episodic novel *The House on Mango Street* (1984), while her fellow Mexican American writer Gary Soto emerged as an important voice representing the Hispanic experience with several collections in the 1980s: *Where Sparrows Work Hard* (1981), *Black Hair* (1985), *Living Up the Street* (1985) and *California Childhood* (1988). Shirley Geok-lin Lim won the Commonwealth Poetry prize for her first collection, *Crossing The Peninsula* (1980) and, as an academic and a poet, became a key figure in Asian American literary culture. Joy Harjo in *She Had Some Horses* (1983) and *Secrets from the Center of the World* (1989), and Leslie Marmon Silko in *Storyteller* (1981) continued the tradition of American Indian poetry established in earlier decades by writers like N. Scott Momaday and Gerald Vizenor. African American poetry, which had a history as long as the settling of the continent and important periods of production coming out of the Harlem Renaissance and the Black Arts movement, one could argue, found its most distinctive shape during the 1980s in hip hop and rap music.

Elsewhere, the predominant mode of poetry, established in the 1970s and cemented in the 1980s, involved the interrogation of representation. What came to be called 'language poetry' gave 'increasing attention to the potential of poetry as a medium for the exploration of language itself.'[53] It is arguable that this has always been one of the objectives of the poetic imagination, but in the US during this period the interrogation of language assumed a position of priority in the writing of some poetry and was so radical in its interrogations that an entirely new incarnation of poetic language emerged. Sharing the same political motives as their predecessors in the 1950s and 1960s, poets working in this mode 'were more interested in using poetry to examine the ways in which language operates within a range of social, cultural, and literary discourses'[54] than they were in expressing their opposition to specific issues. Christopher Beach offers two explanations for this shift in poetic emphasis. The first has to do with the way that the US was becoming an information economy that relied on language in all sorts of different ways, particularly in the media, such that the idea of possessing a neutral or natural language with which to intervene was no longer a trustworthy assumption. The second reason was the circulation in the cultural economy of poststructuralist theories of language that damaged the security of the linkage between signifier and signified and understood language not as a transparent system, but as a referential system of signs whose meanings derived from their relationship with other signs so that definitive meaning was constantly delayed or deferred.

Language poetry developed as a movement, even though its terms of reference were very broad and the work produced under its aegis often very different. $L=A=N=G=U=A=G=E$ was one of the key journals and was edited by Charles Bernstein and Bruce Andrews between 1978 and 1981. Most of the thirteen issues were published as a book in 1984. Ron Silliman's *In the American Tree* (1986) was a key anthology which collected work by language poets such as Lynn Hejinian, Bob Perelman, Michael Palmer, Michael Davidson, Clark Coolidge and Susan Howe, as well as statements from the poets themselves about language and writing. Because of its concentration on the problematic status of meaning and representation, language poetry has a reputation for being opaque. But like a good deal of contemporary art in the 1980s that addressed the boundaries and possibilities of its own representation, language poetry makes more sense when the purpose with which one reads it changes. Language poetry is less concerned with the voice of either a poet or a poem's persona, since in attempting to question the authenticity of language it questions the ability of language to provide access to an authentic subject.

Following in the wake of Roland Barthes' 'Death of the Author' (1967) and Michel Foucault's 'What is an Author?' (1969), language poetry breaks the link between author and text that had been at the base of romantic and even a modernist understanding of poetry and literature. The way in which it self-consciously manipulates language, poetic form and even the layout of the language on the page – often in language poetry the layout is not in clear stanzas but a seemingly random pattern – is reminiscent of the postmodernist strategies of fiction writers who in the 1960s and 1970s in the US were pressing the boundaries of representational forms in fiction. Once this fiction fades from prominence, it is possible to see language poetry inheriting its objectives, but developing them in the genre of poetry rather than fiction and taking them forward in radical experimental forms that surpass the possibilities of fiction. Despite its obscurity, language poetry sold quite respectably. In January 1989, the trade journal *Publishers Weekly* printed an article called 'Publishing Language Poets' in its Independent Publishing section and certainly in academic circles, where many language poets themselves worked, the questions raised by language poetry were taken up, by someone like Jerome McGann, for instance, alongside the French poststructuralism with which it shared its approaches to language. Language poetry, then, replenished the 'literature of exhaustion' once it had become exhausted in fiction.

Chapter 2

Art and Photography

The Art Market

When his painting *Three Flags* (1958) was bought by the New York Whitney Museum for $1 million in September 1980, Jasper Johns offered the following thoughts: 'I was brought up in the Depression, and $1 million is a very important figure to one who grew up at that time. It has a rather neat sound, but it has nothing to do with painting.' Having come to prominence as an artist in the 1950s, Johns, like his friend Robert Rauschenberg, made his reputation as a neo-Dadaist. Taking popular objects and imagery from the public domain – most notably the Stars and Stripes flag – and turning them into works of art, Johns exercised a critical commentary on the status of those objects as they were transposed from one medium to another and transformed in the process. But while the conceptual and aesthetic elements of artistic production may be of primary importance to the artist, at least since the systems of patronage operating during the Renaissance, art has always also circulated in financial markets where monetary value accrues in proportion to perceived aesthetic value. In 1931, Andrew Mellon paid $1.2 million for Raphael's *Alba Madonna*, while Washington's National Gallery paid an estimated $6 million for Leonardo da Vinci's *Ginevra dei Benci* in 1967. What marked the American art world of the 1980s was the degree to which late-nineteenth and twentieth-century art now attracted such sums and the fact that money, business and art became so intimately entwined that the buying and selling of art was as much of a story as the art itself. When *Three Flags* was originally bought by Mr and Mrs Burton Tremaine from the Leo Castelli Gallery in 1959 it cost $900 (plus a $15 delivery charge). To find himself the first living artist to see one of his pieces sell for $1 million may for Johns not have had

much to do with painting; for others in the 1980s, painting
was all about money. By 1989, Johns's *False Start* was being sold for
$17.1 million.

The decade witnessed ever increasing prices being paid for artworks
by European painters like Degas, Renoir, Monet and Cézanne. In 1987
Van Gogh's *Irises* was bought by Australian businessman Alan Bond
at Sotheby's in New York for $54 million, the highest price ever paid
for a painting at that time. To fund the purchase, Bond had to borrow
a substantial proportion of this price from the auction house. When he
defaulted on the loan the painting was sold once more, this time to the
J. Paul Getty Museum for an undisclosed fee. Earlier in the year, Van
Gogh's *Sunflowers* was sold in London for just under $40 million to a
Japanese insurance company. In May 1980, in New York City alone,
$55.8 million was spent on impressionist, modernist and contempo-
rary art,[1] while by 1983 the total New York art market was worth $2
billion.[2] This unprecedented wave of buying and selling was driven by
a variety of factors that put into contact with one another business, an
increasingly entrepreneurial art-dealer network, and a desire to find
and own the next big thing amongst certain elite social classes. In the
US in the 1980s, art became a marker of social status and of cultural
capital like in no other period.

Tom Wolfe was alert to the combination of these forces in the early
1980s when he wrote about an exhibition of Vatican art at the
Metropolitan Museum of Art in New York. Struck by how uneasy the
assembled Manhattan art dealers seemed around religious members of
the audience who had been invited to the opening evening, Wolfe
attributed this discomfort to a sense among the 'culturati' that they
'were being forced to rub shoulders with heathens'.

> That was the way it hit them. For today art – not religion – is the reli-
> gion of the educated classes. Today people look upon traditional reli-
> gious ties – Catholic, Episcopal, Presbyterian, Methodist, Baptist,
> Jewish – as matters of social pedigree. It is only art that they look upon
> religiously.[3]

One of the ways in which Wolfe justifies this claim is to note how,
where once American businesses were happy to give large amounts
of money to churches and religious organizations, in the postwar
world businesses 'pray in public' by supporting the arts. And, Wolfe
notes, 'the worse odor a corporation is in, the more likely it is to
support the arts, and the more likely it is to make sure everybody

knows it.'[4] The hierarchy of public art-giving stretched from naming a whole new museum after a patron – like Joseph H. Hirshhorn – to new wings or floors of existing museums or galleries, to sponsorship of exhibitions.

While businesses undoubtedly saw arts funding as good public relations, in the 1980s they also saw it as part and parcel of their own prestige and status. When the Equitable Life Assurance Society built new headquarters on Seventh Avenue in Manhattan, it included a comprehensive range of artworks in its new layout. As well as buying and refurbishing a mural by American regionalist Thomas Hart Benton and commissioning work by Roy Lichtenstein and Sol LeWitt, Equitable Life opened a branch of the Whitney Museum in its lobby. The *New York Times* reported that executive dining rooms and lobby restaurants would also be decorated with many of America's leading artists.[5] The Chase Manhattan Bank, as well as being one of those corporations who employed their own art curator to buy art, also turned its Soho branch (close to where many New York artists lived and worked in the cheap loft apartments during the 1970s and 80s) into an art gallery, putting on a number of exhibitions each year from its vast collection of art usually only seen by the bank's employees.[6] While Chase Manhattan had been buying art since the 1950s, its efforts multiplied significantly during the 1980s following the appointment of Jack Boulton, former director of the Contemporary Arts Center in Cincinnati, as acquisitions director. In 1984 alone Chase Manhattan acquired 1,300 pieces.[7] If, for Wolfe, this kind of corporate acquisition and patronage of art was a way for organizations to legitimate their wealth and defuse public opprobrium for the huge profits they were making, for the corporations themselves art was considered a sound investment. Spiralling auction prices ensured this, although the circular nature of the art market – since it was only people and businesses with wealth who could afford the high prices in the first place – meant that it was a market that might easily turn into an economic bubble where prices and values fell as rapidly as they rose, especially if the general economic climate grew more gloomy. None of this affected the art market for most of the 1980s, although after Black Monday in 1987 the market quietened noticeably. Some indication of the extent to which corporations entered the world of art can be seen by the appearance of the *International Directory of Corporate Art Collections* in 1983. Published by the International Art Alliance, it listed 500 American corporations which held art collections. Art, then, was a business within business during the 1980s.

Given the close links between art and business during the 1980s, it seems fitting that just as the corporate world of takeovers, mergers and stock dealing which so dominated the shifts in corporate and business structures during the 1980s was dominated by Wall Street and other Manhattan financial institutions, so the art market and the art scene was dominated by Manhattan. According to Tom Wolfe, 'fashions in art are determined by no more that 3,000 people, at least 2,950 of whom live in Manhattan.'[8] But the juxtaposition of Manhattan money and the Manhattan art world was not coincidental. The art critic Robert Hughes, who commented on much that was happening during the 1980s from his column in *Time* magazine, remarked that 'If you want to go in for a crushing but tasteful display of economic power, then even the rawest junk-bond trillionaire knows that art is the best way.'[9] Art became one of the places in which the new money unleashed by economic growth in the 1980s revealed itself through conspicuous consumption. In 1970 there were 200 art galleries in New York City; by the mid-1980s this figure had increased threefold in order to cater for the increased demand for art. The art adviser became a notable figure, helping both private collectors and businesses, and some were even affiliated to banks, such as Jeffrey Deitch at Citibank, which were now willing to accept art as collateral for loans and help finance the purchase of new pieces.

Art dealers played a key role in mediating between artists and the world of finance and were recognized not so much for their ability to spot artistic talent but for being able to turn artefacts into cash. One dealer, Andrew Terner, suggested that 'Most dealers were like commodities brokers' and, furthermore, that 'there was no difference between the collector and the dealer. In a sense, every collector *was* a dealer.'[10] Another dealer, Eugene V. Thaw, was dismayed that art, once turned into financial collateral, 'becomes a commodity like pork bellies or wheat.'[11] The influx of money into the art world also made it more like another arm of the industry of show business. Exhibition premieres attracted famous celebrities and, as a consequence, all sorts of media coverage too. The major auction houses were also sucked into the world of high finance. Sotheby's, a British company with offices in New York, and which had been stumbling along making losses, became the subject of a takeover battle in 1983 between General Felt Industries of New Jersey and Alfred Taubman, a leading developer of shopping malls from Detroit. Taubman emerged victorious and claimed that 'Selling art has much in common with selling root beer. People don't need root beer and they don't need to buy a painting either. We provide them with a sense that it will provide a happier experience.'[12] Taubman had been one of the patrons who provided the funds for the Whitney Museum to buy Jasper Johns's *Three Flags* in 1980.

These new kinds of connections between art and business altered not only the context in which artworks were bought and sold in the 1980s, but also the context in which new artists came to prominence. While Andy Warhol had fashioned a connection between art and celebrity in the 1960s, this had largely relied on his own talents and skills of self-publicity. In the 1980s, dealers and galleries were actively looking for the next big name to unveil to the critics and buyers. With the financial stakes so high, the emergence of artists like Julian Schnabel, David Salle, Robert Longo, Keith Haring and Jean-Michel Basquiat was treated by some as a sign, not of artistic talent, but of opportunism. Robert Motherwell, an Abstract Expressionist painter from the 1950s New York School which also included Jackson Pollock, Mark Rothko and Willem de Kooning, commented:

> There is a lack of subtlety now, an indifference to what are ultimate con-
> cerns, a tendency to improvise rather than think something through
> clearly. When we started out, there were people like Mondrian, who
> regarded art as a calling, something that expressed the world of the spirit.
> People now are quite cynical about that. They have forgotten what art is
> all about. . . One of the criticisms of the whole art scene is that it is rooted
> neither in profound reality nor in the historical origins of modernism.[13]

George McNeil, another of the Abstract Expressionists, suggested that rather than producing great paintings, now 'young artists want to be famous'.[14] More pointedly, Robert Hughes said that 'If [Jackson] Pollock was John Wayne, the likes of Haring 'n' Basquiat resemble those two what's-their-names on *Miami Vice*.'[15]

Jean-Michel Basquiat

Of all the artists who burst onto the art scene of the 1980s, Jean-Michel Basquiat became perhaps the most notorious. While he was the first contemporary African American artist to become an international star, he was dead by the age of twenty-seven. According to his biographer, if the art world of the 1980s was dominated by fame and greed, then Basquiat's career 'cashed in on both'.[16] At the time of his death by a heroin overdose in August 1988, his status had begun to wane following a falling out with his close friend and mentor Andy Warhol. But while some – like Robert Hughes, who dismissed the praise heaped on Basquiat's work by others as 'absurd' – have no time for Basquiat or his work, the fact that he remains one of the figures around whom debates about hype versus quality take place suggest that neither his art nor his impact on the art world can be dismissed so easily.

Born in 1960, Basquiat was the son of middle-class immigrant parents. His father came from an aristocratic Haitian family and worked success-fully as an accountant. It was only when he was seventeen, a year before he dropped out from high school, that Basquiat began leaving his trade-mark tag SAMO (Same Old Shit) and the copyright symbol © on Manhattan subway trains and slum buildings with his friend Al Diaz. But graffiti was only the beginning for Basquiat and he quickly became involved with a New York scene in which art was only one element amongst a whole array of media, many of which were influencing and feeding off one another: 'Artists were mixing up their media,' Phoebe Hoban suggests, and 'music, film, painting and fashion were recombining in innovative ways'[17] at the end of the 1970s and early 1980s. As well as continuing to paint, Basquiat also made the first steps to becoming a media celebrity during this time by appearing on *TV Party*, a public-access cable TV show that ran in New York between 1978 and 1982 and which was co-hosted by Blondie guitarist Chris Stein. Basquiat would often sit in the TV studio and improvise poetry on the screen so it appeared superimposed over the live action.

Basquiat's painting quickly came to the attention of prominent gallery owners and dealers after it appeared in The 'Times Square Show', an exhi-bition sponsored by Collaborative Projects Incorporated (Colab), a New York artists' group, as well as appearing, in 1981, in the influential *Artforum* magazine. It was after this, in 1982–3, that Basquiat had a relationship with a then still aspiring singer, Madonna, and came under the patronage of Andy Warhol. From here Basquiat developed the heroin addiction which eventually killed him. But while he is important as a marker of the way that art and media culture intermingled in the early 1980s, it is sometimes too easy to forget about his work.

Basquiat's paintings were a provocative fusion of figurative images, symbols, and text that foregrounded the issue of race in a traditionally white-dominated art world. Some of his most notable paintings are *Two Heads on Gold* (1982), *Self-Portrait* (1982), *Dustheads* (1982), *In Italian* (1983) and *Flexible* (1984). He represented heroic black sportsmen and musicians – Sugar Ray Robinson, Muhammad Ali, Charlie Parker and Max Roach – in his paintings in startling and abstract ways at a time when main-stream culture stereotyped black characters if it represented them at all. The use of recurring motifs, like the copyright symbol, which for a black artist was as much about not being exploited as it was about commodifi-cation, but also the crown which bestowed a royalty – or 'downtown royalty' – on his figures, and hobo signs from the early twentieth century, gave his work an ideological edge often missing in the work of his con-temporaries. The texture and history of black identity is everywhere in

Basquiat's work. As Hoban writes: 'Many of [Basquiat's] stylistic trademarks are themselves a recognizable part of the continuum of well-established African-American aesthetic traditions, from the iterated drumbeat brought here by men sold into slavery, to the call and response of gospel, the repeated blues refrain, jazz's improvisational riffing, and the sampling technique of rap.'[18]

The failure, both at the time and subsequently, to recognize these qualities in Basquiat's paintings and to concentrate instead on his celebrity lifestyle says as much about the failure of criticism as it does about Basquiat. But it is also a failure to recognize that art in the 1980s was no longer a medium of representation disconnected from other representational forms. Of all the painters of the 1980s, it is not surprising that Basquiat's life was turned into film, by Julian Schnabel in *Basquiat* (1996). If Basquiat's work incorporated his influences from music, from poetry and from TV, then it is hardly surprising that his life touched each of these media in its short and dazzling existence and that they in turn helped to mythologize him in the public imagination.

Figure 2.1 Jean-Michel Basquiat's life turned into film: Jeffrey Wright as Basquiat in Julian Schnabel's biopic *Basquiat* (Miramax, 1996). © Eleventh Street Production/Miramax/The Kobal Collection.

The accusation against many of the new artists was that their work was superficial. The age of the artists themselves – Schnabel, Salle and Longo achieved success by the time they were thirty, while Haring and Basquiat were even younger – together with their popular-culture influences and the speed with which their work was selling for tens of thousands of dollars, all contributed to this feeling. But while such accusations would never go away, the context in which artistic production of all kinds was being understood in the 1980s was also changing. The modernism of which Motherwell spoke was an increasingly distant and, for many young artists, increasingly irrelevant phenomenon in a world where the boundaries between art and popular culture were collapsing thanks in part to the commodification of all areas of cultural production and consumption. High art no longer existed beyond a financial economy.

Postmodernist and Neo-Expressionist Art

If one of the features of the art market of the 1980s, both in the US and elsewhere, was the high prices paid for modernist and twentieth-century art, then this signalled a process whereby modernism had become mainstream. No clearer evidence of this was required than the acquisition of modernist art by large and powerful corporations. According to the American critic Fredric Jameson, high modernism had 'conquered the university, the museum, the art gallery network, and the foundations',[19] and he went on to argue that:

> Those formerly subversive and embattled styles – Abstract Expressionism; the great modernist poetry of Pound, Eliot or Wallace Stevens; the International style (Le Corbusier, Frank Lloyd Wright, Mies); Stravinsky; Joyce, Proust, Mann – felt to be scandalous or shocking by our grandparents are, for the generation which arrives at the gate in the 1960s, felt to be the establishment and the enemy – dead, stifling, canonical, the reified monuments one has to destroy to do anything new.[20]

Jameson's critical intervention was one of many in the 1980s that tried to understand the changing landscape of cultural production and consumption that seemed to have emerged after the 1960s. As a Marxist critic, Jameson saw culture changing in response to economic and social conditions. In 'Postmodernism, or, the Cultural Logic of Late Capitalism' (1984), and drawing on the work of Ernst Mendel, Jameson characterized the period since the Second World War as a time when Western capitalism was entering a new phase – the era of 'late capitalism' – dominated by multi- and transnational corporations and the circulation of financial capital and which gradually saw the absorption of the cultural sphere by the economic sphere. As a result, culture, and cultural products, became commodified in ways unknown in the era of modernism earlier in the twentieth century. In the postmodernist culture that results, according to Jameson, the boundaries between high and popular culture, and the genres and styles connected with them, have broken down to the extent that such distinctions are no longer applicable.

While Jameson's account of postmodernist culture is by no means a definitive one, and certainly not one that can be delimited by the 1980s, it is intriguing because it emerges as a critical standpoint conterminously with artists struggling to create the 'anything new' of which Jameson writes. Prominent critics, like Robert Hughes, remained wedded to high modernism as an authentic aesthetic and part of Hughes' disparaging view of the New York art scene in the 1980s was determined by precisely the failure of the work being produced to measure up to this standard. Jameson's work, however, prompts the question: just how appropriate is this standard any longer?

In the 1960s, Andy Warhol, through the cultural production coming out of 'The Factory', turned the relationship between high and low culture on its head by transforming consumer objects – the Campbell's soup tin being the most obvious example – into art works. Warhol selected these objects not simply because they were consumer objects, but also because they possessed resonance for him, as memories of childhood or home, for instance, and his work was indicative of a more general process whereby not only were the kinds of 'experience' or 'subject matter' considered suitable for representation in art changing, but so too were the rules of composition. The artists who emerged in the 1980s were controversial not just because of the money that circulated around them, but also because of the art they were producing.

Jeff Koons

Described by the writer and sometime conceptual artist Douglas Coupland as 'the quintessential 80s artist',[21] Jeff Koons is also one of the most unfathomable. After more than twenty years, Koons is still attracting the same baffled responses while the value of his pieces soars on the international art market. Unlike the Neo-Expressionists, Koons did not try to revive painting in the 1980s. He can best be described as a conceptual sculptor, although the material he sculpted followed in the pop-art tradition of Andy Warhol by drawing on popular consumer objects. *New Hoover Quik-Broom & New Hoover Celebrity IV* (1980) was two 1950s vacuum cleaners enclosed in a Perspex case, while in *Three Ball 50/50 Tank* (1985) Koons arranged three basketballs so they floated in water in a glass tank. These early works, while similar to Warhol's work in that they transform consumer objects into art objects, are slightly different in that they frame the objects themselves rather than reproducing them as screen prints or lithographs. In this sense, they are not endlessly reproducible, although Koons did produce variations of both the vacuum cleaners and the basketballs. He also reproduced copies of objects – a basketball, a football, a snorkel, an aqualung and a lifeboat – in bronze. The object itself becomes the focus of attention in these works. According to Coupland, 'Readymade objects were once again allowable. Objects no longer had to be pared down to minimal blankness, and nor did they have to be viewed as Pop iconography. They could simply be *themselves* and yet also be charged with talismanic aura.'[22]

The 'aura' of these objects, and the irony with which they were presented, was not visible to everyone, however, and Koons was seen by some as exploiting rather than offering a commentary upon the world of consumer culture that formed the core of his sculpture. Koons certainly understood the relationship between commodities and money, having worked as a commodities broker on Wall Street after leaving college in the late 1970s, but the development of his work in the later part of the 1980s demonstrated a changing attitude towards the appropriation of popular-culture imagery. Koons began to engage with precisely those elements of popular culture that were still unfashionable or beyond redemption: decorative items regarded as either tasteless or sentimental in style and classifiable as kitsch. While the old vacuum cleaners and the basketballs had a retro styling that was both simple and cool and therefore easily assimilated, Koons's 'Banality' period ceramics were more unsettling.

Pink Panther (1988) brought the popular cartoon character together with a semi-naked Jayne Mansfield and entwined them in a metre-tall romantic embrace. Collapsing all sorts of boundaries between animation and real life, representation and reality, and human and animal, this ceramic is at one and the same time a mockery of the public celebrity romance and a sentimental ratification of the pleasures of observing such celebrity romance, all wrapped up in a vibrant and excessive ceramic that overshadows and outdoes the figurines of popular characters available in department stores. Koons's work in this period reached its peak with *Michael Jackson and Bubbles* (1988). A life-size, gold-leaf-covered statue of Michael Jackson sitting down with his pet chimpanzee, whom Jackson had rescued from a cancer clinic in Texas in 1985, this appeared when Jackson was at the peak of his fame, but just as he was also attracting media attention along with the nickname 'Wacko Jacko' for often unsubstantiated claims about his idiosyncratic behaviour. Sold for $5.6 million in 2001, the statue, with its whitening of Jackson's face, pre-empts many of those debates about skin colour, race and bodily transformation that have surrounded Jackson in recent years. The gold leaf makes the statue look like a gold idol and draws attention to the way in which Jackson's status as a pop idol mirrors the worship of idols often considered to be primitive in non-Western cultures. The kitschy nature of the sculpture – the smiles on the faces of both Jackson and Bubbles, for instance – confront the viewer with all kinds of questions about authenticity, self-presentation and image manipulation.

After these sculptures were produced, Koons went on to marry Ilona Staller (the Italian porn star Cicciolina) and produced erotic photographs of the two of them together. In 1992 he was commissioned to create a sculpture for an exhibition in Germany and came up with a fourteen-metre-tall West Highland terrier puppy in flowers on a steel framework. He has also faced various copyright-infringement lawsuits for his use of pre-existing images.

Through it all, Koons has remained one of the most astute chroniclers of the relationship between art and popular culture and one of the liveliest and most provocative commentators on the process of living in a consumer culture that constantly mediates emotional experience.

The label that attached itself to some of these artists was Neo-Expressionism. Marked by a return to traditional paint on canvas, Neo-Expressionism, with its rough and violent use of paint, and its juxtaposition of often disparate objects in paintings, can be seen as a reaction again the minimalist and conceptual art of the 1970s. While it brought attention back to the body, Neo-Expressionism did so in a decidedly abstract and distorted way. Influenced by both American Abstract Expressionism and European Surrealism, Neo-Expressionist artists were criticized for not creating original work, but simply recycling previous styles. Julian Schnabel, who had himself photographed, like Jackson Pollock, working on large canvases on the floor, was, David Blelajac argues, 'harshly attacked as a commercial opportunist for cynically recycling the masculine, action-painting persona of the heroic artist-genius',[23] while Robert Hughes referred to Jean-Michel Basquiat as 'the black Chatterton of the 80s'.[24] Schnabel and Basquiat, along with David Salle, were the most prominent of the Neo-Expressionists. Salle's *Pitcher* (1983) exemplifies the odd juxtapositions in Neo-Expressionist painting. A painting of a naked woman on a beach, Salle attached to the canvas a ceramic water pitcher on a small wooden shelf. While the framing of the objects within the same picture suggests some connection between them, the nature of this connection is so tenuous as to seem arbitrary. Schnabel's signature style was to paint on broken crockery. *Divan* (1979), *Grace High Tower* (1987) and *Joe Glassco* (1988) all use this technique. While the effect achieved is one of fragmentation, a familiar modernist technique, Schnabel fragments the very structure of the picture rather than just the representation. If fragmentation in modernist art served to dislocate the centre of consciousness of a work of art, that centre was recovered by a sense of stylistic and authorial unity. Both Salle and Schnabel, with their arbitrary juxtapositions and structural dislocations, offer no such sense of unity and in this respect their work marks a break with modernist techniques.

The fact that their work was taken up so readily by the New York art market suggests that in the process of destroying the 'reified' monuments of modernism, Neo-Expressionist art offered few of the radical or scandalous qualities associated with modernism. Some critics have tried to distinguish between different modes of postmodernist artistic production. For Lisa Phillips, who produced the catalogue to accompany the second half of the Whitney Museum's two-part exhibition on American culture from 1900 to 2000, one strand of postmodernist art consisted of 'a popular, retrograde from found in much new architecture and the emerging Neo-Expressionist painting' which used only 'a pastiche of historical styles and decorative elements'.[25] The accusation that postmodernist culture in general relied on pastiche was a position articulated by Jameson in the 1980s. Distinguishing pastiche from parody, Jameson argued that pastiche, although similar to parody in that it imitated or mimicked a particular style, is different to parody because 'it is a neutral practice of such mimicry, without parody's ulterior motive, without the satirical impulse, without laughter, without that still latent feeling that there exists something *normal* compared to which what is being imitated is rather comic.'[26] Stripped of this 'ulterior motive', for Jameson pastiche becomes the stylistic accompaniment to a more profound disillusionment with the idea of a 'unique self and private identity',[27] an attitude that drew on structuralist and poststructuralist ideas emerging, particularly in Europe, during the 1960s and 1970s and which became pervasive in the humanities and social sciences. While it may not have convinced conservative writers like Allan Bloom, and others in the culture wars critical of university education, there certainly seemed to be a resonance with the culture that was being produced in the US in the 1980s. The reliance on pastiche, which Jameson identified in both film and literature, certainly seemed apparent in the world of art.[28] David Salle reused images not only from other French and American paintings, but also advertising images from the 1950s and manuals meant to teach people how to draw, while Basquiat mined the iconography of African American art and sculpture for use in his work.

Although Jameson's suggestion that modernism exhausted the combination of possible styles may seem too pessimistic, there is a sense in which, during the 1980s, the recycling of earlier styles became an important mode of cultural engagement. The availability of so many styles – through their commodification and easy reproduction – produced a moment when 'contemporary or postmodernist art is going to be about art itself in a new kind of way . . . one of its essential messages will involve the necessary failure of art and the aesthetic, the failure of the new, the imprisonment in the past.'[29] While art, and culture more broadly, had clearly been self-conscious about its own purpose and production in the past (a modernist novel like William Faulkner's *As I Lay Dying* is clearly an engagement with the nature of fictional form), what Jameson is suggesting is something different: that while self-reflexivity, like other elements of postmodernist culture (fragmentation, juxtaposition, pastiche, for example) can be found in modernism, 'these things have been secondary or minor features of modernist art, marginal rather than central, and that we have something new when they become the central features of cultural production.'[30]

For Jameson, then, the culture of postmodernism, and here one would include the Neo-Expressionist painting of Schnabel, Salle and Basquiat, represents a shift in the mode of artistic production. Whether this shift can be classified as a radical break is more difficult to assess since it really represents a change in emphasis. But if critics like Phillips have been quick to condemn Neo-Expressionism as 'retrograde' in opposition to a 'more profound' postmodernism that 'deconstructed and reconstructed the very nature of representation',[31] this distinction seems not to hold. If the use of pastiche, according to Jameson, does the very job of self-reflexively exposing how contemporary art is imprisoned in the past then this would seem to be precisely the same work as deconstructing and reconstructing 'the very nature of representation'. For both Jameson and Phillips the primary purpose of postmodernist art is the process of referring to its own production. The problem for other critics, and sometimes for art viewers, is that once this becomes the case art works seem only to relay the same idea and lack the differentiation that marked earlier emphases upon content and stylistic individuality. Observing the 1980s retrospectively allows us the benefit of understanding American Neo-Expressionism not simply as the product of a desire for celebrity and fashionable status because of money and commodification. Neo-Expressionism emerged simultaneously in Europe and it is perhaps the case that it marked a necessary transition from a world of modernist principles of composition to a world of late capitalist postmodernity where content and form were reconstituted along different principles.

Art at the Margins

It would be wrong to assume that, as powerful and pervasive as they were, the art galleries and art dealers of New York constituted the entire artistic landscape of the 1980s. While Soho and Greenwich Village in Manhattan attracted aspiring artists in the late 1970s and early 1980s – when loft space was freely available and relatively cheap – so that they were within touching distance of Manhattan's cultural and moneyed elites, other parts of the city also saw developments in art practices completely at odds with those in Manhattan. Fashion Moda was founded by Austrian-born Stefan Eins in 1978 at Third Avenue near 147th Street in the South Bronx. It was located in what Douglas Crimp describes as 'the very heart of an environment that is hard and brutal indeed, the most notorious black and Hispanic slum in the United States.' But it was located there 'not to stand its ground against its environment, but rather to engage with it constructively.'[32] Fashion Moda was the antithesis of the leisured appropriation of art by patrons and consumers that took place in the quiet and often staid environment of traditional gallery and museum culture. It was envisaged by Eins as a space where artists living and working in the South Bronx – an area notoriously underprivileged following the construction of Cross Bronx Expressway during the late 1940s and early 1950s and the building of the Co-op City housing complex in the northeastern part of the borough during the 1960s – could come together, exchange ideas, collaborate on projects and find spaces to exhibit their work and installations. Its cross-race constituency incorporated white artists disillusioned with fashionable uptown Manhattan and the marginalized African and Latin American residents who lived in the area and who were working in a cultural tradition whose material and purpose was beyond canvas and paint.

Fashion Moda was one the first avenues where graffiti art was championed. In the early 1970s, as subway trains became the canvas for young taggers with cans of spray paint, Mayor John Lindsay declared war on graffiti and turned it, overnight, into a political issue. In response, Fashion Moda promoted the work of John Fekner, Jean-Michel Basquiat, Jenny Holzer and Keith Haring and its first graffiti show appeared in 1980, curated by a nineteen-year-old graffiti artist, Crash, who invited eleven of his friends, many of whom were black and Puerto Rican, to produce work for the show. The political dimension to graffiti was one which informed many of Fashion Moda's exhibitions and collaborations. When Ronald Reagan visited the South

Bronx in 1979 as part of his election campaign, Fashion Moda collaborator John Feckner stencilled the words 'Broken Promises' and 'Decay' on walls around the Bronx. Unaware of their origin, Reagan then appropriated and used the walls as the backdrop for his press conferences. In 1980, Lucy Lippard reported on 'The Real Estate Show', which she described as 'a unique combination of art exhibition and guerrilla action'.[33] Fashion Moda took over a derelict building on Manhattan's Delancey Street and occupied the space with 'art protesting absentee landlordism, eviction, developers, the city's waste of space, greed – the whole notion of property in a capitalist society.'[34] This kind of politicized public art was central to the Fashion Moda project. But while its reputation led to invitations to put on exhibitions at big European events like Germany's Documenta 7 in Kassel in 1982, it also quickly attracted the attention of the official art world it was seeking to distance itself from. Some of its early participants – like Basquiat and Haring – moved into the fashionable Manhattan art world and Peter Schjeldahl in the *Village Voice* suggested that while in Fashion Moda he had 'anticipated something fervid, volcanic' it had become instead 'participatory narcissism'.[35]

Other similar groups which existed at this time in New York included Colab and Group Material. Colab's most important event was the 'Times Square Show' which took place in a former massage parlour near Times Square. Lasting for a month, the show featured a mixture of traditional art, conceptual installations, film projections, erotica and photography and addressed various political and sexual themes. Group Material, according to Lisa Phillips the most 'rigorous' of these groups,[36] tackled social issues from a conceptual standpoint. Rather than staging open-ended events, Group Material shows focused on a particular theme. 'People's Choice' (1981) was an anthology of objects brought to the collective's gallery by the local residents of East 13th Street, while 'AIDS Timeline' (1989) was a history of the AIDS crisis that consisted of photography and documentary alongside statistics and facts about the spread of the disease.

Elsewhere in the US, art was responding to the changing nature of the country's ethnic make-up in innovative ways. Picking up on the conceptual and ideological importance of 'Borderlands' – 'the metaphor of choice to designate communal space' in Chicano arts and letters – The Border Art Workshop was established in 1984 as a collective of white, Mexican and Chicano artists who engaged on projects specifically addressed to the US–Mexico border.[37] Based in the San Diego–Tijuana area, the Border Art Workshop put on exhibitions which were multimedia events – incorporating outdoor murals, sculpture, performance pieces and installations – by artists such as David Avalos, Guillermo Gómes Peña and Victor Ochoa which explored the hybrid culture of the border, the tense political ramifications of border life bound up with immigration, as well as how issues such as abortion and AIDS intersected with border life. At the same time, the 'borderlands' metaphor was one that assumed more general significance in the context of a process of globalization where all kinds of geographical borders were being renegotiated.

Photography

By the time the 1980s arrived, photography had secured its place, albeit after a long battle, as an acceptable art form in the US. The work of pioneering photographers from earlier in the century like Edward Steichen, Alfred Stieglitz, Walker Evans, Ansel Adams and the Jewish immigrant Robert Frank, amongst others, helped establish the techniques and the specific genres – notably portraits and landscapes – which dominated photographic art. Robert Frank's *The Americans*, originally published in France in 1958 and then, with an introduction by Jack Kerouac, in the US the following year, was a key text in this process. A travelogue that in eighty-three photographs recounted Frank's journeys across and understandings of the country, *The Americans* was as much artistic illustration as it was documentary and experimented with focus, lighting and cropping to provide the viewer with a defamiliarized version of the meaning of the nation at an important moment in the post-war period. By the 1970s, the photojournalism influenced by Frank had assumed artistic credibility.

One demonstration of the way in which photography became assimilated into the art world is the success of photorealist painting in the late 1960s and early 1970s. It is also called super-realism or hyper-realism and painters like Richard Estes, Denis Peterson, Audrey Flack and Chuck Close often worked from photographic stills to create paintings that appeared to be photographs. Estes, in his urban street scenes, makes great use of reflective surfaces, particularly windows, to add to the appearance of verisimilitude – see, for instance, *560* (1972), *Lee* (1974), *Billiards* (1976) and *Lincoln Center* (1979). The everyday nature of the subject matter of the paintings likewise worked to secure the painting as a realist object. Estes continued to produce his photorealist painting all the way through the 1980s. The photorealist genre, however, is clearly more than just an attempt to replicate the mechanical action of taking a photograph. It also intervened in a debate that was as old as photography itself: to what extent is a photograph simply a reflection of reality, or to what extent does it mediate the reality it is representing? This debate was one that stubbornly refused to go away, and the arrival of other kinds of visual images during the twentieth century, particularly moving images on television and in the cinema and the purposes to which these 'real-life' images were put, meant that photography forever carried with it an engagement with the mode of realism that painting had long since left behind. Because there was a residual understanding of photography as a realistic medium, it was a medium that was forced to perpetually reflect on its own status as the producer of reality. In an art world that was, as I suggested earlier, confronting more self-consciously than ever before the purpose and nature of its own production, photography, which 'had long been considered a stepchild to painting and sculpture . . . would soon move to the center of avant-garde practice and, at the same time, become a vibrant mainstream medium for art making.'[38]

The emphasis in photography falls upon the assembling and constructing, rather than the mechanical taking of, a photograph. One of the most interesting figures of the decade in this respect is Barbara Kruger. After studying under the prominent and successful photojournalist Dianne Arbus at the Parsons School of Design in Greenwich Village, New York, Kruger became a graphic designer for the Condé Nast magazine *Mademoiselle* in 1969. The experience of working in the media industry and being involved on a day-to-day basis with the world of advertising and selling in a medium which fused the textual and the visual would have a huge influence on Kruger, although she spent much of the 1970s working on abstract painting. A poet as well as a keen reader of the sort of European critical theory by Walter Benjamin, Roland Barthes and Theodor Adorno that was making an impression in American intellectual circles during this period, Kruger began to fuse text and photography in a series of images at the beginning of the 1980s in a style that would become her trademark. Rather than taking photographs herself, Kruger reused old black and white photographs from a variety of sources – magazines, annuals, how-to books – and then over the top of these images laid short and ambiguous captions and epigrams, often in white and red typeface. The works have the visual impact of advertising posters, both in their visual clarity and simplicity and in the way that the slogan is meant to be read against the image.

Unlike the advertising of the marketplace, however, Kruger's photographic collages are driven by two main critical points of reference:
feminism and attacks on capitalism. Kruger starts from the position,
which became a critical commonplace in the 1970s, that visual images
in America and Europe privileged the male perspective. 'Most of the
things we see as representations in film and TV and most art,' Kruger
argued, 'are really undifferentiated addresses to a male audience, a male
spectator.' She saw her work as 'a series of attempts to ruin certain representations and to welcome the female spectator into the audience of
men.' An untitled image from 1981 consisted of a photograph of three
hovering razor blades and their ominous shadows, with the caption 'I
am your slice of life' underneath. Another used an old picture of a
shadowed man – signified by his hat – holding his forefinger to his
mouth gesturing for quiet, while the caption reads 'Your comfort is my
silence'. While these images may appear to be unsubtle in their depiction of men's violence against and repression of women, they can also
be read as sophisticated negotiations of the way in which that violence
and repression is not only instantiated in the physical world, but also
relies on images and language for its perpetuation. Kruger's use of the
pronouns 'I', 'You', 'Your', 'We' in virtually all of these photographic
collages mean that they hover between advertising slogans and public
information billboards but also that they raise questions about just
who is included, or excluded, by the pronoun and who is being
addressed by the piece and how they are being constituted as a viewer
and reader. In this sense, the pronouns can be seen as a direct engagement with French Marxist Louis Althusser's notion of interpellation.
For Althusser, interpellation is the process by which an individual
subject is produced or brought into being by ideology rather than
existing in advance of ideology.

Kruger's most famous photographic collage is one that she produced at the end of the decade and which soon entered the popular discourses of contemporary life in all sorts of unpredictable ways. A
picture of a brown paper bag with a black and white photograph of a
hand superimposed on the it, the hand is made to look as if it is holding
a red card, on which is printed the slogan 'I shop therefore I am'.
Humorous, perhaps, in the way it transposes one of the central tenets
of Western Enlightenment thought (Descartes' 'cogito ergo sum': 'I
think therefore I am'), by replacing thinking with shopping Kruger is
also critically assessing the commodification of contemporary experience and the centrality of consumerism to contemporary identity, a
message that fits in with some of her other work, whose slogans

include: 'Who is bought and sold?' and 'Your assignment is to divide and conquer'. Kruger also adapted Joseph Goebbels infamous 'When I hear the word culture, I take out my gun', replacing the word 'gun' with 'checkbook'. However hostile to capitalism, Kruger also believed there was no escape from it: 'I began to understand', she said, 'that outside the marketplace there is nothing – not a piece of lint, a cardigan, a human being. That's what the frames were about: how to commodify them. It was the most effective packaging device.' While this might be interpreted as a realistic understanding of the capitalist penetration of everyday life, it does also mean that Kruger is herself in an ambiguous situation when profiting from the very market forces her work is interrogating. Ultimately, Kruger's photographic collages pick up the postmodernist obsession with appropriation, pastiche and commodification to draw attention to the nature of the art object. Characterizing the 1980s herself, Kruger argued that 'In the art world, when people refer to the '80s they talk about high rollers, high prices, high on drugs, big paintings, art stars, etc. But to me it was also a time when we saw the emergence of work about representation.'

Cindy Sherman

One of the most influential photographers and artists of the late part of the twentieth century, Cindy Sherman started off as a painting student at art college before moving to photography. Part of the New York art scene of the late 1970s that took advantage of cheap Manhattan loft space, Sherman began to use a genre early on in her photography that would not only become her trade mark, but that was also borrowed from, and more readily associated, with painting: the self-portrait. From Albrecht Dürer and Rembrandt, through to Van Gogh, Picasso and Chagall, the self-portrait has been an important space in which artists have contemplated the process of painting and authorship. Although a figurative separation of artist and art object, the self-portrait is at the same time the visual image which for the viewer offers the most obvious starting point from which to examine and understand the artist. The idea of a photographic self-portrait immediately raises questions about the mechanics of photography since for the artist to appear in the photograph means that, whereas the painter or sculptor retains contact with brush or material, the photographer is disconnected physically from the medium of production. In this regard, Sherman is part of the new photographic art movement that emphasizes the making of the photograph rather than the taking of the photograph. Her appearance in her own photographs, while clearly locating her work in the tradition of self-portraiture, also moves the genre into a new technological age.

Sherman produces much of her work in series. *Untitled Film Stills* (1978–80) is her first major self-portraiture collection and consists of sixty-nine black and white images of Sherman, each one staging and constructing what looks to be a film still or publicity picture for a film and each depicting a stereotypical or clichéd version of womanhood and femininity that evoked the 1950s and 1960s. Although produced at the end of the 1970s, these images would achieve critical acclaim and circulation during the 1980s and became important for several reasons.

First of all, the series reflects upon the imagery of popular culture in novel ways. Where Warhol and the pop-art movement had turned popular and mass-produced objects into mass-produced art objects, and where Jeff Koons framed and fetishised the mass-produced consumer object, Sherman was more interested in the codes and performances of popular culture than in the objects of popular culture as a source or raw material. So while the photographs in *Untitled Film Stills* appear familiar – Sherman as a schoolgirl, a seductress, a housewife – they do not reference particular films or original sources; instead they target and reproduce generic gender conventions that have seen women constructed in certain ways. The challenge of the photographs lies in not only interpreting each untitled image to try and understand the dynamics of the pose, the clothing and the artefacts present, but then in linking the photographs together as a collection and seeing that they manage to portray the same woman – Sherman – in so many different ways. The photographs as a collection do the job of abstracting gender from the level of biology to the level of image and performance of a role, and in this way raise questions about the fixed nature of women's, and by association men's, identities. Sherman's photographs do not reveal the artist in the way that self-portraiture has traditionally done, but instead constantly defer that identity.

Sherman's photographs produce a discourse of identity – flexible and performative whilst still politically resonant – that was informing the critical study of gender amongst feminists during the 1980s. At the same time, they are invested in a postmodernist aesthetic that utilizes pastiche as a way not simply of re-using past styles for performative effect, but as a way of showing how our understanding of gender performance is rooted in historically locatable models and codes.

Sherman went on produce several other collections during the 1980s, all drawing on similar ideas, although she moved away from black and white and experimented with colour and light. *Centerfolds* (1981) depicted Sherman in a variety of outfits and poses, but always photographed from above. Responding to the centrefold pictures of women found in pornographic magazines, Sherman's images depicted fear and despoliation as well as ambiguous states of sexual arousal. In the *History Portraits* (1989), Sherman wore costumes and prosthetics to recreate the images of women as they had been represented across four hundred years of Western painting. Combining humour with a rigorous insight into the historical development of gendered bodies, Sherman's work in the late 1970s and 1980s was not only visually arresting, but also critically alert.

Other artists who worked with photography in order to address the issue of representation include Sherrie Levine and Richard Prince. Levine is best known for her collection *After Walker Evans* (1981). In 1936, Walker Evans published a series of photographs depicting poverty during the depression in the American South. The stark portraits of the victims of this poverty and the surroundings in which they lived became iconic images. What Levine did was to appropriate the most famous of these images by re-photographing them from a book of prints and then presenting them with the title *After Walker Evans*. While this seems to be the most basic form of copying, Levine's purpose in titling the pictures *After Walker Evans* is to refer to the established artistic practice of producing work in the style of, or influenced by, a particular artist. What Levine is asking is at what point does being influenced by someone become plagiarism and at what point does a viewer stop seeing a picture and instead see the name of the artist who created it? At the same time she is undermining the notion that works of art must necessarily – at least in terms of form and content – be original or expressive of a personal vision. Her reproductions of Evans' photographs address the very meaning of artistic representation but, by selecting this particular collection, Levine also brings back into the public space images of poverty from a different decade that help read the poverty that, however much the clichés of the decade would suggest otherwise, was a feature for many in the 1980s. So while the images do the work of making us question how representation works, they do so while the artistic process of selection remains important.

Richard Prince, who was trained as a painter, switched to photography in the mid-1970s when he was working in the tear-sheet department at Time-Life. A tear-sheet is a page taken from a magazine and used as evidence to an advertiser that their advert has been published. Working with magazine advertising in this way prompted Prince to relocate many of these advertising images, moving them from the world of mass culture to artistic artefact. While initially he re-photographed adverts for watches, pens, bags and clothes, in 1980 he produced a series of photographs which appropriated images of cowboys from the famous and iconic Marlboro cigarette advertisements. In re-photographing these images, Prince cropped the advertising slogans and branding to leave the cowboy dissociated from the product and thus disconnected the image from its advertising context. Prince is also commenting on the issue of appropriation, since Marlboro themselves had appropriated the image of the cowboy lifestyle in order to give their cigarettes a certain quality that they did not inherently

possess and which was then passed on to Marlboro smokers metonym-
ically: smoke Marlboros and you too can be a cowboy. At the same
time, by re-photographing these images, Prince is, as David Hopkins
suggests, both obscuring the role of artist as author and creator of
images whilst 'obliquely preserving an ironically macho identification
between himself, as artist, and the romantic outsider-figures of the
cowboys.'[39] In 2005, one of Prince's cowboy images became the first
photograph to raise more than $1 million at auction.

If these photographs dealt in a playful way with the parameters of
American artistic representation and authorship, Prince also used
appropriation for more shocking purposes with his 1983 photograph
Spiritual America. Borrowing its title from Alfred Stieglitz's famous
1923 close-up photograph of the haunches of a horse harnessed for
work, Prince makes completely different associations between America
and the spiritual. If in Stieglitz's photograph the work ethic is ambigu-
ously portrayed as both spiritual essence and repression, Prince's photograph of a naked, ten-year-old Brooke Shields, wearing lipstick and
eyeliner and standing provocatively in a bath, exposes the voyeuristic
and sexualized dimensions of a culture that remain taboo but all the
more resonant and disturbing when located in and on the body of a
child. It is surprising that the photograph caused little controversy when
first exhibited, given the increasing surveillance of child imagery in a
cultural climate – both in the US and Europe – increasingly alert to child
abuse and paedophilia. It does, however, reflect the continuing willingness of artists – despite, and perhaps because of, the shift to the right in
politics – to push the boundaries of representational acceptability. This
willingness and the vehemence of neo-conservative opponents led to a
series of battles over imagery and censorship during the 1980s.

Censorship

When, in 1985, Ronald Reagan appointed Ed Meese to conduct a government enquiry into the dangers and effects of pornography in
the US, the implicit intention was to overturn the 1970 Lockhart
Commission report which had found no link between pornography
and sexual violence. Much to the consternation of many of its scientific witnesses who had argued to the contrary, the Meese report did
indeed conclude that there was a causal link between pornography and
sexual violence. Unfortunately for the neo-conservative and religious
Right, the government proved powerless to try and prevent either the
production or distribution of pornography, especially in the video age.

Given the lack of legal options, attempts to restrict access to, or to censor, material considered pornographic, blasphemous or obscene filtered down into the cultural arena and localized campaigns and complaints. Art and photography were affected primarily because of the way that taxpayers' money was used in the support and sponsorship of art by the National Endowment for the Arts (NEA). By the end of the decade a series of controversies saw the NEA coming under increasing pressure to withhold public funding for artists and exhibitions which were considered by some to be offensive.

The intervention of conservative and religious groups in debates about culture and censorship was, of course, nothing new in the US during the 1980s. In 1921, the New York Society for the Suppression of Vice, formed in 1873 by Anthony Comstock whose intention was to protect the morality of the public and who gave his name to the Comstock Law that made it illegal to send 'obscene, lewd, or lascivious' books through the mail, brought a prosecution against *The Little Review* which had serialized James Joyce's *Ulysses*, including the sections where Leopold Bloom is masturbating. The magazine was declared obscene and *Ulysses* was banned in the US until 1933, three years before the Comstock Law was overturned. The McCarthyite witch-hunt of the early 1950s was notable for the way that it targeted Hollywood while, during the same period, the Senate Subcommittee on Juvenile Delinquency was investigating the effects of superhero comic books on the nation's youth as parent organizations publicly burned these comic books. The hysterical nature of these interventions was matched at the end of the 1980s.

In 1988, one of the seven winners of the annual Southeastern Center for Contemporary Art 'Awards in the Visual Arts' was a photograph by the Roman Catholic Honduran-Afro-Cuban artist Andreas Serrano. The photograph, titled *Piss-Christ*, and originally produced in 1987, was an image of Jesus Christ on a crucifix submerged in a glass tank of Serrano's urine. Serrano was awarded $15,000, which was funded by a variety of charitable associations – the Ford Foundation, the Rockefeller Foundation, private and corporate donors – as well as the NEA. While the initial exhibition and success of Serrano's photograph brought little controversy, the following year Serrano and the gay photographer Robert Mapplethorpe became key figures in a battle that reached the floor of the Senate, led to obscenity prosecutions and indelibly affected arts funding by the NEA.

Mapplethorpe, who did not live to see the controversy, died from AIDS in early 1989. He had long been a fixture in the New York art scene and his early work in the 1970s consisted mainly of portraits of his circle of friends and acquaintances – Andy Warhol, Debbie Harry, Richard Gere, Peter Gabriel and Patti Smith – together with still photography of flowers. At the end of the decade Mapplethorpe began to explore sexuality and homoeroticism in his work, resulting in the 'X Portfolio' (1978), a collection of photographic images of male sadomasochism, and the 'Z Portfolio' (1981) which focuses on images of black men. *Man in a Polyester Suit* is one photograph that comes from this period. A picture of an African American man, cropped at chest and thighs, in a cheap three-piece suit with an open fly from which hangs his penis, the photograph has divided critics. While some find the objectification and fetishisation of the black male body degrading and stereotypical, others, like gay writer Edmund White, find Mapplethorpe's homoerotic representation of black men to be passionate and loving.[40]

The gap between the first publication and exhibition of Mapplethorpe's photographs and the controversy around them which emerged at the end of the 1980s is telling of the way that AIDS altered the American cultural landscape in the mid-1980s. If the 1970s saw the emergence and establishment of gay male subcultures in large American cities, AIDS occurred at a time when, as Dennis Altman noted in 1986, 'the generosity of that [American] society to its outcasts is declining to a level previously unknown.'[41] HIV and AIDS, and the early connections made by the media and the 'numerous spokespersons claiming to stand for Christian morality'[42] which linked them to the nature of gay male sexual activity – promiscuity, anal intercourse – meant that cultural production and cultural activism that represented or promoted homoerotic behaviour could easily be victimized in the same way that gay men were victimised. If in the 1970s and early 1980s, work like Mapplethorpe's could pass virtually unnoticed by the self-appointed protectors of the nation's morality, AIDS meant that homoerotic art and culture was targeted not just on the traditional grounds that it was perverted or immoral, but that it also promoted a lifestyle that could bring disease to the entire society.

The art world during the 1980s was particularly badly hit by AIDS. As well as Mapplethorpe and other notable artists such as Keith Haring and David Wojnarowicz who all contracted the disease in the 1980s, AIDS became a pressing issue for many who lived and worked within artist communities in large American cities. Mapplethorpe's work, however, appears to hark back to a different, pre-AIDS culture, and noticeably deviates from the kind of art that someone like Richard

Goldstein argued AIDS would produce: art that would 'transcend the epidemic'.[43] The visceral and consciously homoerotic nature of Mapplethorpe's pictures also seem out of line with those respectable and important, though ultimately, according to Douglas Crimp, passive responses of cultural practitioners to AIDS: fundraising galas. Events like this, Crimp argues, perpetuate 'the idea that art itself has no social function (aside from being a commodity), that there is no such thing as an engaged, activist aesthetic practice.'[44] Mapplethorpe seemed to embody an activist spirit in his bold pictures, though he was himself by no means an activist.

It was the re-exhibition of Mapplethorpe's pre-AIDS pictures and the sensibility they projected that attracted the attention of neo-conservatives in 1989. After opening at the Institute of Contemporary Art in Philadelphia in December 1988 and closing without incident the following January, Mapplethorpe's 'The Perfect Moment' retrospective was due to visit five other cities. The proposed tour, however, coincided with a new campaign instigated by the American Family Association (AFA) to censor 'blasphemous' art. Serrano's *Piss Christ* was one of their first targets and when it became known that 'The Perfect Moment' had also received NEA funding, the cause of the AFA was taken up in the Senate by Republicans Jesse Helms, Alfonse D'Amato and Dick Armey. Helms embarked on a mission to restrict NEA funding of what he called 'shocking, abhorrent and completely undeserving art'. In June of 1989, in the wake of Helms' Senate campaign, the Corcoran Gallery of Art cancelled its showing of 'The Perfect Moment'. In an organized protest, Mapplethorpe's pictures were projected onto the front of the gallery building. The campaign against NEA funding of 'shocking' art led to calls for its entire budget to be cut and there was a longstanding opposition to federal arts funding by many on the Right who did not consider it the proper role of government. While such calls were never likely to succeed, Helms did have an amendment passed to the NEA bill going through Congress, that banned grants for works that 'promote, disseminate or produce obscene or indecent materials, including but not limited to depictions of sadomasochism, homoeroticism, the exploitation of children, or individuals engaged in sex acts; or material which denigrates the objects or beliefs of the adherents of a particular religion or non-religion.'[45] Although this was later diluted so that the judgement of what was obscene rested with the NEA, the events of 1989, which saw Helms destroy on the floor of the Senate pictures by both Serrano and Mapplethorpe, signified a new climate of cultural conflict between the neo-conservative and religious Right and cultural producers that led to the prosecution on charges of obscenity of Dennis Barrie, director of the Cincinnati Contemporary Arts Center, when it exhibited 'The Perfect Moment' in 1990.

Barrie was acquitted after standing trial, but, if the banning of *Ulysess* in 1921 seems to belong to an entirely different cultural era, the Serrano and Mapplethorpe saga is a salutary lesson that US society, like many others, does not naturally move in the direction of greater tolerance and freedom. Writing about New York from the early to the mid-twentieth century, George Chauncey has argued that gay history, in New York at least, does not fall easily into the 'progressive' history of steady liberation. Instead he suggests that

> gay life in New York was less tolerated, less visible to outsiders, and more rigidly segregated in the second third of the century than the first, and that the very severity of the postwar reaction has tended to blind us to the relative tolerance of the prewar years.[46]

If this position changed again during the 1960s and 1970s, the 1980s brought with it an atmosphere altogether more hostile and demonstrated that censorship in the US can never be consigned to the past. It continued in the 1980s and beyond, often unseen, in the complaints of parents and parents' groups, religious organizations and pressure groups, not just about arts funding, but also the screening of films – such as *The Last Temptation of Christ* (1988) – the playing of music – as mentioned in the Introduction – and the stocking of certain books in libraries.[47] For all the 1980s has a reputation for being a decade of excess, the boundaries of acceptability were constantly being policed.

Chapter 3

Film and Television

Hollywood Synergised

The Hollywood that emerged at the end of the 1980s, buoyed by a decade of record box-office receipts, mergers and diversification, was very different to the crisis-ridden industry which ended the 1970s. For Stephen Prince, the 1980s marked a watershed in the history of Hollywood that not only saw its corporate structures change, but also witnessed a fundamental shift in the very nature of Hollywood's purpose: 'Instead of making films, the industry shifted to the production of filmed entertainment, a quite different enterprise that encompassed production and distribution of entertainment in a variety of markets and media.'[1] What Prince is emphasizing is the way that during the 1980s Hollywood began to take full advantage of film's ancillary markets. While the licensing of film products had long been part of film production, it had never generated significant income. During the 1980s, diversification into video, video games, cable television, publishing and various forms of product merchandising provided increasingly important streams of revenue for the industry.

Before these new markets could be exploited, however, there were certain structural problems in Hollywood that needed to be corrected. Like other large industries in the 1970s, the major Hollywood studios and the larger organizations of which many were subsidiaries had become inefficient, vulnerable to rising inflation and lacked the kinds of integrated business focus needed to be successful in an increasingly competitive, global economy. Paramount Pictures, for example, was a subsidiary of the conglomerate Gulf and Western Industries Inc., whose portfolio of businesses stretched from the agricultural sector to manufacturing to car replacement parts and the leisure sector – where Paramount resided and which in 1980 accounted for 20 per cent of

Gulf and Western's total sales.[2] This wide range of interests had been put together by Charles Bluhdorn following his takeover of Michigan Plating & Stamping in 1958. When Bluhdorn died in 1983, he was replaced as Gulf and Western Chief Executive by Martin S. Davis who had worked his way up through Paramount Pictures. Davis concentrated on the leisure and communication sectors, which included book publishing, television, cinema theatres and cable sports entertainment, and proceeded to sell off many of the unrelated businesses. In 1989, so effective were the results of this corporate streamlining, that Gulf and Western was renamed Paramount Communications. It was now an organization whose business interests were diversified in connected and coherent ways.

Similarly, Twentieth Century-Fox entered the 1980s as a stand-alone company with two major areas of business activity: Fox Entertainment, which looked after film, television and music production and distribution; and Fox Enterprises, which was involved in the bottling of soft drinks and leisure-resort management in Aspen and Pebble Beach, California. While Fox Entertainment, with its range of media interests, was usefully diversified, structurally there was little that Fox Enterprises could add to this business and the company as a whole looked weakened by its disparate interests. In 1984 Rupert Murdoch's News Corporation, a media and communications conglomerate with interests in newspapers, book publishing, sports and television, took control of Twentieth Century-Fox which became the News Corporation's film production and distribution wing.

These two examples give an indication of the way in which Hollywood filmmaking was restructured during the 1980s. There were many other instances, too. As each of the major movie studios produced blockbuster hits with all sorts of potential for ancillary spin-offs, so they were all attractive businesses for takeover or merger. The principle driving this shakeout was synergy: a belief that two or more influences or agents can, when acting together rather than independently, create effects which are more than the sum of their parts. In business this meant the vertical integration of economic interests. For a company that produces films it makes much more financial sense to also own the company that produces and distributes the video of the film (as well as the toy company that produces film merchandise and the recording company that releases the film soundtrack) than it does to own a company bottling soft drinks. And for a company that has global media interests outside of film, it makes sense to add film to that media portfolio. Companies and subsidiaries with disparate economic interests changed to become, over the course of the 1980s, businesses with 'a tight focus on entertainment and communications operations in which theatrical film was a small but vital component'.[3]

What was taking place in Hollywood, and more generally in the media industry, was part of that process of national economic restructuring in the US described in the Introduction. Mergers and acquisitions in the media industry were more numerous than in any other sector apart from banking and business services and were worth in total some $89.2 billion over the course of the decade. The process was not always a successful one. Coca-Cola bought Columbia Pictures in 1982 for $692 million in the hope that there was a profitable connection to be exploited between soft drinks and films. In fact, this connection proved not to be economically viable, despite Coca-Cola informing its shareholders that 'In Columbia we have an excellent complement to our traditional businesses – an almost ideal fit with what we are.'[4] Columbia was eventually sold to Sony for $3.4 billion as the Japanese company sought to establish itself as a global hardware and software conglomerate, having already purchased CBS Records the previous year to become world's largest record producer. Other examples of successful, and synergy-driven, mergers and acquisitions are the merger of Time Inc. and Warner Communications which was eventually completed in 1990 and the buyout of MCA by the Japanese hardware manufacturer Matsushita, also in 1990.

If the major producers of American films began the decade as stand-alone businesses or subsidiaries of US-focused conglomerates, by the end of the 1980s all were elements in huge, global entertainment and communications corporations. The only exception was Disney, whose longstanding international success allowed it to avoid merger and buyout and turn itself into a global entertainment corporation. This trend, although it started in the 1980s, continued through the 1990s and continues today, where a handful of corporations – Bertelsmann, General Electric, News Corporation, Seagram, Sony, Time Warner, The Times Group, Viacom, Walt Disney Company – dominate the global multimedia economy. Such concentration of ownership has generated concerns not only about monopolistic business practices, but also about the value of cultural products increasingly controlled by the demands of business and capitalism.[5] The film producer Don Simpson, whose hits of the 1980s included *Flashdance* (1983), *Beverly Hills Cop* (1984) and *Top Gun* (1986), once remarked that filmmakers 'have no obligation to make history. We have no obligation to make

art. We have no obligation to make a statement. To make money is our
only objective.'[6] While statements like this serve to polarise opinion
about the advantages and disadvantages of media control, what is
perhaps more important for thinking about the 1980s is how such
structural changes affected the way in which audiences experienced
and consumed film.

The Video Revolution

In 1980, the new home-video market accounted for just 7 per cent of
film industry revenues while domestic and foreign revenues from
ticket sales generated 52.4 per cent. By 1990 the home-video market
generated 38.6 per cent of revenues, more than the income from
domestic and foreign ticket sales and network television rights combined. In money terms, the home-video market was worth $280
million in 1980 and $5.1 billion in 1990. The irony of the growing
importance of this sector to the film industry is that for much of the
late 1970s and early 1980s, two of the major film studios – Universal
and Disney – were locked in a court battle with Sony, claiming that
Sony video machines assisted the infringement of film copyright. At
the heart of this case was a more general fear in the film industry that
new video-recording technology, and its location in households across
the country and the world once cheap hardware became widely available, would drain Hollywood of income:

> The home video boom was a nightmare come true for the Hollywood
> majors. Studio executives lay awake at night, sweating and trembling.
> They pictured families across America watching video movies taped
> from cable television and loaning those videos to friends, or worse yet,
> pictured families with two VCRs hooked together, making video copies
> of other tapes. To the majors, everyone with a VCR was now potentially
> a pirate.[7]

In 1984, the Supreme Court, although only by a split decision, eventually ruled in favour of Sony. What saved Sony was the fact that 'the
sale of copying equipment, like the sale of other articles of commerce,
does not constitute contributory infringement if the product is widely
used for legitimate, unobjectionable purposes.'[8]

As the revenue figures demonstrate, the fear of home video was
misplaced. Cinema ticket sales rose by 20 per cent during the 1980s
(from 1.02 billion in 1980 to 1.26 billion in 1989)[9] while the number

of cinema screens increased from 17,590 to 23,132.[10] Rather than replacing film and the watching of films in cinemas, home video added a whole new consumer market for the film studios to service, although it took them a while to realize that the real opportunities lay not in video rentals but video sales. Because of the first-sale doctrine, an exception to US copyright laws which allows the purchaser of a product (such as a video rental company) to transfer a legally acquired copy of protected work without permission, film studios received no royalties each time a video was rented. The industry tried to overturn this exception with the Consumer Video Sales/Rental Amendment of 1983, but the bill was defeated. The result was that in the early years of home video, the sale price of videos was prohibitively high, since the studios tried to maximize their income from sales to video-rental businesses. What the film studios found, however, was that once they started to lower the retail price of videos there was a clear consumer demand. People wanted not just to see a film in a cinema, but also to buy their favourite films on video in order to watch them again at home. When Steven Spielberg's 1982 hit *E.T.* was eventually released on video in 1988, it sold 15 million copies within the first year, generating revenue of $175 million, almost as much as the $187 million that its cinema release had produced. Revenue of this order ensured that video was the most lucrative of the new markets for film in the 1980s.

Top Gun (1986)

The biggest box-office film of 1986, *Top Gun* was the product of a collaboration between British director Tony Scott (brother of Ridley) and producers Don Simpson and Jerry Bruckheimer. For much of the 1970s and early 1980s, Scott made television commercials. One of these was for SAAB, the Swedish car and aircraft manufacturer, and featured a SAAB 900 Turbo racing one of the company's fighter jets. Impressed by this, as well as Scott's commercially unsuccessful modern vampire film *The Hunger* (1982), Simpson and Bruckheimer offered Scott the *Top Gun* project, which was based on a magazine article Bruckheimer had read about pilots at the Miramar Naval Air Station, San Diego. As well as catapulting Tom Cruise and Kelly McGillis to stardom, *Top Gun* epitomized the 'high concept' and synergy-driven nature of contemporary Hollywood studio production.

Top Gun's plot is straightforward: brilliant but flawed fighter pilot 'Maverick' (Cruise), haunted by the memory of his lost father who was shot down in Vietnam, conquers his personal demons and the death of his best friend by using his brilliance in the cockpit to protect his country and ensure that he gets his girl, Charlotte (McGillis). The combat scenes in the film are shot with all the slickness Scott developed in his advertising work and such was the success of these sequences that the film inadvertently buoyed US Navy and Air Force recruitment. The soundtrack also played a key role in the film's popularity. Spawning three major hits, the most notable was Berlin's ballad 'Take My Breath Away', which reached number one in the US *Billboard* chart and won its writers, Giorgio Moroder and Tom Whitlock, the Academy award for Best Song and the Golden Globe award for Best Original Song in 1987. The video that accompanied the song cut scenes of Berlin singer Terri Nunn wandering amongst decommissioned aircraft with those scenes from the film which tell the story of Maverick and Charlotte's romance. 'Take My Breath Away' reached number one in the UK charts in the same the month the film was released in the UK, while the soundtrack album sold several million copies for Sony. In the 1980s, then, music video became a way of selling films while films became a way of selling music.

Another successful film–music combination was *Flashdance* (1983), directed by Adrian Lyne. The story of a woman who welded by day and disco-danced at night, the marketing strategy for the film was driven by the music. The title track was released before the film and was a hit by the time the film came out. Lyne also produced videos for the other single releases from the film and, like 'Take My Breath Away', utilized clips from the film for the MTV audience to whom the videos were played before and after the film's release.

Top Gun came into its own, however, with its video release. Selling 2.5 million copies in the first week, it became not only the fastest-selling video at that point, but also took advantage of marketing strategies that would later become common practice in the industry. While video rental outlets and the major studios had often been at loggerheads over rental income from videos, the release of *Top Gun* showed that they could work together since many of its sales were through rental outlets. In addition, *Top Gun* was the first video release ever to contain commercial advertising. The first thing that viewers saw as they sat down to watch the video was an advert for Pepsi featuring a group of pilots with names like the characters in the film and performing the same kind of aerobatic stunts that take place in the film. Shot in a similar style to the film and with a similar soundtrack, for Steven Prince, the 'ad achieves perfect synergy with the film, its style and thematic content blending seamlessly with the film's imagery . . . creating a symbiosis of the two products.'[11]

Other spin-offs included the *Top Gun* video game which was released in 1987 for PC, Commodore 64, ZX Spectrum and Nintendo Entertainment System. Subsequent versions followed in the 1990s and as recently as this year Nintendo released a new version for its dual-screen handheld game console. The Ray Ban sunglasses that Cruise wears in the film boosted sales of that particular design by 40 per cent.

Figure 3.1 Tom Cruise as the clean-cut hero backed by patriotic technology in the high-concept *Top Gun* (Tony Scott, Paramount Pictures, 1986). © Paramount/The Kobal Collection.

If video altered where and how people viewed films, the technology on which it relied also altered the way people managed their film and TV viewing. Video cassette recorders (VCRs) were the first piece of home technology to allow viewers to time-shift – to choose when they watched film and network television. No longer tied to television schedules, viewers were able to programme their viewing requirements in advance. This feature of VCR technology, in comparison to videodiscs – a competing technology at the end of the 1970s which was of much higher quality than video but which was not recordable in the home – ensured that VCRs were rapidly taken up as a must-have piece of equipment. In 1980 only 1.9 million US households had a VCR. By 1989 this figure was 62.3 million, or two thirds of all US households.

The portability and ease of access to video more than made up for its inferior quality and it also changed the way films were made. The opportunity to quickly review a take on set during filming – known as a video assist – could slow down the shooting process, but it offered the kind of instant feedback unavailable with traditional technology and helped reduce post-production costs. It also gave impetus to electronic editing and the digital-effects revolution which would take off during the 1990s.

There were also a couple of unforeseen spin-offs from the arrival of video. The first was the stimulus it provided for independent film-making. While the major studios produced dozens of films, there was clearly a demand for films, particularly in the video market, with which they could not keep pace. The money that was pouring into the film industry through video made independent projects more viable, whether they were distributed by the major studios or by some of the new distribution companies that were establishing themselves in the 1980s, such as Miramax, New Line, Vestron, Island and Cinecom. Some of the most important directors of the decade who emerged via the independent route were: Jim Jarmusch – *Stranger Than Paradise* (1982), *Down By Law* (1983), *Coffee and Cigarettes* (1986), *Mystery Train* (1989); Joel and Ethan Coen – *Blood Simple* (1985), *Raising Arizona* (1987); Steven Soderbergh – *sex, lies, and videotape* (1989); and Spike Lee – *She's Gotta Have It* (1986), *Do the Right Thing* (1989). Lee was notable for being one of very few successful black film direc-tors in the wake of the waning blaxploitation trend so important to filmmaking in the 1970s.

Even more unexpected, and in the context of the neo-conservative climate of the 1980s all the more alarming for the Christian and polit-ical Right, was the dramatic upturn in the production of pornographic films. Previously restricted to adult cinemas or unwieldy and poor-quality 8mm projectors, pornography quickly took advantage of video. Films could be shot straight to video now that video cameras were readily available, while VCRs created a massive potential audi-ence. The increased visibility of pornography resulted in an anti-porn backlash from both the religious Right and the feminist movement, an uneasy alliance which was successful in drawing government attention to pornography – Attorney General Ed Meese set up a Commission on Pornography and a National Obscenity Enforcement Unit was established to help assist prosecutions under obscenity laws – but which singularly failed to prevent the porn industry from thriving over the course of the decade. By the late 1980s, and mainly from its bases in California's San Fernando Valley, the pornography industry was releasing over a thousand videos each year and generating revenues of around $400 million. The industry even managed to survive AIDS and the death of some its biggest stars from the disease (notably John Holmes and the gay porn stars Casey Donovan and Eric Stryker) and began to regulate itself through the regular testing facilities offered by the Adult Industry Medical Health Care Foundation, set up by former porn actress Sharon Mitchell.

If Steven Prince is right that 'in the eighties film *was* video',[12] then video was also the epitome of the way in which Hollywood, like other longstanding industries, was looking to regenerate itself, not by simply reviving existing markets, but by exploiting entirely new markets opened up by advances in technology. The corporate restructurings which marked the 1980s meant that video was at the forefront of an integrated assault upon eager consumers only too happy to participate in a new media and communications landscape where film, video, soundtrack and video game were all part of the film experience and allowed the film to live on long after its cinematic release.

Blockbusters

In many ways the blockbuster film was central to this whole integrated process. While video, soundtrack and supplementary merchandising opportunities might help recoup money on films struggling to break even, the blockbuster film was guaranteed to generate profits in all its various markets. The 1980s was the decade of the 'high concept' film industry whose principles determined many of the most successful blockbusters (as well as many of the unsuccessful attempts to produce blockbusters).[13] Relying on relatively straightforward and easily categorized characters and familiar plots that could be described briefly, high concept films were high on stylish and slick production qualities and sold themselves not only through their acting stars, but also the publicity which accompanied them. The epitome of synergised film production, high concept films came with soundtracks, video tie-ins and promotional merchandising in fast-food chains. The release cycle for each element – film, soundtrack, video, cable television, network television – was carefully managed to stimulate and maximize audience appeal. Films which the studios thought would have mass appeal were given an initial saturation release, opening simultaneously in cinemas across the country. An expensive exercise given the number of film prints that had to be manufactured, saturation releases – like *The Empire Strikes Back* (1980) *E.T.* (1982), *Ghostbusters* (1984) and *Batman* (1989) – were accompanied by a marketing and promotion blitz that became essential in order to produce the intense public visibility for a film in a competitive leisure and consumer marketplace. Alternative strategies were used for less obviously popular films. They were released to only a select number of cinemas and then rolled out elsewhere as feedback and initial box-office receipts indicated the potential appeal. The multi-Oscar-winning film *Amadeus* (1984), a biopic of the composer Mozart, opened in just twenty-five cinemas in September of 1984 but by May 1985 was playing in 802 cinemas across the country.[14] Other Oscar-winning films that gradually built up audiences in this way included *Ghandi* (1982) and *Driving Miss Daisy* (1989).

While blockbuster movies covered a range of genres and styles, the most popular during the 1980s were science-fiction and fantasy-adventure films. George Lucas and Steven Spielberg cemented their reputations as Hollywood's most bankable directors with a series of huge successes in this genre. Lucas released *The Empire Strikes Back* (1980) and *The Return of the Jedi* (1983) – both the bestselling film in their respective year – while Spielberg, in addition to *E.T.*, fulfilled the promise shown in his seventies hits *Jaws* (1975) and *Close Encounters of the Third Kind* (1977) with the Indiana Jones trilogy: *Raiders of the Lost Ark* (1981), *Indiana Jones and the Temple of Doom* (1984) and *Indiana Jones and the Last Crusade* (1989). (The Indiana Jones and Star Wars films made Harrison Ford, by some distance, the biggest box-office star of the 1980s.)

Popular science-fiction products of the 1950s and 60s – *Superman* and *Star Trek*, for instance – were repackaged for a 1980s audience and went through various sequels as well spinning off into successful TV series (*Star Trek: The Next Generation* which launched in 1987, and an animated *Superman* series launching in 1988 with *Lois and Clark: The New Adventures of Superman* following in the early 1990s). *Ghostbusters* (1984), *Gremlins* (1984), *Back to the Future* (1985) and *Honey, I Shrunk the Kids* (1989) were part of a sub-genre that combined science fiction and fantasy with comedy, while at the other end of the scale films like *Alien* (1979), and the first of its sequels, *Aliens* (1986), along with *The Thing* (1982) and *Terminator* (1984), used science fiction to create more unsettling and dystopic films.

The prevalence of these genres, together with the staples of comedy and horror, among the list of the decade's most popular films has been seen by some as a sign that Hollywood produced only conventional and conservative offerings during the 1980s. This argument is often combined with an attack on the ideological content of blockbuster films which are seen to mirror Reagan's America. Writing in the middle of the decade, Andrew Britton identified 'a general movement of reaction and conservative reassurance in the contemporary Hollywood cinema' and argued that 'it is difficult to think of any mainstream American film released since the spring of 1982 which is even of moderate distinction.'[15] Britton is concerned with what he calls 'Reaganite entertainment', a ritualized, formulaic and self-referential style of entertainment that offers escape from, rather than a critical dialogue with, contemporary society and culture: 'Entertainment tells us to forget our troubles and to get happy.'[16] One can see how the prevalence of science fiction and fantasy as key genres of the 1980s might fit into this paradigm, but, more invidiously for Britton, the treatment of technology in film of the 1980s is unquestioning in its devotion and simply eases the transition from industrial to high-tech capitalism that requires new social structures in order to flourish:

> It is hardly surprising, in a period in which the contradiction between the general interest and the interests served by modern capitalist technique is being exposed with relentless clarity, that capitalist popular culture should be so fundamentally preoccupied with the ecstatic celebration of technology . . . Reaganite space-fiction is there to tell us that the future will be a thrilling replay of the past – with special effects.[17]

More recently, Alan Nadel concentrates on the way that Ronald Reagan made use of cinematic references and clichés in order to secure his political legitimacy. In a culture where 'the narratives of contemporary America rely on unspoken reference to the virtual community created by the cinematic conventions that television has deployed ubiquitously since the end of World War II',[18] Reagan's political success was achieved by showing not only his familiarity with these narratives, but also by his ability to deploy them at key moments during his ascendancy to power and his presidency. For Nadel 'cinema triumphs over economics as the primary producer of social realities'.[19]

Both of these approaches are problematic and make assumptions about a consistent Hollywood project that is supposed to be ideologically coherent. While there is no doubt that blockbuster movies, produced and marketed for maximum financial gain, dominated the box-office successes for each year of the 1980s, if one looks at films that actually did very well below this top level then there are some surprises which raise questions about the kinds of assumptions Britton and Nadel make. In 1980, for instance, *The Empire Strikes Back* was the box-office hit, but ahead of a varied group of films that included: *Kramer vs Kramer*, a story about marital breakdown starring Dustin Hoffman; *Airplane*, a spoof film based on the disaster movies of the 1970s; *Coal Miner's Daughter*, a biopic based on the life of country singer Loretta Lynn; and Stanley Kubrick's *The Shining*, a horror movie starring Jack Nicolson as the psychopathic caretaker of an isolated hotel. In 1986, the year that *Top Gun* topped the box-office charts, James Cameron's *Aliens* offered a very different version of the kinds of encounters that technology might produce than the ones Tom Cruise deals with in his Grumman F-14 Tomcat. Steven Spielberg's adaptation of Alice Walker's *The Color Purple*, a novel about the brutal experiences of a young African American woman, was also well placed in this year.

To attempt to link these films together, along with the hundreds of other films viewed and rented during the course of each year, by way of an ideological common denominator is to produce an account of ideology that is so general as to be virtually worthless. *Top Gun* may well epitomize certain elements of 'Reaganite entertainment' in its patriotic swagger and faith in the superiority of American technology, but the same can hardly be said of *Aliens*. The variety of Hollywood's production and the diversity of the audiences to which it had to appeal in order generate revenues meant that to be ideologically prescriptive would only limit the potential market. Whilst Hollywood's corporate structure may have been monolithic, although less so in the 1980s, perhaps, than other decades, the passing of so much visual information to so many audiences ensured there was no way in which its ideological position could be uniform. The problem with Britton and Nadel's approach is not so much that they want to identify certain trends during the 1980s, but that these trends are used to define rather than illuminate a context. There were films that worked within a Reaganite context but which cannot necessarily be considered to simply represent a Reaganite world view.

Nightmare Visions

John Carpenter described his film *The Thing* (1982) as 'the exact opposite of *E.T.*'[20] Although both films were made by Universal Pictures, they offered radically conflicting representations of alien encounters. While *E.T.* tells the story of a benevolent alien botanist stranded on earth and befriended by children who help him escape back to his own kind, *The Thing* recounts the devastation that an alien predator wreaks in an isolated American research centre after being buried in the Antarctic ice for hundreds of years. Capable of assuming the physical characteristics of the animals and humans it devours, the alien predator has no intention of returning home. Whereas *E.T.* humanizes and infantilizes the figure of alien, and correspondingly reduces its capacity to shock or disturb the world of its viewers, *The*

Thing provides nothing but shock and fear, and this is dramatized most evidently in its use of special effects which are particularly visceral and bloody.

A remake of the 1951 film *The Thing from Another World*, John Carpenter's reworked version emphasises the inability of the research-centre workers to cooperate in order to defeat the alien. This is due both to the difficulty of seeing exactly where the alien is and to the distrust that spreads amongst the workers and which begins to drive them apart. The film ends with only two men left in the station, each thinking the other is the alien. The only solution is to destroy themselves. As an image of a social community trying to deal with danger, *The Thing* is bleakly pessimistic. The fact that one of the survivors is white and one black only heightens the impression that *The Thing* is rooted in a contemporary cultural context, not of cooperation and forward-looking revivalism, but of a historically deep-rooted conflict and fear. Because the alien passes from one host to another invisibly, like a virus, the film also raises questions about the discrepancy between appearance and reality and about the reliability of visual performance. If the 1980s was a moment when acting and politics never had closer connections, then these kinds of issues raised by a film like *The Thing* ultimately offer feedback of the kind that writers like Britton and Nadel have argued is absent in American film production during the period.

Wolfen (1981), similarly, offers an interesting early 1980s take on the business of Wall Street that will come to preoccupy the decade. Starring Albert Finney as a New York detective investigating the murder of wealthy industrialist Christopher Vanderveer and his wife, the film offers differing interpretations of the mysterious wolf-like creatures causing havoc in the city. While official bodies suspect a political terrorist group, with Vanderveer's radical niece a prime suspect, Finney learns that the wolfen are actually spirits from Native American folklore taking revenge on modern society. Other horror films such as *Poltergeist* (1982) – scripted by Steven Spielberg – and *Pet Sematary* (1989) – based on a Stephen King novel – also deal with the haunting of contemporary society by Native American spirits whose land has been desecrated.

In many ways, the horror genre is well suited to the task of articulating discontent since its recovery and representation of the repressed, the abject and the uncomfortable is always likely to unsettle a cultural dominant that would sooner see these elements contained. The tension between these conflicting desires is witnessed by the fact that, although a popular and successful genre during the 1980s, horror also generated various moral panics which sought to censor it or condemn it because of its supposedly evil social effects. The slasher movie genre was central here. Growing out of the horror tradition in the late 1970s and early 1980s, films like John Carpenter's *Halloween* (1978) and Sean Cunningham's *Friday the 13th* (1980) instigated a rush of movies in this genre, such as *Slumber Party Massacre* (1982), *Sleepaway Camp* (1983) and *A Nightmare on Elm Street* (1984), many of which had numerous sequels. With low budgets and driven by simple plots that usually consist of young people (although especially young women) being murdered by psychotic, masked attackers whilst away from adult supervision, slasher films rode the video boom and found an eager audience. The ready availability on video of these and other horror movies with explicit violent and sexual content led to them being termed 'video nasties' in Britain and a new, stricter classification of such titles under the Video Recordings Act 1984. In the US, slasher films were attacked by the political Right and Left and by film critics. While there was no formal political intervention as in Britain, the Motion Picture Association of America (MPAA), the film industry's representative body, came under increasing pressure to alter its classification categories, particularly for video releases which often kept their cinematic rating even though material cut from the original cinema release was included in the video release. The Left, and particularly feminists, objected to the violence perpetrated against women in many of the films, while the Right included the film industry in its larger moral crusade against pornography and violence on screen. Both Left and Right were concerned that violence on screen resulted in violence off screen. The MPAA responded by bringing in a new classification system in 1984 which distinguished between PG and PG-13 films, the latter requiring special parental guidance for children under the age of thirteen. The R and X categories remained unchanged, however.

The larger argument about the off-screen effects of slasher and violent horror films is ongoing, but some of the initial critical reaction against such material has been tempered by more subtle understandings of how film operates in dialogue with its audience. Mark Jancovich, for instance, takes issue with one particular objection to slasher films: that they present the monstrous as the essence of evil rather than as a product of American social life, and in so doing offer no leverage with which to critique America and its institutions. Rather, Jancovich argues, it is precisely their apparent lack of motivation which makes them horrific and fascinating for the viewer:

These figures captivate their audiences because they are driven by relent-less and compulsive types of behaviour over which they have no control. The tendency to refer to these figures as 'killing machines' is therefore highly appropriate. They lack subjectivity and seem to act like pro-grammed automatons. The fears associated with these serial killers are similar to . . . other form of contemporary horror. They are fears that human identity is being erased by forms of rationalized behaviour.[21]

Neither is the supposed misogyny of the films straightforward. While women are often the victims, it is not always – as is sometimes assumed – female promiscuity which is being punished. Often, as in *Halloween*, the female who survives is strong and independent. There are even examples, such as *I Spit on Your Grave* (originally released in 1978 but re-released in 1981 after certain cuts), of women playing the role of killer. If women and femininity are a problem for the men both portrayed in and viewing slasher films, then this is just as much a signal of the anxieties about masculinity the films are exploring as it is straightforward misogyny. As mentioned in the Introduction, Susan Faludi sees the 1980s as a period of cultural backlash against women. But in constructing a discourse complaining about the success of fem-inism and its consequences for women, this backlash was also indica-tive of an uncertainness and concern about the place of men in American culture. While fears of feminization go as far back as the late nineteenth century, when Henry James has Basil Ransome in *The Bostonians* complain that 'the whole generation is being womanized',[22] the response in the 1980s to this fear was the construction of a manli-ness that not only reasserted a sense of cultural and social authority, but that was also hypermasculine. Action-movie heroes were a staple of the decade. The two most successful were Sylvester Stallone, who continued his Rocky movies – *Rocky III* (1982), *Rocky IV* (1985) – while also portraying one of the decade's most recognizable film roles, John Rambo in *First Blood* (1982), *Rambo: First Blood Part II* (1985) and *Rambo III* (1988), and Arnold Schwarzenegger, who found Hollywood fame with performances that utilized his bodybuilding past in films such as *Conan the Barbarian* (1982), *Conan the Destroyer* (1984), *Terminator* (1984), *Commando* (1985), *The Running Man* (1987) and *Predator* (1987). Films in this action genre represent reas-suringly masculine (and often patriotic) men, but while as spectacle they might offer 'ordinary' men a vicarious sense of masculine success, they also present images of masculinity – the 'hard bodies' about which Susan Jeffords writes[23] – that are wholly unattainable and which may serve only to remind their audience how far distant from them is this image of manhood.

The same can be said of films which re-imagine the past. Part of the neo-conservative agenda of the 1980s was not only a determination to get over the cultural crisis of confidence that Ronald Reagan called the 'Vietnam syndrome' in his First Inaugural Address of January 1981, but also a nostalgia for a time before the 1960s, a decade synonymous for many neo-conservatives with events – civil rights, multiculturalism and feminism, for instance – that signalled a wrong turn in American history. The attempt to recover the 1950s often formed around a rhetoric of contented domesticity and so-called 'family values' of respect, monogamy and simplicity.

Back to the Future was the highest-earning film of 1985 and provides a reading of the 1950s, and its relationship to the 1980s, which complicates much of this rhetoric despite having been held up as a film that does the job of neo-conservative ideology. Reagan, in his 1986 State of the Union address, claimed that 'Never has there been a more exciting time to be alive, a time of rousing wonder and heroic achievement. As they said in the film *Back to the Future*, "Where we're going, we don't need roads."'[24] This referencing of the film in support of technological progress seems downright ironic when one of the central technological elements of the film – the DeLorean car used by Marty (Michael J. Fox) to travel backwards and forwards in time – was one of the biggest hi-tech failures of the 1980s. Eventually going bankrupt in 1982, the DeLorean Motor Company was set up in Northern Ireland by American engineer and inventor John DeLorean in 1978. His new concept car – stainless steel body, gull-wing doors – proved to be an ignominious failure. *Back to the Future* is also one of the films cited by Alan Nadel as following a Reaganite logic in its formal construction:

> Banking on quick returns, on an infinite supply of credit, on not running out of time, on not getting caught – in other words, banking on all the cinematic powers that facilitate Doc and Marty's adventures in *Back to the Future* – thousands of financiers, traders, speculators, and public officials disrupted the space–time continuum through insider trading and leveraged offers. They went, so to speak, back to the futures.[25]

While there may be an element of truth in this assessment, it does little to resolve some of more ambiguous aspects of the film. First of all, at the beginning of the film, the 1950s is depicted as a time when the

Figure 3.2 Marty (Michael J. Fox) goes back to the 1950s and meets his mother (Lea Thompson) and father (Crispin Glover) in *Back to the Future* (Robert Zemeckis, Universal, 1985). © Amblin/Universal/The Kobal Collection.

future for Marty's parents is determined not for the better, but for the worse: Marty's mother, Lorraine, is an alcoholic and his father, George, is Biff Tannen's lackey. Marty's trip back to the 1950s becomes a re-arranging, albeit accidentally, of events that produce a much more successful and happy family: at the end of the film Lorraine is beautiful and glamorous and George a successful author with Biff his gopher. This rewriting of the script of the 1950s with the hindsight of the 1980s has more than a hint of being a commentary on the way the 1950s is constructed ideologically in the rhetoric of the New Right. Second, the determination Lorraine shows in trying to seduce her future son adds a whole new dimension to the accusation that some 1950s men were mummies' boys. The oedipal connotations of this storyline and Biff's attempted rape of Lorraine at the Enchantment under the Sea dance suggest more complex – and much less chaste – attitudes towards sex and sexuality than those sometimes associated with the 1950s.

If *Back to the Future* has fun at the expense of the way some Americans conceive the 1950s and the discrepancies between 1950s and 1980s life (who could believe that Ronald Reagan would be pres-ident, that life preservers would be fashionable, that black music would have such an influence on the next generation of kids?), David

Lynch's *Blue Velvet* (1986) strikes at the heart of the idea that the 1950s was an idyllic time in national history. Set in the small town of Lumberton, even though the date of the action is never revealed, Lynch uses a series of visual and audio cues to recreate the feel of the 1950s and early 1960s: the film opens with the camera panning from clear blue skies to white picket fences and gardens with blooming roses and tulips; over these images plays Bobby Vinton's 1963 version of 'Blue Velvet', originally a hit for Tony Bennett in 1951; a distinctly ancient-looking fire engine with a waving fireman rolls past. This idyll is soon shattered when the father of central protagonist Jeffrey Beaumont (Kyle MacLachlan) suffers a stroke while watering his garden. The camera closes in on the myriad bugs and insects which live in the lawn and the film begins to impart its main ideological tenet: that beneath the veneer of what looks like an idyll resides another world that is much more discomforting. Jeffrey is led into this world when he finds a severed ear in a field after visiting his father in hospital. Jeffrey's girl-friend, Sandy Williams (Laura Dern), is the daughter of the detective investigating the case of the severed ear, and the romance between Jeffrey and Sandy is depicted as a pastiche of 1950s teen romances: they walk along quiet suburban sidewalks, hang out in the local diner and drive around in Jeffrey's convertible, while Sandy dresses in a series of retro dresses, blouses and knitwear.

All this sits uncomfortably alongside the world of crime and sexual violence Jeffrey encounters as he tries to find his own solution to the severed ear. The way the camera travels into the ear, and does not come back out until the end of the film, suggests that what takes place in the intervening period is as much a psychological as a social exploration, and the way the film fuses these two elements – through its use of film noir and stylized representations of the past – makes it such a success. Jeffrey is drawn into the world of Frank Booth (Dennis Hopper), a sadistic killer who controls nightclub singer Dorothy Vallens (Isabella Rossellini) after murdering her husband and kidnapping her son. The most memorable scenes in the film are when Jeffrey watches from Dorothy's closet as Booth extorts sadistic sexual favours from her while inhaling amyl nitrate. Jeffrey's relationship with Booth is com-plicated – with their desires implicitly connected – when he embarks on an affair with Dorothy himself before finally shooting Booth dead. The ending of the film returns the viewer to the idyll with which it started. Jeffrey and Sandy are reunited, the Beaumont and Williams families are about to eat lunch together and Sandy spots a robin with a bug in its mouth perched on the kitchen window-ledge. What is

Figure 3.3 Frank Booth (Dennis Hopper, right) reveals the violence and sexual exploitation of suburban life to the innocent Jeffrey Beaumont (Kyle MacLachlan) in *Blue Velvet* (David Lynch, De Laurentiis, 1984). © De Laurentiis/The Kobal Collection.

fascinating about this moment is the purposely artificial nature of the robin, which turns its head mechanically like an automaton. The artificiality here undercuts the rosy ending to the film and stands as a reminder of how the ideological reconstruction of cultural memory might, likewise, be artificial. *Blue Velvet* reinserts into this cultural memory the possibilities and human practices – uncomfortable, unpalatable and nightmarish – that are often elided in the rush to define an era and to define experience. After the failure of his previous film, *Dune* (1984), *Blue Velvet* marked a return for David Lynch to the world of the grotesque and surreal that he explored in *Eraserhead* (1977) and *Elephant Man* (1980) and remains one of the most important films of the 1980s.

Wall Street (1987)

Oliver Stone's *Wall Street* was released in December 1987, two months after Black Monday saw the second-largest one-day percentage decline in stock market history. Even before this, public confidence in Wall Street practices and the yuppie lifestyles that went along with them had been hit by the first wave of insider-trading allegations. Although it received mixed reviews on release, Stone's depiction of ruthless financial trading created a figure – Gordon Gekko (Michael Douglas) – who stood as the epitome of all that was wrong in the corporate and financial world that had developed so rapidly in the 1980s. While the role won Michael Douglas an Oscar, it is perhaps notable that in the American Film Institute's list of top fifty movie villains, Gordon Gekko comes in at twenty-six, ten places higher than *Blue Velvet*'s sadistic murderer Frank Booth.

Wall Street and American corporate business have provided an easy target over the years. Indeed, as Emily Stipes Watt has pointed out, 'Most businessmen depicted in post-1945 television and serious literature are still characterized as greedy, unethical, and immoral . . . whether they are JR of William Gaddis's *JR: A Novel* or J.R. of "Dallas".'[26] The same can be said of American film, from Charlie Chaplin's *Modern Times* (1936), through *The Hucksters* (1947) and on to *Glengarry Glen Ross* (1992). While *Wall Street* provides perhaps the greatest of all corporate villains, Stone's film is interesting because of the grounds on which it chooses to indict Wall Street and American capital. The film revolves around the relationship between the legendary Gekko and ambitious young stock trader Bud Fox (Charlie Sheen). After eventually getting to see him, Bud ingratiates himself with Gekko by passing on information he has learnt from his father, Carl (Martin Sheen), who works for Bluestar airline. Gekko uses this information – the not-yet-public news that Bluestar will be cleared of negligence in a crash investigation – to buy shares in the company. When the news is made public the price of the shares rises and Gekko makes a quick profit. While Bud learns the secret of successful trading, inside information, his blue-collar origins are also used in the film to distinguish between the right and wrong ways to create wealth. Gekko's methods are exposed in one of his speeches:

> The richest one percent of this country owns half our country's wealth, five trillion dollars. One third of that comes from hard work, two thirds comes from inheritance, interest on interest accumulating to widows and idiot sons and what I do, stock and real estate speculation. It's bullshit. You got ninety percent of the American public out there with little or no net worth. I create nothing. I own.

The conflict between predatory wealth that owns but does not create and a more traditional concept of 'hard work' is the central ideological conflict the film explores. Because of his upbringing, his father and his current job, Bud has a foot in both sides of the conflict. As he becomes part of Gekko's inner circle of associates, he becomes very wealthy and begins to enjoy the trappings of a yuppie lifestyle. There comes a moment, however, when he is forced to choose between the relative values represented by Gekko and by his blue-collar, union-leader father. This moment occurs when he discovers that Gekko is organizing a hostile takeover of Bluestar as part of an asset-stripping plan. Using the tricks of insider trading he has learnt from Gekko, Bud manages to foil the takeover, but as a result is arrested for breaking trading laws.

Stone's film is clearly an indictment of the Wall Street the American public had fallen out of love with. But it achieves its critical purchase on this phenomenon by way of an overly idealistic representation of the values associated with Bud's father Carl and the blue-collar world to which he belongs and which has shaped Bud's moral ideology. In some ways, this idealization is symptomatic, not of any radical political agenda, but of the very partial cultural memory that was used in the 1980s by neo-conservatives in their representations and reconstructions of the past. The one issue not raised by the film is that blue-collar workers, especially blue-collar men, were strong supporters of neo-conservatism, especially its economic policies after the malaise of the 1970s. The so-called Reagan Democrats – blue-collar workers who traditionally voted Democrat but who switched to Reagan in 1980 and 1984 – are the absent presence of *Wall Street* and might make us consider that condemnations of corporate mal-practice which pit the moral against the immoral often simplify complex networks of ideological affiliation.

Figure 3.4 Ambitious young broker Bud Fox (Charlie Sheen, left) pays close attention to his corporate-raider mentor and hero Gordon Gekko (Michael Douglas) in *Wall Street* (Oliver Stone, 20th Century Fox, 1987). © 20th Century Fox/The Kobal Collection.

The Rise of Cable Television

On 1 January 1980 the US was due to have a new cable television network. Called Premiere, it was set up by four of Hollywood's major film studios – Columbia, Paramount, MCA and Twentieth Century-

Fox – and had exclusive rights to the films it showed for nine months after their release to the network. This move by the film studios was an indication of the burgeoning revenues available in the cable television market and demonstrated their keenness to diversify into areas connected with film production and distribution. Unfortunately for the studios involved, their entry into cable television was belated and driven by a fear of Home Box Office (HBO) which was owned by Time Inc. and had, during the late 1970s, established a very strong position in cable while the major film studios had chosen to ignore it. As Stephen Prince points out, this was one of 'a number of miscalculations and errors' the studios made 'in their attempts to implement strategies for dealing with new markets'.[27] What irked the studios was that HBO bought the cable rights to films in advance of their cinematic release. This meant that if the studio found they had a major success on their hands, they could not negotiate licensing deals based on the popularity and box-office success of a film. What complicated this situation was that they also needed HBO's money to help finance the films they were making. HBO, for instance, provided more than a third of the $12 million required to make *Sophie's Choice* (1982).[28] By the time the major studios realized the potential of cable, HBO already had 60 per cent of American cable subscribers and the $2 billion market that it constituted.[29] Premiere was Hollywood's way of fighting back. They also launched a legal assault on HBO, claiming its position was monopolistic and that because it financed, produced and showed films on its own cable network, this represented a restraint of trade. Instead of indicting HBO, however, the Justice Department accused the four studios behind Premiere of acting together to restrict competition, or, in other words, of violating American anti-trust laws. Premiere admitted defeat and the new cable service was abandoned.

The battle between HBO and the Hollywood studios signalled how important cable television had become by the beginning of the 1980s. From relatively humble origins in the 1940s, when the first cable networks were set up in Arkansas, Oregon and Pennsylvania to service local communities eager to take advantage of the increased availability of cheap television sets but where ordinary aerial reception was limited, cable television has gradually eroded the place of traditional broadcast or terrestrial television in the US provided by ABC, NBC and CBS. Whereas cable had initially been used to allow access to these network channels, it soon became a means of distributing local programmes, while cable-only networks, like HBO, took advantage of new satellite technology in the 1970s to establish themselves as nationwide providers. Indeed, much of the important groundwork for cable expansion was laid in the 1970s. Just as it was in the late 1970s that the air traffic and gas industries were deregulated, and it was Jimmy Carter who appointed Paul Volcker as Chairman of the Federal Reserve 1979, so the appointment of Charles Ferris to the chair of the Federal Communications Commission (FCC) in 1977 introduced a new perspective on regulation and the FCC began licensing thousands of new stations in an effort to replace behavioural regulation with the forces of competition. Within the cable industry itself, the event that is spoken of most consistently as the catalyst for the growth of the sector is an event that took place in the middle of the 1970s: Muhammad Ali and Joe Frazier's heavyweight bout, the Thriller in Manila, of October 1975. This was the first time a TV channel, in this instance HBO, had used a geosynchronous satellite transmission to broadcast a pro-gramme to its cable subscribers. By doing so it relayed a live sporting event to the entire country and showed the possibilities for a cable TV industry that had been stagnant for much of the 1960s and early 1970s.

The consequences of cable and satellite television in the 1980s were manifold. In terms of quantity, cable and satellite dramatically increased the number of channels available. Whereas broadcast televi-sion sent a signal via a radio wave which contained information about only one channel, co-axial cable and satellite technology allowed the transmission of dozens of different channels in one signal that was then decoded via a box at the viewer's end. Cable and satellite also gener-ated various forms of dedicated content. Rather than providing a range of material – from drama to comedy to film to news – like the broad-cast networks, cable channels developed specialist niches. Before it diversified into a multi-channel network with different kinds of pro-grammes, MTV (Music Television) showed nothing but music videos after it launched on 1 August 1981. CNN (Cable Network News) launched as a single-channel, dedicated news station on 1 June 1980 and introduced rolling, twenty-four-hour news coverage to American, and, later, world audiences. ESPN (originally an acronym for Entertainment and Sports Programming Network) launched in September 1979, and although it started off primarily as a sports news channel and showed marginal sporting events, by mid-decade it had rights to show live National Football League games on a Sunday night, and by the end of the decade had secured rights to show live baseball as well, making it the most pre-eminent cable sports channel in the US.

Cable also opened up whole new areas to television and altered the very purpose of television. The Home Shopping Network originally launched on local cable television in Florida in 1982. Within three years it had become the first national shopping channel. The QVC (standing for Quality, Value, Convenience) shopping channel began transmitting the following year and by 1987 was available twenty-four hours a day. Developments such as this show that just as filmmaking in the 1980s was increasingly aware of the ancillary markets which would change the very nature of its artistic and business focus, so television was embarking on a period of development that involved both creating new markets and increasingly targeting viewers with specialized content. Specialization and niche marketing ensured that many different genres and tastes were catered for. As well as religious television networks, during the 1980s various racial and ethnic groups began to utilize the opportunities offered by cable and satellite. Black Entertainment Television, aimed at a predominantly urban, African American audience, began in January 1980 and was showing programmes twenty-four hours a day from 1983. The rise of genre cable channels was also a notable feature of the decade. The Discovery Channel was launched in 1985, A&E Networks, owners of The History Channel and The Biography Channel, was formed in 1983, while the same year also saw the launch of Disney's first cable television channel. The fragmentation of the television-viewing experience, which was aided by the availability of the VCR, was further enhanced by the increasing plethora of cable and satellite offerings. While Bruce Springsteen might complain on his 1992 album *Human Touch* about there being '57 channels and nothing on', the reality was that not only were there many more channels than fifty-seven available, but also people were finding something to watch. While basic cable networks may have relied on repeat screenings of shows and non-original programming, the premium pay-cable channels – like HBO, Showtime, and Encore – offered fresh, exclusive content, especially film, drama and sport, that had mass appeal.

One final legacy of cable television was its public-access ethos. As cable developed in the late 1960s and early 1970s, the FCC decreed that all new cable systems should offer public, educational and government (known as PEG) access to cable technology, usually paid for out of the fees cable companies received. This arrangement was based on a long-standing principle that the airwaves belonged not to companies but to the American people and that public access was only fair when companies were running their cable through and underneath public land. Although the FCC decision was overturned in 1977, such was the competition among cable companies to make agreements with local authorities that public-access rights were often used as part of their negotiating strategies and now from part of most cable agreements. While public-access television is almost always low budget, it is one of the few places where local members of the community can make their own programmes using equipment provided by the cable companies. While these were often made in the spirit of community broadcasting, public-access television was also used more controversially. In New York, *The Ugly George Hour of Truth, Sex and Violence* became a cult cable TV show. There was little truth or violence in the programme, however, which mainly consisted of the show's creator and presenter 'Ugly' George Urban coaxing the women of New York to remove their clothes for the camera. Extremist political groups like the Ku Klux Klan have also used cable television to make public-access programmes. While the 1984 Cable Franchise Policy and Communications Act allowed cable television monopolies to exist in each community in exchange for a percentage being given to communities to provide public-access programming, the Act also prevented cable operators from exercising editorial control over the content of public-access programming.

The low-budget ethos and makeshift quality of much public-access TV was mocked by Mike Myers in his *Wayne's World* sketches, which first appeared on the TV show *Saturday Night Live* in February 1989. The sketches, along with the film that followed in 1992, can also, however, be seen as offering a vindication of public-access TV, with its ramshackle production qualities and community-oriented values, in the face of the increasingly market-driven, corporatized and predatory entertainment industries of the 1980s and 1990s.

Television Genres: Soaps, Crime Dramas, Sitcoms and Talk Shows

If cable television was altering the delivery and diversity of small-screen programming during the 1980s, it wouldn't be until the late 1990s that premium cable networks began to produce the kind of critically acclaimed and popular drama shows with which we are now familiar. In the last ten years, HBO has been responsible for *The Sopranos*, *Six Feet Under* and *Sex and the City*, but during the 1980s did not produce any of its own drama programmes, showing instead sitcoms, syndicated shows and films. The relatively expensive nature of drama production also put such investment beyond the reach of any other cable networks during this decade. It was left to the major networks – ABC, NBC and CBS – to produce the most popular primetime shows.

Soap operas, with their open-ended structure, domestic and family settings and familiar categories of characters had been a staple of American radio and television since the 1930s. Aimed squarely at a female audience they dominated daytime scheduling and, with the exception of *Peyton Place* which ran for five years in the 1960s, made relatively little impact on primetime schedules which were geared towards shows with restricted runs lasting only a few months at a time. This situation began to change at the end of the 1970s, and the 1980s was notable for the rise of what became known as the 'primetime soap'. The working model for this genre was *Dallas*, which ran for fourteen series on CBS between 1978 and 1991. While still shown in series form (each series consisted of between twenty-four and thirty episodes), *Dallas* began to employ many of the traits of daytime soap operas but adapted them for the demands of primetime. While daytime soaps were usually low-budget affairs filmed in limited locations and often in studios, *Dallas* used glamorous settings, wardrobes and lifestyles and combined them with the sensational material of adultery, alcoholism, murder, business intrigue and family feuding to mould a template that would influence many imitators during the 1980s. It also utilized the open structure of the daytime soap by having plots carry over from one episode to another, and even from one series to another, and by making the lives of its characters, as well as the audience's association with them, transcend the boundaries of the individual storyline that marked each week's episode. The final episode of series three, 'A House Divided', broadcast on 21 March 1980, was a landmark in the way primetime television shows began to make use of the soap tactic of the cliff-hanger. The episode ended with the iconic villain of the series, J. R. Ewing, being shot. Not knowing whether he would live or die or who was responsible for the shooting, television audiences were forced to wait until the beginning of the next series, which was delayed until November following an actors' strike, for a resolution. Public interest was such that when the next series began, the first episode received the highest viewing in US television history to that point, as well as sparking a whole ancillary trade in 'Who shot J. R.' merchandising.

Dallas was the first- or second-ranked television show for the first five years of the 1980s. Part of the show's appeal was that as well as utilizing soap elements that had traditionally attracted a female audience, it also appealed to men because of the centrality of the oil business to the extended Ewing family, all of whom lived in the same house, and the ranching mentality that its Texas setting facilitated. Few of the principle male characters were to be seen without their Stetsons at some point in the show, and J. R.'s combination of business suit, cowboy boots and cowboy hat became an iconic image from the show. The longevity of the show, and the demands of actors leaving and joining, also meant that the pioneering past of Jock Ewing and his originating feud over oil and Jock's wife, Miss Ellie, with Digger Barnes, could be explored in ever increasing degrees of intricacy. Some aspects of the ongoing storylines, however, tested the audience's patience and provide examples of the problems that primetime soaps generated in seeking to extend their dramatic runs whilst retaining audience loyalty. In 1984, Barbara Bel Geddes, who played the role of Miss Ellie and who remains the only actress to win an Emmy award for a role in a primetime soap, left the show to have heart surgery, although her character remained and was played by Donna Reed for one season. When Bel Geddes was well enough to return, Reed was fired and successfully sued the show's production company. More infamous was the way in which series nine (1985–6) was retrospectively turned into a dream of one of the characters, Pam Ewing, played by Victoria Principal. This ploy was used entirely to facilitate the return of Pam's husband Bobby Ewing, played by Patrick Duffy, who had been killed off at the end of series eight.

Although it remained in the list of the top twenty-five programmes for the rest of the decade, *Dallas* never really recovered from these mid-decade glitches. As a genre-defining show, however, it did influence other successful shows of the 1980s, most notably *Dynasty* which was ABC's response to *Dallas* and another show about an oil family, this time located in Denver. Both *Dallas*, with *Knots Landing*, and *Dynasty*, with the less successful *The Colbys*, produced spin-off shows. They were both also enormously successful overseas and marked a new phase in the export of American television to a global audience. Soap operas had become a global form and by utilizing the basic components of the soap, *Dallas* worked in translation in many different locations.

Such was the success of the primetime soaps that drama series also began to incorporate soap elements. Ensemble casts, open-structure plots and fuller development of characters were mixed together with the staples of episodic programming. What had distinguished the drama series from the soap until this point was a small number of central characters and storylines that were resolved each week. Rather than ending with a cliff-hanger that prompted the viewer to watch the next episode, drama series worked by dealing with a discrete issue each week. Even *The Waltons*, with its large cast, followed this pattern. One

Figure 3.5 J. R. Ewing (Larry Hagman) of *Dallas*, the most recognized face on worldwide television during the 1980s. © Lorimar/The Kobal Collection.

of the most successful drama series of the 1970s (running from 1972 to 1981 and the antithesis of the materialistic world of *Dallas* and *Dynasty*), the ending to each episode was always the same: the whole family saying goodnight to one another. This signalled precisely the kind of resolution and self-contained, episodic quality that marked out the drama series.

In the 1980s, however, drama and soap began to merge. The crime drama, which was especially suited to the series format, since each episode could revolve around the solving of a case, was at the forefront of this shift. Although never a particularly popular show, the multi-Emmy-winning *Hill Street Blues* set the template that other shows followed. *Cagney and Lacey*, which ran for six series on CBS between 1982 and 1988, not only changed the genre by having two female detectives as its central characters, but also in the way that it incorporated soap elements. Mary Beth Lacey (Tyne Daly) was frequently shown at home with her family, often discussing her work and the cases she was involved with, and her increasingly strained relationship with husband Harvey (John Karlen) was centrepiece of the show. The birth of her third child was also a major storyline. In contrast, Christine Cagney (Sharon Gless) was a single woman struggling to find a man and trying to face up to her alcoholism. *Cagney and Lacey* combined these continuing storylines with traditional crime-solving, but the whole show was always inflected by the social issues of the day. The position of two professional women in a male-dominated organization was an ongoing concern, as was the way that gender affects the whole process of solving crime. Showing women dealing with violence, guns and the criminal world – traditionally marked as male and masculine domains – forced audiences to think about issues not usually part of the crime genre. *Cagney and Lacey* also took on controversial issues. In 1985, the plot of 'The Clinic' saw Cagney and the five-months-pregnant Lacey investigating the bombing of an abortion clinic by a pro-life activist and several television networks affiliated to CBS refused to show this episode. 'The City is Burning', shown in September 1987, was based on a real-life incident in Howard Beach the previous year when three African Americans were brutally beaten by a groups of white men. In the final season, Cagney endures date-rape while Mary Beth is forced to confront her own prejudices when she learns that one of her son's classmates has AIDS.

Hill Street Blues (1981–7)

Although it was never a popular success, appearing on the list of the twenty-five most watched shows only once – at number twenty-one in 1982–3 – *Hill Street Blues* was one of the most influential drama serials of the 1980s. Its distinctive features not only earned it the Outstanding Drama Series Emmy each year between 1980–1 and 1983–4, as well as numerous awards for the show's actors, but also changed the genre of the drama serial. The creators and writers of the show were Steven Bochco and Michael Kozoll. Bochco was an experienced writer who had worked on successful 1970s crime dramas such as *Ironside*, *Columbo* and *McMillan and Wife*. Knowing the formulas of the crime drama meant that Bochco was in a strong position to change them, and both he and Kozell took a major role in the conception, writing and production of the show. *Hill Street Blues* retained an episodic integrity which was the staple of the crime drama. If *The Waltons* ended in the same fashion each week, then *Hill Street Blues* began in the same fashion, with early-morning roll call at Hill Street police station and Sergeant Phil Esterhaus (Michael Conrad) – until his death in 1984 – outlining the list of cases the police officers should be working on, always ending his briefing with the warning 'Let's be careful out there'. Each episode also stretched across just one day.

What Bochco and Kozoll added to this formula, however, was a large list of around twenty central characters. This ensemble quality meant that the show never revolved around one or two individuals, like other crime dramas which often took their titles from their leading detective. While precinct captain Frank Furillo (Daniel J. Travanti) became the key player in the battle between the officers on the streets and the Public Defender's office and the other forms of bureaucracy which impacted on the police department, there was simply too much going on around him for him to become the centre of consciousness of the show. Using a large ensemble cast like this was completely new in serial drama. It meant that there were often several storylines running alongside one another and the show complicated this process further by resolving some storylines within individual episodes and having others span several episodes. While clearly presenting continuity and storyline difficulties, the problem was handled partly by pairing off some of the central characters – often ones whose characters were very different – so that relationships provided one path of continuity for the viewer.

Another innovation was the way that the show followed its characters away from work into their private lives, demonstrating not only how the two were intimately connected, but also personalizing and humanizing the decisions that had to be made in the day-to-day world of police work. Furillo, while having run-ins with his fiercest adversary, Joyce Davenport (Veronica Hamel), a lawyer in the Public Defender's office, was also having an affair with her and shows often ended with the two of them at home or in bed together contemplating their conflicting feelings about each other and about the legal system.

Perhaps more important than any of these factors, however, and what made *Hill Street Blues* truly genre-breaking, was the style in which the show was shot. Hand-held cameras, extraneous dialogue and a compositional lens that wandered and cut quickly from one angle to another gave a feeling not of staged drama but of documentary. Combined with the shambolic and chaotic nature of an urban police station, the show almost had a quality of *cinéma vérité*. Blending elegantly with its content – often hard-hitting social and urban problems and their influence on crime in the 1980s – this style contributed towards *Hill Street Blues* attempting to mould a more realistic form for television drama. One of the reasons that NBC kept the show going, despite its lack of popular success, was precisely this innovative aesthetic approach which not only went down well with critics, but also appealed to a key demographic group that network television stations could never ignore, given their reliance on advertising revenues: both male and female young, urban professionals. The legacy of *Hill Street Blues* was a whole raft of television shows in the later 1980s and 1990s which borrowed both the narrative strategies and the look and feel of Bochco and Kozoll's masterpiece, including *St Elsewhere* (1982–8), *L.A. Law* (1986–94), *thirtysomething* (1987–91), *Law and Order* (1990 to present), *NYPD Blue* (1993–2005) and *ER* (1994 to present).

Elsewhere in drama, very few shows responded to the arrival of the yuppie as a social phenomenon in the 1980s. The exceptions here were *L.A. Law*, created by Stephen Bochco, which ran from 1986 to 1994, and *thirtysomething*, created by Marshall Herskovitz and Edward Zwick and which ran between 1987 and 1991. While *L.A. Law* drew on the work setting of a Los Angeles legal practice in a similar way to *Hill Street Blues* in order to generate its drama–soap synergy, *thirtysomething* used an ensemble cast of friends who all lived and worked in Philadelphia to more self-consciously address the conditions of upwardly mobile life in the 1980s. Working variously as advertising executives, college lecturers, illustrators, freelance photographers and graphic artists, the characters are reminiscent of those in Lawrence Kasdan's 1983 film *The Big Chill* in that they often yearn nostalgically for a time before work and other responsibilities have taken over their lives. As well as extending the soap-drama form to incorporate a group of friends rather than extended biological or working families, *thirtysomething*, from its lower-case title to its narrative techniques, which often utilized flashback, fantasy and daydream, had artistic ambitions which pushed the soap-drama format into new areas. Although accused of not dealing with social issues outside of the show's limited world view, *thirtysomething* was certainly topical in its depiction of the 'new man' – a more emotional and domesticated kind of man interesting the media at this time – and in the way it drew on a therapeutic discourse to think through the difficulties of personal and sexual relationships. It was also the first American television programme to show two men in bed together.

If drama was changing shape in the 1980s, then sitcoms seemed more resistant to innovation. As successful and long-running shows

Figure 3.6 The ensemble cast of groundbreaking drama *Hill Street Blues* (1981–7).
(© NBC-TV/The Kobal Collection).

like *Taxi* and *M*A*S*H* came to an end in the early 1980s, there was no sense of a flood of new shows ready to take their place. Two sitcoms did emerge, however, and both, for very different reasons, were important developments of the genre. *Cheers*, which ran on NBC from 1982 to 1993 and produced the successful spin-off show *Frasier*, used a Boston bar as its situation and for its comedy utilized the ensemble cast. *Cheers* was notable, then, for drawing on the ensemble device that was influencing drama and the merging of soap and drama in the 1980s. A critical and popular success, *Cheers* won the Outstanding Comedy Series Emmy in 1983, 1984, 1989, 1991 and 1992. The popularity of *Cheers*, however, was outdone by *The Cosby Show*, the most-watched television show in the US in the last five years of the decade. For a show that had as its central focus a middle-class African American family, this was a remarkable achievement considering the relative absence of African American shows in mainstream US television until this time, notable exceptions being *Good Times* (1974–9) and *The Jeffersons* (1975–85). Telling the story of the Huxtable family, with Bill Cosby playing a successful gynaecologist and his wife a successful lawyer, the show created black characters that fell well beyond often-seen stereotypes. Cosby is a strong father figure and the family is, at heart, strong too. An emphasis on education runs through the show. The eldest daughter is a student at Ivy League Princeton University, while the next youngest daughter eventually goes to an all-black college. This latter storyline points to an understated racial pride that runs through the show and is evidenced by the African American art on the walls of the Huxtable house and the jazz score which is woven into the transitions between scenes. None of this quite explains the popularity of the show, however, particularly among a white audience. Here the conservatism of the show is perhaps more important. The long tradition and popularity of black performance for white audiences might suggest that the values represented by the Huxtables in some way make them safe black characters. In this way they absolve a white audience from thinking either about the chronic racial inequality which marked the 1980s, or about their responsibility for the racism that perpetuates such inequality. Ultimately, *The Cosby Show* is interesting precisely because it managed, through sophisticated significations and storylines, to appeal to both black and white audiences at the same time and to allow the issue of race to be, depending on the viewing position of its audience, both an obvious and invisible element of its comedy.

Chapter 4

Music and Performance

CDs, MTV and the Music Business

In 1979, the US phonographic industry entered its first recession for more than thirty years. Sales of vinyl records dropped 11 per cent and wouldn't show an upturn until 1983.[1] As an industry that relied on disposable income being spent on leisure items, the record business fell victim to the stagflation of the late 1970s as well as the recession affecting the rest of the economy during the early 1980s. But while this national situation may explain away some of the industry's problems, there were other more immediate factors impinging on the popularity of music at this time. There was certainly increased competition from other markets entering the leisure sector. Computer games were increasingly finding their way into households with the arrival of cheap consoles and popular games like *Space Invaders* and *Pac-Man*. Home video and the burgeoning cable sector competed both for time and resources. Larry Starr also argues that the fashion for disco at the end of the 1970s helped sustain record sales, but that its decline in popularity was not compensated for by a similarly popular replacement.[2] The combination of these factors meant that not only were sales falling, but so was revenue from sales.

The total sales figures, however, hide emerging trends that help in an understanding of just how, by the end of the 1980s, the situation would recover to the extent that the values of sales had doubled from a 1980 base point. The major trend here was the decline in sales of vinyl, both singles and, even more dramatically, LPs. In 1980, the US market saw sales of 164 million singles and 323 million albums. By 1990 these figures were 28 million and 12 million respectively. By 1992 the sales of vinyl LPs had dropped to just 2 million units. The market for vinyl, then, a material and a product which had dominated the production of records since the 1950s, collapsed within the space of a decade. It was replaced by two other formats, one – the analogue pre-recorded musicassette – which had been around since the 1960s, and another – the compact disc (CD) – that entered the commercial market in Asia in 1982 and the rest of the world in 1983, bringing with it for the first time a portable digital audio product. The market for music formats in the 1980s, however, was not simply one where CDs gradually replaced vinyl. Sales of CD albums did not outstrip their vinyl equivalent until 1988. Musicassette sales outstripped vinyl in 1983 and continued to outsell CDs until 1992.

The popularity of the musicassette was driven in the 1980s by the availability of portable cassette players, the most famous of which was the Sony Walkman. The original silver and blue Walkman, branded as the Soundabout, was first produced in 1979 and immediately changed the possibilities for listening to music. Traditional restrictions imposed by musical hardware no longer applied with the Walkman and now it became possible to listen to music in virtually any situation. The economic impact on the music industry was more or less immediate. Sales of musicassettes in the US increased threefold between 1980 and 1984. While initial predictions of sales for the Walkman by Sony were modest, the reality was that there appeared to be a market ready and waiting for the opportunity of portability offered by the Walkman. The jogging and fitness crazes of the 1980s, stimulated by Jim Fixx's 1977 bestseller *Complete Book of Running* and Jane Fonda's incredibly popular workout videos released from 1982 onwards, were often solitary activities made less arduous by having some form of musical accompaniment. The musicassette, like the CD that would follow it, also had all the advantages of portability and could be moved from the home stereo system to the car stereo and to the Walkman in turn.

If the economic impact of the Walkman was to create a new market for musicassettes and to generate renewed interest in music sales generally, its cultural impact might be measured by the degree to which portability in all areas of cultural consumption have become a feature of contemporary life. From iPods and laptop computers, to mobile phones and Sony's Playstation Portable, the distinctions between leisure spaces and domestic, public and work spaces have become increasingly blurred as hardware developments allow the movement of technology across these boundaries. The Walkman was one of the earliest instances of this phenomenon and has also been held responsible for creating the 'cocooning' effect that some have noted is one of the consequences of personalized portable audio products. Because listening to music through earphones requires the blocking out of the auditory landscape of one's surroundings, the retreat into this world might be seen as a way of disengaging with the public world of conversation and with other people. These accusations are similar to arguments that watching television is a vicarious and mediated experiencing of the world rather than a material engagement with it. While the literal act of wearing earphones could be read as shutting oneself off from one's surroundings, it can also be argued that portability allows greater and more prolonged access to culture and the information it carries. Listening to music need not be, no matter what the context of that listening, a passive experience. The boombox or ghettoblaster, which also encouraged the surge in the sale of musicassettes in the 1980s, is in Spike Lee's film *Do the Right Thing* (1989) one piece of portable hardware which has consequences that are only too public. When Radio Raheem takes his stereo into Sal's pizza parlour and refuses to turn down the sound, the race riot and police violence which follow testify not only to the important political resonances of music, but also to the way in which portability does not necessarily diminish or erode them but instead can displace them.

Despite its popularity, audio-cassette technology was a creature of the analogue and magnetic-tape world of the 1960s. While its portability and the availability of portable technology ensured its popularity, deficiencies in sonic quality were highlighted by the emergence of digital technology in the 1980s. Developed during the 1970s, digital audio discs became a commercial possibility following the collaboration of Philips and Sony and their production of what was known as the 'Red Book', the standardized technical specifications for all CD formats. The Compact Disc Digital Audio trademark that one finds on CDs indicates adherence to these specifications, which set the physical parameters and properties of a CD, acceptable deviation and error rates and the form of digital audio encoding. Smaller and with more capacity than a traditional vinyl LP, CDs were also more robust, less fragile and delivered a sound quality beyond that available with vinyl on all but the best hardware. What initially held back the sales of CDs, however, was the fact that they required completely new hardware on which to be played and were also more expensive than their vinyl equivalent. Only the availability of cheaper hardware – Sony released its first portable CD player in 1984 – provided consumers outside the niche classical and audio enthusiast markets to make the shift from analogue to digital on a mass scale. Once this began to occur, backed by an enthusiastic music industry, one major trend that developed was

Figure 4.1 Music is at the heart of the Bedford Stuyvesant neighbourhood in *Do the Right Thing* (Spike Lee, Universal, 1989). © Universal/The Kobal Collection.

the replacement of vinyl albums in one's record collection with CD versions. This trend was a major factor because of the wider demographic base of audio consumers that had developed by the 1980s. The teenagers of the 1950s and 1960s for whom music had been a vital element of the popular culture in which their growing up was rooted were now the more affluent middle-aged consumers whose disposable income could afford the new hardware and CD prices. While, by re-releasing their back catalogue on CD, music companies 'managed to sell people music that they already own',[3] consumers were only too happy to buy this re-released material in order to re-listen to it and preserve it in a more sustainable format for future re-listening.

The new CD market was, therefore, one way that the music industry found to expand its reach during the decline of sales in the late 1970s and early 1980s. Digital CD technology, along with the concept of portability that produced new hardware, can be seen as structural changes whose effect was to revivify a failing market. The market was also stimulated by the emergence of new forms for promoting music in the 1980s. I have already discussed the way that films such as *Top Gun*, and one might also include *Fame* (1980), *Flashdance* (1983) and *Dirty Dancing* (1987), were used almost as music videos to promote their soundtracks. But one other medium was crucial to this phenomenon. When MTV launched on August 1 1981, the first video it played was for the song 'Video Killed the Radio Star', by British band The Buggles which had reached number one in the UK charts in 1979 (although only number forty in the US). While this choice proclaimed MTV's newness and its desire to replace the stars of more traditional technological forms, the arrival of MTV is perhaps better understood as the addition of one more outlet to a series of outlets – including the burgeoning radio sector – that, in conjunction with one another, co-promoted music across an increasingly broad terrain.

As a venture of Warner Communications, one of whose subsidiaries was the Warner Music Group, the importance of MTV lies partly in its symbiotic relationship with the music industry and partly in the stimulus it provided for the genre of the music video. The early videos shown on the channel were mostly promotional clips and films interspersed with live concert footage. The success of the channel meant that music companies began to see that it was in their own interests to provide better and more elaborate videos to promote their artists. Perhaps the most notable of these attempts came with the series of videos made to promote single releases from Michael Jackson's 1982 album *Thriller*, culminating in the fourteen-minute video of the title track which was first shown on television by MTV in December 1983. Directed by John Landis, whose Hollywood films included *The Blues Brothers* (1980), *An American Werewolf in London* (1981) and *Trading Places* (1983), the video cost $800,000 to make, featured the voice of classic horror actor Vincent Price and completely rearranged the music to fit the demands of the video. While the single and album track featured a traditional verse–chorus progression, in the video all the verses are sung first while all the choruses come at the end. The 'Thriller' video marked a new stage in the efforts of record companies to

Figure 4.2 Michael Jackson with Ola Ray in the landmark music video for 'Thriller' (1983).
© The Kobal Collection.

promote their music and their star acts. Although the video could not propel 'Thriller' to the number one position in the US singles chart – it peaked at number four – it certainly did contribute to the iconic status of the album and helped it stay in the top-ten album chart for eighty consecutive weeks. Globally, *Thriller* is also the biggest-selling album of all time, outsold in the US only by The Eagles' *Their Greatest Hits 1971–1975*. A documentary, *The Making of Thriller*, was released on video in 1984 while Michael Jackson went on to have Martin Scorsese direct his 1987 video 'Bad'. NBC introduced its own music video show, *Friday Night Videos*, in 1983 and the first video it showed was Jackson's 'Billie Jean', also from the *Thriller* album. In 1989, in honour of Michael Jackson and his contribution to the production of music video, MTV renamed its 'Video Vanguard Award' to the 'Michael Jackson Vanguard Award'.

These achievements outlast and, in financial terms, outweigh the chart success of any particular single. Video, through the conduit of MTV, helped to turn music performers into national and international stars in a way which had not been possible in the 1970s. One of the biggest-selling bands in the US during that decade, and the fourth biggest-selling band in US history – behind The Beatles, Elvis Presley and Garth Brooks – Led Zeppelin refused to even endorse singles released by their record company, Atlantic, and steadfastly avoided television appearances. In the 1980s, the cultivation of a superstar image through promotional video was a key ingredient to success and many stars, notably Madonna, continually refined and reinvented their image with each album and video performance.

Madonna

Born in Bay City, Michigan in 1958 and raised by Italian-American and French-Canadian Catholic parents in Detroit, Madonna Louise Veronica Ciccone is arguably, along with Michael Jackson, the most important pop artist of the 1980s. This reputation is based only partly on her music. What Madonna epitomizes is the 1980s superstar recording artist whose career is also a story of stylistic innovation, self-promotion, scandal and public visibility. While this visibility persists through to the present day, Madonna is notable now more for her attempts to evade the public eye when, during the 1980s, she took every opportunity to entertain, affront and seduce her broad audience of admirers.

Although she did have music lessons from an early age, Madonna's background was in dance and performance. She received a dance scholarship to attend the University of Michigan, but left before completing her course and moved to New York in 1977 to pursue a dance career, working with dance companies and touring as a dancer with bands while supplementing this work with various temporary and part-time jobs. A regular on the New York club scene, Madonna soon began to form her own bands – Breakfast Club and Emmy – producing disco and dance songs, which eventually led to a recording contract with Sire. After a couple of hits from her first, self-titled album – 'Holiday' and 'Lucky Star' – Madonna's career shifted to a different level of success and notoriety following the release of her second album, *Like a Virgin*, in 1984. This album, which generated various video, tour, guest appearance and film spin-offs, cemented Madonna's position as the premier female recording artist in the US.

The album's title immediately makes provocative links between her own religious name – Madonna is the Roman Catholic title for Jesus' mother, Mary – and the Christian concept of the virgin birth. The title song of the album clearly alludes to this too, but does so in a way that overtly sexualizes Christian imagery and iconography. After all, the persona of the song is not a virgin: 'I was beat incomplete / I'd been had, I was sad and blue'. Instead, it is the sexual experience with a new partner that makes the persona 'Shiny and new / Like a virgin / Touched for the very first time'. The album's cover also adds to the mixed messages of the song. Reclining on silk sheets, with a bouquet on her lap and wearing what appears to be a wedding dress, on closer inspection Madonna's image is highly fetishised and sexualized. The heavy make-up, pouting lips, and despoiled hair, along with the tight-fitting bustier and full-arm lace gloves, turn her into a figure not of virtue, but desire. This point is emphasized by the belt she is wearing, the wording on which is just visible: 'Boy Toy'. The ambiguity, and much of Madonna's appeal at this point in her career, is based upon the fact that she presents herself not just as an object of desire, but also as a desiring female subject.

The video that accompanied the single, filmed partly in New York and partly in Venice, follows through with the theme introduced on the album cover. Shown on a gondola wearing black, punk clothes and jewellery, Madonna also appears in the wedding outfit. The video was first shown on MTV in July 1984 and Madonna appeared at the first MTV Video Music awards the same year. Her performance of the song at this event, again wearing the wedding outfit and the Boy Toy belt, was anything but virginal as she rolled around on the stage and simulated masturbation. While these elements of her performance might easily be dismissed as publicity stunts, like her kiss with Britney Spears and Christine Aguilera at the MTV Video Music Awards nearly twenty years later in 2003, the consistency with which Madonna complicated the paradoxical demands often imposed on women – that they be virtuous mothers and carers but also sexually available – suggests a side to her performances that is much more culturally engaged.

'Material Girl', another single from the *Like a Virgin* album, might be read as a simple parody of 1980s consumerism, but both the cover of the single and the promotional video suggest that issues of gender are the primary concern of the song. On the cover of the single, an uncomfortable-looking Madonna appears naked on a bed, in what appears to be a post-coital state, clutching a sheet against her body. If the implication is that she has been used for sexual gratification, the video reverses this situation. Mimicking the performance of Marilyn Monroe in the 1953 film *Gentlemen Prefer Blondes*, Madonna is surrounded by a group of eager young men vying for her affection while she teases them by telling them, as the lyrics declare, 'the boy with the cold hard cash / Is always Mister Right'.

The inescapable narrative here is one of female agency. While it may operate as a fantasy narrative in its pop setting, what pop music allows is the circulation of this narrative in a wider cultural context. And while this narrative may have appealed particularly to her female audience, there was enough of a heterosexual allure about Madonna for this appeal to spread even further. Her undermining of gender stereotypes also made her, from an early stage in her career, an icon in the gay community and she cemented this position by speaking out about the need for money for AIDS research. In many ways, too, the development of her career seemed to crystallize the messages of her songs and videos. Playing the feisty, independent and cool character of Susan in the feature film *Desperately Seeking Susan* (1985), Madonna is the role model for bored housewife Roberta, played by Rosanna Arquette, whom she initiates into an urban culture of pleasure and freedom. While Madonna's acting career never really took off, her performance in this film, and the success of 'Into the Groove' which is used in the film although only a B-side to the single 'Angel', helped Madonna appear to be the consummate all-round singer/dancer/actress. Her first US tour, The Virgin Tour (1985), confirmed the iconic status she had achieved through the *Like a Virgin* album, and in this respect Madonna, along with other star solo performers like Prince, Michael Jackson, Whitney Houston, Bruce Springsteen and Phil Collins, marked the way in which the supergroups of the 1970s were being replaced by bankable individual superstars capable of supporting an entire record label. While the *New York Times* dismissed Madonna's live singing abilities and *Billboard* magazine declared that she would be forgotten within six months because of the way that her image overshadowed her music, this ignored the crowds of Madonna fans who copied her every dance move and imitated her fashion choices of ripped T-shirts, fingerless gloves and lace bras.

By treating video, film, fashion and dance as equal partners in her pop career, Madonna created not only a sound but also an image with which her audiences could engage. While this combination of image and music may not have been entirely new, Madonna was certainly one of the first artists to fully utilize the changing landscape of music production and distribution during the 1980s. Her later albums in the 1980s – *True Blue* (1986) and *Like a Prayer* (1989) – and their associated spin-offs were notable for the way in which Madonna continually modified her image and re-invented her self-presentation, leaving behind the heroine of *Like a Virgin* for different models of womanhood.

Figure 4.3 Madonna carries her pop persona across into film in *Desperately Seeking Susan* (Susan Seidelman, Orion, 1985). © Orion/The Kobal Collection.

The changes taking place in the production, promotion and marketing of music in the 1980s were doing so in a context much like that affecting the film industry. Just as the 1980s saw the merger and takeover of film studios so that they became part of global media conglomerates, so music labels were being brought under the umbrella of a handful of powerful multinational organizations driven by the same synergistic principles affecting all dimensions of the media world. By 1992, five organizations owned 93 per cent of US music sales. The largest of these were Warner and Sony, with 27 per cent and 25 per cent respectively, followed by EMI with 15 per cent, MCA with 12 per cent and BMG with 5 per cent. Independent companies accounted for the remaining 7 per cent. The fact that of these, only two, Warner and MCA, were based in the US – Sony is Japanese, EMI British and BMG German – gives some indication of the way in which the US market was becoming part of a global cultural economy in the 1980s. Robert Burnett characterizes the 1980s as a period of 'historically high' concentration in the US market, by which he means very few organizations are controlling music sales, as well as suggesting that despite this, the diversity of material offered by these organizations also is historically very high.[4] Refuting the idea that the concentration of cultural production in an advanced capitalist economy necessarily leads to the homogenization of the culture offered to the consumer, Burnett argues that based on a simple statistical measure between decades in the postwar US, the 1980s saw more new records and artists achieving chart success. While this crude measure does little to differentiate amongst the styles and genres emerging in the 1980s, Burnett's more convincing arguments have to do with the state of music manufacturing as the industry reaches what he describes as its 'mature' phase.[5]

Part of the transition to this stage includes the takeover and merger of producers as the battle for market share in a period of declining sales and profits like that of the late 1970s and early 1980s leads to companies attacking one another. But influences like the changing consumer demographic – notably more consumers and their generational differences in tastes – mean that the industry has to cater for a broader range of demands. Although the Warner Music Group may control a quarter of the US market, it does so not under one label but dozens of different labels, each with their own branded identity and roster of acts. Sire Records, which Warner acquired in 1976, is just one example. In 1976, punk band The Ramones released their self-titled first album with Sire, who, six years later in 1982, signed pop princess Madonna and then, in 1986, gangsta rapper Ice-T. Alongside bands and artists as stylistically diverse as Depeche Mode, k. d. lang, The Pretenders and Talking Heads, these artists suggest something of the range of material available and the same could be said of other Warner subsidiaries such as Atlantic Records (Abba, AC/DC, Phil Collins and Foreigner) and Elektra (The Cars, Tracy Chapman and Mötley Crüe). Just as importantly, and as already shown, the processes of manufacturing, marketing and distributing music undergo structural change such that the availability of music itself – on television, on radio, as soundtracks to films, on video – and the means of listening to it – Walkmans, musicassettes, CDs – dramatically increase the penetration of music into more and more areas of consumer and leisure activity. The diversity of their artist portfolios meant that the major music producers could withstand the vagaries of fashion, and it is also the case that major and independent producers were no longer in competition with one another. Instead, there was co-operation, 'with indies often moulding new acts and then making licensing and distribution deals with the majors.'[6] For Burnett, then, the industry changes of the 1980s have a 'liberating effect on the creative process', giving the lie to the idea that mass culture is incompatible with diversity.

Rock Rolls On: Metal, New Wave and Alt

A familiar narrative that is retold about British guitar-based music in
the 1970s is that towards the end of the decade, the arrival of punk and
new wave finished off the dinosaur rock acts who had dominated the
earlier years of the decade. These would include hard rock bands such
as Led Zeppelin, Deep Purple and Black Sabbath and progressive rock
bands such as Pink Floyd, Yes, Jethro Tull and Genesis. In the US, this
narrative is mirrored except that in place of The Sex Pistols, The
Buzzcocks and The Clash, one finds The Ramones, Patti Smith,
Television and Talking Heads usurping all those British bands as well
as the likes of The Doobie Brothers, Steely Dan, Lynyrd Skynyrd and
the Allman Brothers. There is only a modicum of truth in this description of events and several problems with it.

First of all, it mistakes generational shifts in music styles and the rise
and fall in the popularity of certain bands for battles between competing genres. People did not stop listening to the progressive rock or
hard rock produced in the 1970s during the 1980s; it was that these
people got older and less visible as consumers. While the introduction
of CDs manifestly relied on older consumers re-buying digital copies
of their old vinyl recordings, the marketing departments of music businesses were keen to present a public face that associated them with the
next big thing and were busy targeting the next generation of music
consumers. Second, punk and new wave music should not be understood as something which suddenly emerged in opposition to rock
music. While it may have presented itself as having no investment in
the musical past, certainly in the US new wave bands drew on the
garage band subculture of the 1960s and proto-punk and glam rock
acts such as Iggy and the Stooges, The Velvet Underground, MC5 and
the New York Dolls. Additionally, John Covach suggests that while it
rejected the rock music that chronologically preceded it, 'New wave
never completely sheds the practices of hippie rock'.[8] Comparing the
song structures of new wave band The Cars and soft rock band
Foreigner, Covach identifies a striking likeness that means younger listeners hearing this music many years later 'are more likely to hear the
similarities . . . than the distinctions upon which new wave depended'.[9]
It is only by situating the songs in regard to different musical traditions
that listeners are able to hear them differently. For Covach, then,
the listening process is about more than just hearing musical notes
and sounds; it is a cultural act of distinction. At the same time, a strand
of rock music that while distinct from 1970s rock still wanted to

explicitly appropriate a musical past emerges, in the shape of artists like Bruce Springsteen and Tom Petty.

Finally, rock music was beginning to change itself even as punk and new wave emerged. Bands such as Boston, Journey and Styx released material that was more radio-friendly and accessible, and while they were often accused of being sell-out corporate or adult-oriented rock bands, there is little doubt that they injected US rock with a sharper edge. Perhaps more importantly, however, heavy metal unearthed a new guitar hero in the figure of Eddie Van Halen who rewrote the technique manual and altered the sonic range and potential of the instrument with his trademark tapping, harmonics and use of the tremolo. Van Halen's famous 'brown sound' and his lightning pedal-tone riffs and guitar solos made the guitar work of earlier rock bands seem thin and pedestrian in comparison. At the same time, the influence of earlier West Coast bands could be heard in the swagger of singer Dave Lee Roth and the band's vocal harmonies. The eleven songs on their first album, *Van Halen* (1978), came in at just over thirty five minutes in total, indicating their desire to be a songwriting band rather than a collection of virtuoso musicians.

The confluence of these various trends at the end of the 1970s produced a guitar music scene in the 1980s that was more diverse than in any previous period. The heavy metal market began to fracture into a series of sub-genres. Glam metal bands like Mötley Crüe, Twisted Sister, Ratt, W.A.S.P., Dokken and Quiet Riot drew musically on their 1970s hard rock antecedents while mixing in sounds similar to those pioneered by Van Halen. The image of glam metal relied heavily on tight spandex and big, teased and back-combed hairstyles – a 1980s phenomenon that stretched from the world of metal to the fashion magazines – and its visual appeal played well on MTV, although also led to it being dismissed by some as 'hair metal'. Lyrical content often failed to pass beyond sex, drugs and partying, although the occult – a staple of heavy metal since Black Sabbath in the 1970s – did receive some attention. Not as much, however, as in thrash metal, an important sub-genre that began to develop after 1983 and the release of Metallica's first album *Kill 'Em All*. Influenced by British bands like Judas Priest and Motörhead, who were renowned for both the speed and volume of their music, Metallica fashioned a metal sound that relied on fast and complex, detuned multi-layered guitar riffs and solos that were played at high speed and often used neo-classical techniques such as sweep picking and fluid legato. Former Metallica guitarist Dave Mustaine formed Megadeth, and along with bands such as Slayer and Anthrax they formed the core of a thrash metal scene that gathered momentum all the way through the 1980s, attracting a good deal of controversy along the way from Christian pressure groups who objected to what they considered to be blasphemous lyrics in songs such as Slayer's 'Altar of Sacrifice' and 'Jesus Saves' from their *Reign of Blood* album. Slayer also attracted criticism for using Nazi references in songs like 'Angel of Death', a song based around Nazi doctor Joseph Mengele. The anxiety about heavy metal lyrics and graphical content reached its peak in the US in 1990 when Judas Priest were unsuccessfully accused in a civil action of prompting the suicide of two teenage boys by way of a subliminal message on their 1978 album *Stained Class*.

There were other sub-genres like death metal and progressive metal, although these did nothing to help take metal into the mainstream. Amongst a core constituency of young white men, however, the collection of metal genres was an important feature of 1980s music. Popular hits like Survivor's 'Eye of the Tiger' (1982), the theme tune to the Sylvester Stallone film *Rocky III*, the synth-metal crossover of Van Halen's 'Jump' (1984) and ZZ Top's *Eliminator* album (1983), that produced three major hits on the back of popular videos featuring a Ford hot rod and several glamorous women, ensured that less extreme metal products did achieve chart success. Indeed, the cluster of these releases had a remarkable impact on sales of heavy metal material. Accounting for just 8 per cent of sales in 1983, the following year this figure had risen to 20 per cent.[10] By 1986, MTV's *Headbangers' Ball* became the channel's most popular show,[11] the same year that metal crossed over with rap music in a big way for the first time in Run D.M.C.'s cover version of Aerosmith's 'Walk This Way'. Re-recording their parts for the song and appearing in the video, Aerosmith also built a comeback on the success of this song.

The new wave music emerging at the end of the 1970s was less generically identifiable than much of metal's output. One of the features of the music of a band like Talking Heads, for example, was an eclecticism that fused punk with pop, funk and world influences. Added to this was an anti-establishment sensibility that was a legacy of many of its performers' art school backgrounds. Talking Heads singer David Byrne first met drummer Chris Frantz and bassist Tina Weymouth at the Rhode Island School of Design in the early 1970s and the albums *More Songs about Buildings and Food* (1978), *Fear of Music* (1979) and *Remain in Light* (1980) were all co-produced by Brian Eno, who had worked with art-rock artists like David Bowie and Roxy

Music in the 1970s. While their chart success was limited, although it improved with their later albums of the 1980s, Talking Heads were influential because of the way in which they experimented with musical styles and saw their music as one element of their cultural production. The songs 'Once in a Lifetime' (1980), which features David Byrne talking rather than singing the lyrics, and 'Road to Nowhere' (1985) both used innovative videos, the former of which – with David Byrne dancing like a string puppet – was notable for being exhibited in the New York Museum of Modern Art.

If Talking Heads grew out of the New York scene at the end of the 1970s, there were other bands emerging around the country whose fusion of punk and rock was less esoteric and contributed to a serious alternative rock genre during the 1980s, although it too had its roots in an anti-establishment, art school background. The most successful of these bands was R.E.M., although their superstar status did not materialize until the end of the decade and into the 1990s. Formed in 1980, the band members met at the University of Georgia, where singer Michael Stipe was studying photography and painting, and from their covers of garage and punk songs they found a sound reminiscent of folk-rock band The Byrds but that had a pared-down quality taken from punk. Their first five albums were released on the independent label IRS Records before they signed for Warner Brothers in 1988 and they put much of their efforts into an old-school approach to building an audience and fan base, spending much of their time touring and in the recording studio rather than chasing public visibility through video. Critical acclaim followed in the music press. Guitarist Peter Buck's arpeggiated chords and riffs, together with Johnny Marr's similar style for Manchester indie band The Smiths, produced a whole host of imitators, while Stipe's melancholy and often mumbled vocals performed a gloomy, brooding sensibility that was in many ways the antithesis of the kind of optimistic, up-tempo pop of someone like Madonna. *Life's Rich Pageant* (1986) marked something of a turning point for the band. More upbeat than their earlier albums, Stipe's lyrics also began to address ecological and environmental issues. 'Cuyahoga' is about a polluted river in Cleveland, while on the bottom half of the album's cover is a herd of buffalo.

Like R.E.M., the Minneapolis band Hüsker Dü, formed by Macalaster College graduate Bob Mould in the 1970s, released their first five albums on an independent label, SST Records, before signing for Warner Brothers. Beginning as a hardcore punk band on the live *Land Speed Record* (1982), they changed tack completely with the

1984 double album *Zen Arcade*. As an album whose conceptual structure owes more to the progressive rock of the 1970s than to hardcore punk, *Zen Arcade* also mixes together jazz, psychedelic, folk and pop influences. The band's next album, *New Day Rising* (1985), was more streamlined and eliminated all vestiges of their hardcore origins, concentrating instead on Mould's distorted guitar and tightly structured, melodic songs. The balance between accessibility and experimentation marked out another key alternative rock band of the 1980s, Sonic Youth. Altered guitar tunings, the use of feedback and other kinds of white noise on their albums made their music difficult listening. But through their 1980s albums – *Bad Moon Rising* (1985), *EVOL* (1986), *Sister* (1987) and culminating with the double album *Daydream Nation* (1988) – they gradually modified the balance between noise and melody. One interesting Sonic Youth spin-off was the band Ciccone Youth. Part tribute to, and part parody of, Madonna, the band released a cover of Madonna's hit 'Into the Groove' (1986) in classic Sonic Youth style. Although recorded at the same tempo as the original, 'Into the Groove(y)' was a hardcore copy with heavily distorted guitars and laconic vocals which made it sound like a much-sloweddown version.

One artist whose blue-collar background is very different from the backgrounds of some of the artists working in the new wave and alternative scene of the 1980s is Bruce Springsteen. Along with singer-songwriters and guitar players like Tom Petty and Bob Seger, Springsteen is sometimes categorized as 'Heartland Rock', a style of music associated with the white working-class regions of the Midwest and the rust belt. Drawing on folk, country and western, blues and rock roots, the music of Springsteen can be by turns anthemic and soulful. His early success in the 1970s with *Born to Run* (1975) meant that by the 1980s Springsteen was already a star name, writing songs for other performers and ready to follow his instincts on his own recordings. *Darkness on the Edge of Town* (1978) was a much more sombre album and Springsteen premiered parts of the double album *The River* (1980) at the 1979 No Nukes concerts at Madison Square Garden, a series of shows organized by Musicians United for Safe Energy (MUSE) in the wake of the nuclear accident at Three Mile Island, Harrisburg, Pennsylvania.

As well as Springsteen's commitment to political themes in his songs, he has been a meticulous documenter of working-class life and, in ways reminiscent of the 'Dirty Realist' writers discussed in Chapter 1, he is often attracted to the sadness which lurks in the mundane dimensions of everyday life and the quest for happiness. In 'Hungry Heart', Springsteen's first top-ten single in the US, he writes:

Got a wife and kids in Baltimore, Jack
I went out for a ride and I never went back
Like a river that don't know where it's flowing
I took a wrong turn and I just kept going

I met her in a Kingstown bar
We fell in love I knew it had to end
We took what we had and we ripped it apart
Now here I am down in Kingstown again

Everybody needs a place to rest
Everybody wants to have a home
Don't make no difference what nobody says
Ain't nobody like to be alone

This melancholy dimension to Springsteen's music was emphasized in *Nebraska* (1982), a stark, mainly acoustic album recorded without his usual band and whose title song narrates the story of the serial killer Charles Starkweather. Springsteen followed this album two year later with his most successful album, *Born in the U.S.A.* Completely different in tone to *Nebraska*, it was the first Springsteen album to feature synthesizers and its mixture of anthemic and melodic songs ensured it became popular on the radio and in the stores (as well as being the first commercial CD to be pressed in the US). Producing seven top-ten hits, the most famous of these was the title track, a story of soldiers killed in Vietnam and veterans neglected by the government on their return. Although the video that accompanied the release of the single was hardly groundbreaking in terms of style, its use of live concert footage interspersed with scenes of working-class life – Vietnam veterans, assembly lines and oil refineries – pushed home the song's message in an election year and after the full effects of economic recession had been borne by the rust-belt cities of the North East and Midwest. Springsteen's use of 'U.S.A.' in the title and his use of the US flag on the album cover and in the video to the title song is ambiguous, just as the anthemic choruses of the song stand at odds with the misery of the verses. While there is little to suggest that Springsteen does not think a sense of national pride and community important, there is much in his lyrics that suggests the state of the nation when he was writing the song, and the way it was being run, did not meet his approval.

Guitar-based music in the 1980s, then, was a varied and fragmented genre. It also had a specific demographic appeal that, while an important element of the music-buying public, was not representative of the way music was developing in the 1980s. Alongside guitar music, black musical forms that had – with jazz, blues, soul and r 'n' b – been so influential in US musical culture all the way through the twentieth century were also changing and fragmenting in new directions.

Rap and Hip Hop

The origins of rap music are multifaceted and multinational. Delivering an oral story or poem over a drum beat has been common cultural practice in West Africa for centuries. It was from these parts of the continent that many Africans were transported into slavery to North American and the Caribbean. Jean-Michel Basquiat depicted such storytellers, or *griots*, in some of his paintings, including 'Grillo' and 'Gold Griot' (both 1984). In Jamaica during the late 1960s and 1970s, the phenomenon of DJs 'toasting', or adding their own vocals over the music they played on sound systems at parties, became common and they often used the same boastful, rhyming style associated with rapping. In the US, the legacy of vocal styles used in jazz – such as scat singing (the improvisation of vocal sounds over an instrumental backing) and vocalese (the singing of lyrics over previously instrumental passages) – provided an African American tradition in extemporized vocal performance. The convergence of these traditions emerged mainly in New York City during the 1970s. Caribbean immigrants to the city, like Kool DJ Herc and Grandmaster Flash, played a key role as rap developed partly as a reaction against the commercialization of disco and its mainstream acceptance amongst a white audience, and partly because the DJs working at block-parties in the black neighbourhoods were working to isolate and repeat the most danceable percussion breaks of disco, funk and soul records. While DJs controlled the turntables, the Master of Ceremonies, or MC, would work the audience with their vocal performances which eventually turned into rapping.

The music that grew out of this meeting of DJ and MC – hip hop – had assumed a measure of popularity by the end of the 1970s, as well as a range of techniques which formed a grammar and a vocabulary of a similar order to that used by musicians on more traditional instruments. Scratching, needle drops, cutting, phasing, beat juggling and slip queuing are all central elements in the work of the DJ, while for the MC or rapper the use of rhyme, alliteration, cadence, prosody and improvisation is what distinguishes one's style. In these early stages of its development, however, hip hop was very much music of the street and had not crossed into commercial record production. The essence of hip hop at this time was its live, performative quality and its place within an often politically aware young black community. DJ Afrika Bambaataa formed the Universal Zulu Nation in the 1970s, bringing together reformed street-gang members, rappers and graffiti artists, and organized the first hip hop tour of Europe in 1982. In the same year he also released the single 'Planet Rock', an influential song that mixed hip hop beats and rhythms with European sources such as German electronic band Kraftwerk's 'Trans-Europe Express'. The first evidence of hip hop entering popular consciousness came with the release of The Sugarhill Gang's 'Rapper's Delight' in 1979. Touching the fringes of the top forty, the song recycled the bass line from Chic's 'Good Times', a big disco hit, and led to a legal confrontation with Chic's Nile Rogers who claimed copyright infringement. This was the first of many battles over the technique of sampling and ultimately paved the way for legal precedent that meant all sampled material should only be used under licence. Also important to the commercialization of hip hop at this time was Blondie's 1980 number one US hit 'Rapture'.

Following in the wake of these initial commercial successes, more established DJs from the black street scene began to release material. Grandmaster Flash, born in Barbados but brought up in the Bronx, played at illegal parties in the 1970s along with Kurtis Blow and Lovebug Starski. Grandmaster Flash joined forces with five MCs to form Grandmaster Flash & the Furious Five and, after signing to Sugarhill Records in 1980s, the band released a series of seminal hip hop tracks: 'Freedom' (1980), 'The Adventures of Grandmaster Flash on the Wheels of Steel' (1981), 'The Message' (1982) and White Lines (1983). Kurtis Blow became the first rap artist to release an album on a major label, *Kurtis Blow* (Mercury, 1980), and although it was considered by the record industry in general to be a passing trend, hip hop established itself as a viable musical form. But in many of the early hip hop records, the spirit of disco lived on in its good-time feel and attention to the activities of dancing, performing and partying. Grandmaster Flash's 'The Message' marked a change of approach by actively taking on life in the 'ghetto':

Broken glass everywhere
People pissing on the stairs, you know they just
Don't care
I can't take the smell, I can't take the noise
Got no money to move out, I guess I got no choice
Rats in the front room, roaches in the back
Junkies in the alley with a baseball bat
I tried to get away, but I couldn't get far
'Cause the man with the tow-truck repossessed my car

Don't push me, cause I'm close to the edge
I'm trying not to lose my head
It's like a jungle sometimes, it makes me wonder
How I keep from going under

'White Lines', meanwhile, is an anti-drugs song, but though the lyrics of these tracks represent the tough conditions of urban life for many African Americans, the music maintained a soft edge that fitted it for radio and nightclub alike. Yet hip hop, along with many other forms of black music, failed to make much impact on the white-dominated MTV. By the mid-1980s, although hip hop had crossed over into the mainstream, it began to fragment into a series of sub-genres whose impact would drive hip hop into a position of musical influence that completely undermined the notion that it was a passing trend.

The formation of Def Jam Records in 1984 by Rick Rubin and Russell Simmons was a key development. The first independent hip hop label of note, Def Jam released early material by LL Cool J, The Beastie Boys and Run D.M.C. These artists were all more hardcore than earlier rappers. Disco bass lines were less evident, while drum machines and heavy scratching came to the fore and the rhythms were more aggressive. Overall, these hip hop recordings had a less lush feel and a harder edge to both their vocals and their music. Run D.M.C.'s *Raising Hell* evidenced this shift and also gave impetus to the rock/hip hop crossover sub-genre. Rubin, who had once performed in a punk band, helped push this crossover with the Beastie Boys too (and he would also co-produce thrash metal band Slayer's *Reign of Blood* in 1986) but it was with Run D.M.C., one of whose members was Simmons' brother, that this sub-genre reached its apogee. The band sampled The Knack's rock-pop hit 'My Sharona' on *Raising Hell*'s second track 'It's Tricky', but their cover of Aerosmith's 'Walk This Way' proved to be a huge hit, backed up by a video which depicted

Aerosmith and Run D.M.C. on opposite sides of a wall which is then broken down as both bands come together. The two genres worked so well together because they shared a musical aggression and an anti-pop attitude and competing styles of 'cool' that brought into confrontation, without entirely bridging, issues of racial difference.

These issues lay at the heart of gangsta rap, which emerged at the same time. The lyrics of this sub-genre shifted to the urban lifestyles of gang members and the violence, crime and racism that were so much a part of this world. Ice T, although better known now as an actor, was at the forefront of this shift, as was Schooly D, whose hardcore rap style was littered with expletives that had to be edited from radio versions of his releases. Gangsta rap also marked that point when hip hop and its successors stopped being a predominantly East Coast, and mainly New York, phenomenon. Although born in New York, Ice T grew up in Los Angeles, and it was here that N.W.A. were formed in 1986. Their second album, *Straight Outta Compton* (1988) defined the genre and is overtly confrontational in its treatment of race politics and withering in its attack on white racism and brutality. 'Fuck tha Police' sets up a mock court where the police department is put on trial:

Fuck tha police, coming straight from the underground
A young nigga got it bad 'cause I'm brown
And not the other color, so police think
They have the authority to kill a minority

Without a gun and a badge, what do you got?
A sucker in a uniform waiting to get shot,
By me, or another nigga
And with a Gat it don't matter if he's smaller or bigger

In general, a greater politicization of lyrical content marks rap at the end of the 1980s, whether this was the gangsta rap of Ice T and N.W.A. or the softer jazz rap of a band like De La Soul, whose *3 Feet High and Rising*, according to Nelson George, 'marked a whimsical new direction for hip hop' with its 'fanciful names . . . playful, intricate rhymes . . . and delightfully layered beats and samples.'[12] While De La Soul's liberal hip hop avoided the charges of misogyny and homophobia levelled at many hardcore rap artists in the gangsta rap tradition, it was this latter style that would propel the genre into the 1990s, as artists like Dr. Dre, Ice Cube, Snoop Doggy Dog and Tupac Shakur released a series of critically acclaimed and commercially successful albums that lingered over the violence and ghettoization of contemporary African American experience, the model for which had been set by New York band Public Enemy.

Public Enemy

Formed in Long Island, New York in 1982, the core of Public Enemy during the 1980s was its two MCs, Chuck D and Flavor Flav, and their DJ, Terminator X. In later years the band became more of an ensemble, incorporating S1W – originally a security organization which provided their services at hip hop parties – and The Bomb Squad – a hip hop production crew renowned for its dense layering of beats, guitars and spoken word. The driving force behind the band was Chuck D, whose performance on a demo tape initially brought him to the attention of Rick Rubin and Russell Simmons at Def Jam. What is notable about both Chuck D and Flavor Flav is that, unlike many later rappers who emerge from the street and gang culture of New York and Los Angeles, they both came from the small town of Roosevelt and first met when they attended Adelphi University. While Flavor Flav is a classically trained pianist, Chuck D took a graphic-design course. Although Roosevelt might not be considered part of the ghetto, it is one of the few majority African American communities on Long Island and has higher degrees of poverty than surrounding areas. As Nelson George points out, while Long Island – or 'the Velt' – produced one African American 'genius' during the 1970s, the basketball player Julius Erving, during the 1980s it produced several, including Eddie Murphy, De La Soul, the rapper Rakim, in addition to Public Enemy.[13] When thinking about Public Enemy's music, this information is important because it suggests that rather than simply a documentary retelling of life on the street from those whose experience might be considered in some way authentic, rap music is a much more sophisticated musical and lyrical aesthetic performance, through which young African American men, in particular, consciously engage with what it means to be young and black in a society that does not value or nurture them, especially during the 1980s when the civil rights movement had long since failed to deliver the changes it dared to hope for.

Part of this performance is clear on their first album, *Yo! Bum Rush the Show* (1987), which trades in the imagery of car and gun culture, sex and criminality and discusses them all with the braggadocio with which rap is now so associated. But it does so in a way which is neither straightforward nor documentary in style. The song 'Miuzi Weighs a Ton', for instance, may well refer to the Uzi machine gun – supposedly the weapon of choice for the most powerful street gangs – but it does so in a figurative way in a song that is all about lyrical performance and the power of this performance. The narrator may be 'public eye enemy' and 'wanted in 50, almost 51 States where the posse got me on the run', but 'Lyric to lyric, line to line' he has a reputation not for crime but a 'reputation for rhyme'. He dodges not bullets but 'microphone thunder' and asks the listener to 'Understand my rhythm, my pattern of lecture / And then you'll know why I'm on the run'. With 'Rightstarter (Message To A Black Man)', Public Enemy begin to hint at the broader political impetus which undergirds their musical performance:

> You spend a buck in the 80s, what you get is a preacher
> Forgivin' this torture of the system that brought 'cha
> I'm on a mission and you got that right
> Addin' fuel to the fire, punch to the fight
> Many have forgotten what we came here for
> Never knew or had a clue, so you're on the floor
> Just growin' not knowin' about your past
> Now you're lookin' pretty stupid while you're shakin' your ass

The referencing here of a slave past 'forgotten' by many is the stimulus driving Public Enemy's racial politics and which becomes even more evident on their next album, *It Takes a Nation of Millions to Hold Us Back* (1988), although the band also take on the media's role in the racist stereotyping of African Americans, as in 'Don't Believe the Hype':

> Some media is the whack
> You believe it's true, it blows me through the roof
> Suckers, liars get me a shovel
> Some writers I know are damn devils
> For them I say don't believe the hype
> Yo Chuck, they must be on a pipe, right?
> Their pens and pads I'll snatch
> 'Cause I've had it
> I'm not an addict fiendin' for static
> I'll see their tape recorder and grab it
> No, you can't have it back silly rabbit
> I'm going' to my media assassin
> Harry Allen, I gotta ask him
> Yo Harry, you're a writer, are we that type?
> Don't believe the hype

Again, the emphasis on the misleading representation of African Americans here makes the self-representation of Public Enemy especially important. Their strategy is to assume the role in which they are stereotypically cast – violent, criminal, drug users – and then from that position fashion a voice and style which resists those stereotypes by using them as the medium for a much more politically engaged discourse. It is through the figurative performance of the black outlaw that Public Enemy both counter white racist stereotypes and appeal to their fellow African Americans. The apocalyptic tone of much of their material on *It Takes a Nation of Millions to Hold Us Back* and *Fear of a Black Planet* (1990) is made even more politically charged by the culture wars of the late 1980s and early 1990s and the battles raging over multiculturalism and narratives of national decline. For Nelson George, *It Takes a Nation of Millions to Hold Us Back* is 'central to a moment in black youth culture when wearing African medallions and Kente fabric from West Africa and using the term "African American" is not simply politically correct, but hip.' But more than this, as AIDS and crack addiction was creating a sense of crisis in many American cities, the need was 'for a fresh critique of racism and this nation's policies'. For George, '*Nation* puts these ideas on radio and on MTV.'[14]

With Spike Lee's film *Do the Right Thing*, Public Enemy also put such ideas in the movie theatre. Their song 'Fight the Power' is one of the band's most vitriolic denunciations of white racism and oppression, summarily dismissing white icons:

Elvis was a hero to most
But he never meant shit to me you see
Straight up racist that sucker was
Simple and plain
Mother fuck him and John Wayne
'Cause I'm Black and I'm proud

Its place in the film as not just the introductory music, but also the music on Radio Raheem's ghettoblaster to which pizzeria-owner Sal takes objection, and the violent nature of this objection leading to Raheem's murder and a riot, signal the central position of hip hop music to racial and ethnic politics in the 1980s.

The measure by which the success of rap and hip hop might be judged is twofold. Firstly, nearly thirty years after becoming established in New York, it is still the most vibrant popular music genre in the United States and beyond. Secondly, the degree to which rap and hip hop have seeped across genre boundaries to become part of other genres of music, especially mainstream pop performance, is unmatched during this period. Like rock and metal, rap and hip has spawned numerous crossover sub-genres. Despite the early doubters, and in terms of impact on American music, rap and hip hop have firmly established their position as a musical form alongside the blues, soul and jazz traditions.

Broadway Musical Blockbusters and Political Performance

Rap and hip hop, as well as rock and metal, rely upon a performative vocabulary – of aggression, violence, outlandishness, sexual promiscuity, coolness – that attaches itself to particular artists and genres of music, such that those artists and genres must come to permanently inhabit that vocabulary. For a rap artist, the performance of a persona cannot cease at the edge of a stage or be confined to the limits of a CD track or music video. The persona must become an enduring identity if it is to convince and attract an audience and is carefully constructed, however wittingly, through appearances and interviews and the music itself. Even for someone like Madonna, who has been so adept at mutating from one persona to another, each of those personas must be linked to a different stage of identity development. Popular music performance, then, might be considered the very antithesis of traditional theatrical acting which requires that actors move from one persona to another without the need to link these performances into a coherent identity. Clearly film and television complicate this process by linking actors to particular character types – the action hero, the villain, the romantic lead – but nowhere is the link between performance, lifestyle and identity perceived to be so continuous as with the contemporary music star. While one might argue that this situation is the by-product of a 1980s culture where consumption became equated with lifestyle and ultimately identity, this would ignore the popularity of theatrical performance, particularly in the Broadway musical, and the political energy with which dramatic productions still offered critical leverage on the social context of the 1980s.

The Broadway musical went through its golden era between the 1940s and 1960s, when shows like *Oklahoma!* (1943), *Carousel* (1945), *South Pacific* (1949), *The King and I* (1951), *My Fair Lady* (1956), *The Sound of Music* (1959) and *Hello, Dolly!* (1964) sometimes ran for several years and made actors, writers and composers household names. In the late 1960s and 1970s, the Broadway musical was boosted by a series of 'rock operas' such as *Hair* (1968), *Jesus Christ Superstar* (1971) and *Godspell* (which arrived on Broadway in 1976 after being a long-running Off Broadway hit). The 1980s signalled a series of new developments that would change the nature of Broadway musical production in ways which fitted the models of cultural production transforming the film and music businesses. While two new musicals – *42nd Street* (1980) and *Barnum* (1980) – rooted in the US past opened the decade, it was to be an improbable musical about Eva Peron, the wife of former Argentine President Juan Peron, which opened on Broadway in 1979, that would offer better evidence of what was to come. Composed and written by British duo Andrew Lloyd Webber and Tim Rice, *Evita* was a follow-up to their transatlantic hit *Jesus Christ Superstar*. Like this earlier musical, the songs

were released originally as an album, achieving chart success in Britain
and the rest of the world, although not proving as popular in the US.
The musical was, however, a success both in London and on
Broadway and cemented Lloyd Webber's status as a pre-eminent
musical force and enabled him to launch a transatlantic assault that
saw the stage musical raised to the level of corporate, multinational
money-spinner.

 Cats, based on T. S. Eliot's collection of poems *Old Possum's Book
of Practical Cats*, opened in London in 1981 and on Broadway the following year with the same team of director, producer and choreogra-
pher. What *Cats* lacked in terms of plot and character development, it
made up for in terms of theatricality. Utilizing the latest aerobic dance
techniques and high-impact special effects, especially at the beginning
and the end, the large cast of feline characters confounded critical
assessments of the play to make the musical, by 1997, the longest
running in US stage history. It eventually closed on Broadway in
September 2000 after 7,485 performances. This longevity was not
achieved simply through the quality of Lloyd Webber's songwriting
talents or the visual display of the production. *Cats* was a crucial
moment in the history of Broadway musical production because of the
way in which Lloyd Webber, along with Cameron Mackintosh, under-
took to market the show as vigorously as possible. The show was
branded like any other consumer product – its logo was two cats' eyes
each with a dancing figure within them – and this branding then
applied to all manner of merchandising. Elizabeth Wollman points out
that making money out of Broadway musicals is nothing new, and that
producers on Broadway have long been capable of deflecting the most
hostile criticism.[15] And Steve Nelson suggests that there is an 'often
unexamined tradition of spectacle on the American commercial stage.
Many . . . forget the opulent production values of the classic 1920s
revues and the lavish spectacles favored by later Broadway impresar-
ios such as Billy Rose, Mike Todd, and David Merrick.'[16] But the sheer
degree of corporate backing that a musical like *Cats* could deploy did
mark a different order of economic and cultural interaction. Woollman
concludes that

> The birth of the Cameron Mackintosh-produced, internationally fran-
> chised 'megamusical' in the 1980s proved . . . that musicals like *Cats*, *The
> Phantom of the Opera*, and *Les Misérables* could, despite tepid reviews,
> be made into international commodities through strategic marketing
> campaigns designed for widening audiences.[17]

The business synergies used by corporate production companies certainly developed in intensity during the 1980s, with a succession of blockbuster hits that often led to spin-off shows touring the country to provide access to those members of the consumer world who could not make New York. And while Nelson might be right about the American tradition of spectacle, what marked the success of many of these musical productions was not only their transatlantic, but also their global appeal. Based on international stories (*Evita* is about Argentina; *Les Misérables* (1987) is an adaptation of French writer Victor Hugo's novel; *The Phantom of the Opera* (1986) is an adaptation of a novel by French writer Gaston Leroux; *Me and My Girl* (1986) is set in World War II London), popular musical successes in the 1980s in the US were unmoored from national contexts and now needed to navigate global waters. While Stephen Sondheim, protégé of Oscar Hammerstein and lyricist of *West Side Story* (1957) and *A Little Night Music* (1973), continued to write, the critically acclaimed work he produced in the 1980s – *Sunday in the Park with George* (1984) and *Into The Woods* (1987) – never achieved anywhere near the commercial success of the 'megamusicals'. *The Phantom of the Opera*, having taken over as the longest-running stage musical of all time, has, according to Lloyd Webber's company's website, played in 119 cities and to audiences of over 80 million people. It has taken $3.3 billion at the box office, which is nearly twice as much as the highest-grossing film of all time, *Titanic*.

By the beginning of the 1990s, it was clear that Broadway musical production had changed irrecoverably. As if to signal this, Bret Easton Ellis made *Les Misérables* one of the cultural touchstones of his 1990 novel *American Psycho*, recovering the poverty which was the subject of Hugo's original novel, both to highlight the state of contemporary New York and to contrast it with the glitzy and musical performance of the story and its transformation into a commodity avidly consumed in all its forms by New Yorkers. Seeing the lucrative potential and opportunities for synergy with its existing products, Disney moved into the production of theatrical musicals in 1993 when it signed a lease on The New Amsterdam Theatre and then staged *Beauty and the Beast* at the Palace Theatre in 1994, a production which is still running.

The new commercialization of theatre in the 1980s marks a change from the 1950s and 1960s when Arthur Miller and Tennessee Williams were able to shape their careers on Broadway. According to Chris Bigsby, Broadway 'was then, as it assuredly is not today, the originator of drama.'[18] The consequence was that theatrical performances moved Off-Broadway, or even further Off-Off-Broadway, while Broadway reacted to them 'like a rich man employing food tasters. If such flourished the plate was snatched away; if they died it was rejected.'[19] Regional theatre also became more important, with its lower overheads and lower expectations of success. But while much good drama was produced during the 1980s, it was also evident that theatrical performance had lost the public and critical attention it enjoyed in the 1940s through to the 1960s.

The victim of a changing cultural climate where film and television and their media spin-offs were increasingly greedy in their demands on leisure time, there were no playwrights working during the 1980s who were capable of achieving the intellectual and public successes of Miller and Williams, largely because of circumstances beyond their control. The closest, perhaps, was David Mamet, whose Pulitzer and Tony-winning *Glengarry Glen Ross* (1984), a relentlessly attritional and claustrophobic play that puts the principles of American business through the grinder of colloquial language to offer up an indictment of its myths and practices, opened in Chicago before moving to Broadway six weeks later. The most important African American dramatist of the decade was August Wilson, who achieved critical success on Broadway with his Pittsburgh cycle of plays which chart African American experience decade by decade through the twentieth-century. *Fences* (1985) and *The Piano Lesson* (1986) both won the Pulitzer prize, while *Ma Rainey's Black Bottom* (1982) and *Joe Turner's Come and Gone* (1984) both transferred to Broadway. Increasingly, theatrical performance fragmented and there was certainly no shortage of work staged during the decade, often by small theatrical groups with particular interest in the representation of gender, race and sexuality.

Split Britches Company

Formed in 1981 by Lois Weaver, Peggy Shaw and Deb Margolin, Split Britches takes its name from the underwear worn by Virginian female workers that allowed them to urinate while standing up in the fields where they were working. The origins of the name suggest something of the way in which, as a theatre company, Split Britches has constantly affronted the assumed naturalness of gender performances and stereotypes and the simplistic understanding of sex and sexuality on which those stereotypes are often built. Emerging out of the WOW (Women's One World) Café, a lesbian performance venue on New York's Lower East Side, Weaver, Shaw and Margolin have performed their own material and collaborated with many other feminist and lesbian performers during their careers. Their work is concerned both with performing different kinds of womanhoods and sexualities, but it is also – in the spirit of much work emerging in literature and art – about the process of representation itself. Rather than relying upon a realist style in order to expose and denounce the inequalities of gender and sexuality that structure US society, Split Britches deploys a range of performance techniques to re-imagine feminist and lesbian experience.

Jane Wagner's *The Search for Signs of Intelligent Life in the Universe*, the one-woman show that opened on Broadway in 1985, starring lesbian actress Lily Tomlin, presented lesbian characters to its audience and raised issues of feminist concern. According to Kate Davy, however, this play 'falls into a trap of its own design. While Wagner and Tomlin insistently fore-ground feminist and lesbian issues, the core problem – the representational frame from which their message emanates – remains intact.'[20] The core problem remains intact because the assumed spectator is heterosexual; in other words, what one finds in Wagner's play is the visual consumption of lesbianism by a heterosexual audience. With Split Britches, and in the other new lesbian theatre emerging in the 1980s, what one finds is a willingness to 'undercut the heterosexual model by implying a spectator that is not the generic, universal male, not the cultural construction "woman," but lesbian – a subject defined in terms of sexual similarity.'[21] In *Upwardly Mobile Home* (1985), for instance, one of the play's monologues describes how the char-acter once met a fat woman at a circus. Jill Dolan suggests that the love the character declares for the fat woman is not based on some wrangle with an internal search for self, but is 'paradigmatic of the lesbian viewing experience. The recognition of mutual subjectivity allows the gaze to be shared in a direct way', such that 'the visual economy is now under lesbian control.'[22]

The unsettling of the realist theatrical frame and the return of the lesbian to the position of viewer is achieved through the interruption of often detailed monologues by surreal episodes, such as sudden bursts of energy – *Split Britches* (1983) – or by characters addressing the audience (*Upwardly Mobile Home*), while gender roles are constantly illuminated and made problematic by the presence of lesbian desire in the plays,[23] since this makes one reassess the purpose of gender in a terrain of sexual desire which no longer relies upon heterosexuality and its implicit oppositions of male/female and man/woman. The constant re-representation of butch and femme images and iconography, and the way in which characters switch between butch and femme roles in the work of Split Britches, also does a similar job of blurring the distinctions of gender upon which these images rest.

Split Britches, and other lesbian and gay performance groups, are not unique in that they address these issues of gender and sexuality. The crit-ical work that has been influential in the way that culture has been studied over the last thirty years would alert us to the ways in which cultural pro-duction in general is constantly grappling with questions based upon an understanding of gender and sexuality. What it is important to remember about a company like Split Britches is that their self-conscious performance is a critical intervention in a way in which much cultural production is not. While Split Britches draw on popular forms, of performance and of representation, their purpose is to realign understanding of these forms, not to recycle them. If one of the earlier rallying cries of the women's movement was that feminism is the theory and lesbianism the practice, what the 1980s showed was that theorists and practitioners were moving towards similar conclusions. Feminist theorist Judith Butler's immensely influential *Gender Trouble* (1990) seems to reiterate the idea that Split Britches had spent the decade illustrating: that gender, sex and desire are rooted in the repetition of stylized performances, the visibility of which are obscured by discourses about nature and biological sex.

At its most engaged, theatrical performance can ask its audience to what extent there is a gap between those roles performed on a stage and the performances of everyday life. While the 'megamusical' which dominated Broadway during the 1980s might initially demand that different questions are raised – such as to what extent do the influx of corporate models of production and marketing alter the nature of the product watched by audiences – Off-Broadway theatre, Off-Off-Broadway theatre and the regional and small touring group theatre can also help to reflect on what it is about performance itself that continued to draw people to theatres – even if only to see blockbuster musicals – during the 1980s.

Despite the market logic driving musical production, and despite the disparate and often improbably obscure sources for many of the successful musicals, it might be the case that the staged performance itself remains a vital way in which audiences not only defer the performative nature of everyday life, as outlined by someone like Judith Butler, to theatrical actors, but also that by observing that process on stage are not simply passive consumers but thinking participants in a performance. In doing so, they may be more like the music stars for whom performance and identity become so closely linked.

Chapter 5

American Culture and Globalization

Cultural Imperialism

If globalization is taken to mean the proliferation of connections and dependencies between different geographical locations across the world, or what John Tomlinson has called 'complex connectivity',[1] then this proliferation should not necessarily be understood to be a development of recent date. Even if globalization were considered to be driven by modernity, the problem arises of how to date that modernity and whether modernity itself should be reduced to a series of social and political changes such as industrialization, urbanization and the rise of the nation state; or whether globalization as it has developed in the twentieth century marks a historical break with modernity and a new phase of social experience. These are complex issues about the conceptualization of history and periodization in which the place of any single decade recedes into the background. For the purposes of this book, one particular strand of the debates around globalization can help to clear the way to think about the US in the 1980s. This is the idea that globalization, certainly in the post-World War II period, is synonymous with a process of Americanization in which the US attempts to exert its control and influence across the globe by cultural as well as economic, political and military means.

The historical back story to this process can be seen in recent developments in the study of US culture that increasingly emphasize the imperialist tendency of US national consolidation in the nineteenth century and the way in which the settling of the continent during this period relied upon the violent acquisition of territory – by the displacement of Indians and the US-Mexican War (1846–8), for instance – supported by ideological justifications for this process, particularly the doctrine of Manifest Destiny. Culture played an important part in

the way that various stages of the settlement were naturalized and jus-
tified, or sometimes contested. A writer like George Lippard, for
instance, who was both a journalist and novelist as well as a political
activist, supported the war with Mexico on the grounds that the settlement of new territory would provide the white working class with
a way of escaping the corruption, poverty and exploitation of the big
cities in east. His newspaper columns in the Philadelphia paper *The
Quaker City Weekly* and his fictional treatments of the war – *Legends
of Mexico* (1847) and *Bel of Prairie Eden: A Romance of Mexico* (1848)
– served the purpose of circulating imagery and ideas about Mexico
and the war and contributed to the discourses and ideologies through
which those events were understood. More generally, Lippard was
part of that process whereby what Benedict Anderson calls print-
capitalism contributed to the cultural roots of nationalism and the construction of the nation state as an imagined community.[2]

By the end of the nineteenth century and into the twentieth century,
however, the idea of conquering territory outside of what is perceived
to be the nation's natural borders proved to be a contentious issue in
the US. In his book about cultural imperialism and American culture
before World War II, John Carlos Rowe claims that ' "Americans" '
interpretations of themselves as a people are shaped by a powerful
imperial desire and a profound anti-colonial temper.'[3] What one finds
in the anti-colonial discourses objecting to further territorial expansion beyond continental America is an implicit argument that
'American' values – independence, self-government, democracy – are
best exported by economic rather than military means.[4] If the technical origin of the word Americanization in the nineteenth century came
from the way that manufacturing in the US was more machine-driven
than in Britain, as the twentieth century has gone on and culture has
become ever more tightly bound up with the economics of production
and consumption of culture in a global system where the US is the
primary economic superpower, Americanization has become confused
with globalization. One of the fears that has emerged from this situation is that the US is using its economic pre-eminence to exercise a
form of cultural imperialism, and that 'a global culture is in one way
or another liable to be a hegemonic culture'.[5]

The elements of this hegemonic culture are the iconic brands of the
American cultural landscape – Disney, Coca-Cola, McDonalds, Levis,
Nike – and the producers of the culture which is increasingly visible –
Hollywood and the multimedia conglomerates. Behind them all lies an
economic model of expansion driven by US multinational capitalist

corporations whose objective, Marxist theorists like the American Herbert Schiller claim, is dedicated to the absorption of national and local cultures into the culture of global capitalism. Certainly in the 1980s, the shift in the corporate structure of film, television and music production and the corporatization of the art market can be seen to contribute to the increasing power of multinational corporations in determining cultural output. The rapid deployment of new digital technology that helped the world's financial markets interact and which drove the mergers and acquisitions frenzy of the decade are all implicated in the rise of the power of the multinationals. Also in the 1980s, these multinationals were also joined by a company whose future development would extend the influence of capitalism into entirely new areas of consumption and leisure. Microsoft, originally founded in 1975, opened its first international office in Japan in 1978 and its first overseas production base in Ireland in 1985. The same year, Microsoft released the first retail version of Windows and spent the rest of the decade releasing early versions of the software for which they are best known: Microsoft Works, Microsoft Office and SQL Server. Microsoft's global reach onto virtually all desktop computers and the phenomenal revenues the company has generated, making Bill Gates the world's richest entrepreneur, are by now a familiar story. Even from its early days, though, Microsoft was accused of monopolistic business practices and of acquiring ideas and technology from others rather than innovating. But its rise to prominence was only the most famous in a computer software sector that would prepare the way for the kind of 'digital capitalism' of which Dan Schiller writes, helping to open up whole new markets for capitalist activity.

What worries critics of global capitalist culture is that capitalism promotes and reinforces itself through the circulation of the culture it produces and distributes. For John Tomlinson, this totalizing approach to the relationship between culture and multinational capitalism remains persistent because of 'the sheer inescapable evidence of the steady advance of the power and influence of transnational capitalism in the contemporary world.'[6] However, while this evidence demonstrates the increasingly close links between commerce and culture, and an unparalleled commodification of culture, Tomlinson is not convinced that this is the same evidence needed to justify the claim that 'a single hegemonic "homogenized" global culture is emerging'.[7] What Shelley Streeby shows in her study of George Lippard's nineteenth-century writing is that despite its overt politicized and ideological intentions, as culture it does not work so monolithically: in other words, that the process of cultural production and consumption was 'diverse rather than routinized'.[8] Similarly, for Tomlinson the fact that people in different parts of the world consume the same cultural products and travel the globe via identical-looking airport terminals does little but suggest 'the power of some capitalist firms ... to command wide markets around the world' and that to suggest otherwise is 'utilizing a rather impoverished concept of culture – one that reduces culture to its material goods.'[9]

The audience is thus crucial to the way in which culture works and the export of a cultural product from one location to another – unless one assumes that the world is already homogenized – necessarily undergoes a process of translation and appropriation which is neither predictable nor uniform. During the 1980s, as cultural-studies work turned its attention to the consumption of cultural products, Ien Ang conducted research into the audience reception of *Dallas* in the Netherlands (published as *Watching Dallas* in 1985). While her methodology relied upon soliciting letters from an advert in a newspaper, the things that her respondents said about the television show illustrate the divided and surprising nature of their relationship with it. While some dismissed it as rubbish but watched it anyway, out of habit as much as anything, others were much more forthcoming about the pleasures they found in watching *Dallas* which did not indicate they were being incorporated into the global capitalist model of the ideal consuming citizen. Some spoke about how certain storylines and characters enabled them to better understand and negotiate their own situations, while others highlighted the melodramatic nature of the soap form more generally. Rather than working at the level of realism, then, *Dallas* and soap operas are enjoyed at the emotional level so that 'what is recognized as real is not knowledge of the world, but a subjective experience of the world: "a structure of feeling."'[10] Even those who dismissed *Dallas* in Ang's study as the epitome of worthless American mass culture found personal self-justification and security in their ability to spot something they considered culturally inferior. These reactions suggest a whole different terrain on which consumers interact with cultural products and that culture itself is more than simply a commercial loop of production, distribution and consumption automatically geared to benefit the interests of an abstract and anonymous multinational corporation. This terrain was being mapped out in the 1980s in tandem with the process of globalization itself.

One further factor to consider, and one that would apply particularly to the 1980s, is that to mistake multinational capitalism for US multinational capitalism is itself a mistake. The 1980s is notable for the way in which non-American corporations, such as Sony, not only consolidated their global economic position, but did so through the acquisition of US multinationals. Sony took over CBS Records from the CBS corporation in 1988 and the following year took control of Columbia TriStar Motion Picture Group from Coca-Cola. The status of the cultural products distributed by these corporations now becomes ambiguous: are they classified as American because the company is based in the US, or Japanese because the economic reins of the company are held in Japan? Similarly, how does one classify bands who may be neither American nor Japanese, but whose music was distributed by CBS Records when it was American-owned but subsequently was distributed by Columbia outside the US, Canada and Japan? Columbia was the name that Sony acquired the rights to from British company EMI. When it bought CBS it only bought a temporary license for the CBS Records name. These are just some of the complications of national origin that arise in an era of tightly integrated global financial networks. And while this may seem a trivial example, it was certainly true that in the 1980s there was a discourse emerging within the US which manifested itself as a fear over the penetration of US markets by non-US multinationals and non-US brands and might help question the narrative that tries to equate global capitalism with Americanization.

William Gibson's dystopic vision of a cyber future in *Neuromancer* (1984), for example, does not see US capital as the dominant force in cyberspace. The novel, as well as being predominantly set in Japan, uses terminology drawn from Japanese business culture. The protagonist, Case, avoids a 'dark-suited sarariman' in Ninsei.[11] 'Sarariman' is the Japanese version of 'salaryman', someone who works for the 'zaibatsus, the multinationals that shaped the course of human history' and which 'had transcended old barriers'.[12] The novel also imagines that Mitsubishi – the Japanese industrial giant – has absorbed the United States genetic engineering company Genentech,[13] while Mitsubishi has also established the Mitsubishi Bank of America.[14] The novel draws here on some of the thoughts, outlined in the Introduction to this book, present at the end of the 1970s and the beginning of the 1980s: that the Japanese and other Asian economies were overtaking and outperforming the US economy, and, crucially, that they were more technologically advanced. The arrival in the US of Japanese computer, audio and digital products added to these beliefs. Even the Atari 2600, released in 1977 and the first truly successful games console, used a Japanese word – 'atari' is Japanese for 'go' – although the console itself was manufactured in the US by a US company. Of course, many of the games it ran – such as *Galaxian* and *Pac-Man* – were developed by the Japanese company Namco. In a similar vein, Bret Easton Ellis' withering portrayal of wealth and consumerism in the 1980s is replete with non-US brands. Patrick Bateman's television in Ellis' *American Psycho* (1991) is made by Toshiba TV, his video recorder by NEC, while his Rolex watch comes from Britain, his A. Testoni loafers from Italy and he goes to see the Irish band U2 in concert. The novel creates a sense that the Americanness of the world in which Bateman lives is being diluted by the forces of global consumer culture.

Despite concerns about the reach of American capitalism and the 'McDonaldization' or 'Disneyization'[15] of non-US cultures, US cultural imperialism remains a dystopic fear rather than an actuality. While consumers continue to be alert and active, and cultural flows move in more than one direction, this situation is likely to remain the case. The more interesting questions to pursue are how US culture itself, in and beyond the 1980s, has been changed by the forces of globalization.

CNN

When Ted Turner took over the family billboard business after his father's suicide in 1963, the world of global media networks was in its infancy. A year earlier, Marshall McLuhan had published *The Gutenberg Galaxy: The Making of Typographic Man* and recycled Wyndham Lewis's concept of the 'global village', although, in decidedly un-prophetic ways, McLuhan had not imagined the domination of visual modes of communication and cognitive interaction in the coming decades and preferred instead to highlight the importance of oral and aural interactions.

Turner began his media empire with a local UHF station in Atlanta, but in 1976 pioneered the national cable business when he took advantage of the new orbiting C-band satellites to distribute what was now WTCG (the TCG standing for Turner Communications Group) across the nation. Although HBO began in 1975, it was a pay-cable service, whereas WTCG was a free service. In the wake of Turner's success in the national cable market, CNN launched on 1 June 1980 as the first twenty-four-hour rolling news television station. While Turner's role as pioneer is important, it is CNN's impact on newsgathering and the viewer's relationship with that news and the world from which it is drawn which is of lasting significance.

CNN has been followed both in concept and format by many other rolling news stations around the world, although most did not begin until the

1990s. The first war with Iraq in 1991, particularly in its early stages, left many stations relying on coverage provided by CNN since CNN had reporters on the ground ready to broadcast. For while the national avail-ability of the news channel was a key to its success, so was its ability to draw coverage from around the globe. It quickly established bureaus around the world, and because of its rolling format these bureaus needed to be ready to move as soon as news broke, rather than knowing that a report could be filed for a scheduled news bulletin.

The format of CNN is, therefore, crucial to its interaction with global news. The channel relies on hosts or anchors in its Atlanta headquarters who are in dialogue with reporters around the world following particular news events. The effect of this format is twofold. First of all, it creates a sense of contemporaneity for the viewer. No longer does news suffer a time lag between occurrence and reporting. Second, it allows the vicarious con-sumption of 'real' events beyond the immediate geographical location of the viewer. Made possible by satellite and digital technology, viewing events in actual time creates a sense of immediacy that is clearly part of that process of time/space compression so symptomatic of globalization. In January 1986, for instance, CNN's live news coverage captured the seventy-three second flight of the Space Shuttle *Challenger* before it exploded, killing all seven crew members. Coverage of this event provided the impetus for a sense of national and international mourning, since it is not often one sees death live on television. But the spectacle of the event and its relaying to national and international audiences also created a new kind of interaction between the media and disaster. The process by which the media coverage of an event, and the ratification as truth and reality that this coverage provides, also leads to criticisms of CNN and rolling news coverage, not just for reporting, but also for creating news.

CNN executive Ed Turner (no relation to Ted Turner) may have described CNN as 'town crier to the global village',[16] but news coverage always relies upon selection and representation. So influential has the CNN format become, and so vigorously has CNN modelled itself as the breaker of news – one of its slogans is 'Be the first to know' – that Edward Said has commented that 'News is what CNN broadcasts, and what CNN broadcasts is therefore news.'[17] It is at this point that CNN's role as a newsmaker might suggest that it has hegemonic control in the global news economy and that its legion of imitators, in utilizing the same format, commit themselves to supporting this hegemony. Said sums up this kind of approach when he says:

> The troubling thing is that CNN's broadcast represents all that one needs to know about the world, reduced, packaged, and delivered without a trace of conflict or contradiction. Its thought, its sensation, what it sees are insidi-ously substituted for what the spectator might himself see, feel, think about. This gradual replacement of a private and personal process with a ready-made, manufactured and processed system is nothing less than a hijacking of the mind by a sophisticated apparatus whose purpose is, I believe, deeply ideological.[18]

Whatever reasonable fears this opinion articulates, its own representation of the CNN audience as passive is equally problematic. This is certainly not how international audiences have understood CNN and news media coverage. In May 1989, the reformist president of the Soviet Union, Mikhail Gorbachev, was due to embark on a state visit to China. Aware that this visit would attract the global news networks such as CNN and the BBC, Chinese students and intellectuals took the opportunity to protest against the Chinese government at precisely this moment when the cameras of the world would be fixed on the Chinese capital Beijing. The subsequent protests in Tiananmen Square were transmitted across the world and gave rise to one of the iconic images of the 1980s: the figure of a lone protester standing in front of a line of Chinese army tanks. With banners and signs clearly designed for an international audience, the protesters had calculated the damage they might do to the Chinese government through their protests. CNN defied the Chinese government's demand that it stop broadcasting during the military suppression of the protests and carried on reporting via telephone links, to be silenced only when the Chinese government closed down satellite links. Rather than CNN making the news in the Tiananmen Square protests, then, it was more a case of the protesters using CNN to reach a global viewing public whom they did not assume to be passive consumers of news.

Transatlantic Circulations

The links between US and British culture, despite the so-called 'special relationship' borne out of colonial rule, revolution, independence and a common language, have long been a source of unease. While the transatlantic route should have eased and facilitated the flow of cultural products, this has not always been a straightforward process. If in the nineteenth century there was some reluctance on the part of British cultural elites to acknowledge US culture – Sydney Smith famously asked in the *Edinburgh Review* in 1820, 'Who reads an American book? Or goes to an American play? Or looks at an American picture or statue?' – there was a corresponding desire from some Americans to self-consciously produce a national literary culture worthy of attention. In his 1842 essay 'The Poet', Ralph Waldo Emerson claimed that 'We have yet had no genius in America, with tyrannous eye, which knew the value of our incomparable materials', but that 'its ample geography dazzles the imagination, and it will not wait long for metres'.[19] Herman Melville, in 'Hawthorne and His Mosses' (1850), called for America to 'first praise mediocrity even, in her own children, before she praises . . . the best excellence in the children of any other land.'[20] But in 1916, Randolph Bourne was still complaining vehemently about English influence:

The truth is that no more tenacious cultural allegiance to the mother country has been shown by any alibi nation than by the ruling class of Anglo-Saxon descendants in these American States. English snobberies, English religion, English literary styles, English literary reverences and canons; English ethics, English superiorities, have been the cultural food that we have drunk in from our mothers' breasts. The distinctively American spirit – pioneer, as distinguished from the reminiscently English – that appears in Whitman and Emerson and James, has had to exist on sufferance alongside of this other cult, unconsciously belittled by our cultural makers of opinion. No country has perhaps had so great indigenous genius which had so little influence on the country's traditions and expressions.[21]

From a contemporary perspective these concerns seem antiquated, given the esteem in which US literary culture is now held in Britain. In his first collection of essays on US literature and culture, British novelist Martin Amis touches on the reversal of the 'big novel' syndrome that so dominated British writing in the nineteenth century and which is inherited by the US in the twentieth. And there is a healthy admiration in Amis' conclusion that 'perhaps it is an inescapable response to America – twentieth-century America, racially mixed and mobile, twenty-four hour, endless, extreme. Superabundantly various. American novels are big all right, but partly because America is big too.'[22] Amis' own big novel of the 1980s, *Money* (1984), is itself a transatlantic dialogue between the shambolic and disintegrating John Self and the culture industries of the US whose slick, neurotic and bottom-line practices Self struggles to cope with, and in many ways a homage to the 'bigness' of the US.

In more abstract and theoretical terms, the transatlantic literary world has also recently been reinterpreted as a realm which might help in an understanding of national cultural traditions. For Paul Giles, 'America . . . introduces an element of strangeness into British culture, just as British traditions, often in weirdly hollowed out or parodic forms, shadow the democratic designs of the American republic.'[23] The purpose of thinking about these kinds of relations is not only to destabilize the traditional narratives of national cultures, but also 'to appreciate the assumptions framing these narratives and the ways they are intertwined with the construction and reproduction of national mythologies.'[24] While Giles deploys writers estranged, exiled or marginalized in the transatlantic world in order to offer readings of their work which precisely demonstrate this intellectual project, there is at times less of an interest in the shifting historical formations in which those estrangements are located. By the 1980s, for instance, the qualitative experience of estrangement is markedly different from that faced by Herman Melville in the middle of the nineteenth century and Henry James at the beginning of the twentieth century. The compression of time and space which twentieth-century globalization produced, not only through faster travel but also the rapid transmission of information around the world, means that the parameters within which culture operates are very different. Having said this, as a novel like *Money* demonstrates, there is still sufficient cultural strangeness to generate – even to an author whose wife is American, whose son is half-American and who considers himself to be 'fractionally American' – a dialogue with national cultures within a transatlantic paradigm. For his next novel, *London Fields* (1989), Amis uses an American narrator, Samson Young, through whom to articulate a sense of decline which is national – 'I always felt I knew where England was heading'[25] – as well as being apocalyptically global in its millennial overtones. And it is also a novel of cultural usurpation – 'America was the one to watch'[26] – but where the American narrator is himself about to die.

While the literary contact between the US and Britain should not be underestimated, the second half of the twentieth century was dominated by the diffusion into British markets of US popular culture. Particularly in the field of music, however, the exchanges between Britain and the US have produced some of the more obvious ways in which US cultural consumption is influenced by cultural movements beyond its increasingly nominal borders. The export of Elvis, rock 'n' roll and rhythm and blues music in the 1950s had a deep impact on music in Britain. The revitalization of the British music scene in the early 1960s produced the first wave of bands to return these musical influences, after filtering them through the prism of British culture, back to the US. The main impact here came from The Beatles, but other bands like The Rolling Stones, The Animals, Manfred Mann, Freddie & the Dreamers, Herman's Hermits, The Dave Clark Five and The Troggs all had number-one singles in the US between 1964 and 1966. Blues guitar music became a major influence later in the 1960s and, partly thanks to the fact that Jimi Hendrix was developing his music career in Britain, a rock scene developed out of which emerged bands like Led Zeppelin, still one of the biggest-selling bands in US music history. Much of the transatlantic rock scene of the early to mid-1970s was visible on the album rather than the single charts – as pointed out in the previous chapter, Led Zeppelin refused to endorse the singles released by their record company – and on the kinds of tours of big American city-venues that became the source for humour in the 1984 film mockumentary *Spinal Tap*. But although less visible than Beatlemania and the British invasion of the 1960s, and what would follow it, one of the reasons that rock crossed the Atlantic was because it grew out of the blues music that found its way to Britain.

While punk and new wave in the late 1970s proved to be the next important import to the US, it really only built on a scene that was already emerging of its own volition, particularly in New York with bands like the New York Dolls and The Ramones. The Sex Pistols, as in much of what they did, were important for the mythology surrounding them rather than anything they produced or performed. They travelled to the US soon after what would prove to be their final gig in Britain, on Christmas Day 1977, and followed this six weeks later with their very last gig, in San Francisco, after which John Lydon quit the band, disillusioned following the short, badly organized tour. It would take several more years for British artists to enjoy unparalleled success on the US music scene.

Looking back from the present day, the level of this success seems hard to believe. Between 1990 and early 2006, only eleven singles by British artists have topped the US *Billboard* chart. Of these, four were by either George Michael or Elton John. In July 1983, by comparison, eighteen of the top forty singles on the *Billboard* charts were by British artists, more than at any time in US chart history, including the 1960s. Sixty-two singles by British bands topped the US singles chart during the decade, covering many different genres of music, from the pop-metal of Def Leppard, the prog rock of Pink Floyd, the techno-pop of The Human League and The Pet Shop Boys, the New Romantic sounds of Culture Club and Duran Duran, through to various ageing rock acts like Phil Collins, Steve Winwood, Peter Gabriel, David Bowie, George Harrison and, with his trademark video from 1986 of a glamorous all-woman backing group on 'Addicted to Love', Robert Palmer.

The popularity of British music in the US also helped with one of the biggest transatlantic cultural events of the decade, the Live Aid concert which took place on 13 July 1985 at Wembley Stadium in London and JFK Stadium in Philadelphia. A massive test of satellite-link technology, the concert was such a huge success not only because of the worthy cause it was supporting – famine relief in Africa – but also because of the musical heritage shared across the Atlantic. While it was noticeable that no American bands played at Wembley, a whole array of British bands played at the JFK concert: Black Sabbath, Judas Priest, Mick Jagger, Simple Minds, Eric Clapton, Led Zeppelin and Duran Duran. Phil Collins, ex-Genesis drummer, and one of the biggest transatlantic artists of the decade, appeared at both concerts, flying to Philadelphia by Concorde after his Wembley performance.

The explanation for this level of popularity of British music in the US is probably down to two major factors. First of all, the punk and new wave movement at the end of the 1970s had a mainstream pop pay-off in British music that was not replicated in the US. With the exception of Blondie, and a few minor Talking Heads hits, most of the new wave scene in the US remained clustered in New York, underground and away from commercial reach. In Britain, the regional music scene, with its intense rivalries and hard-core bases in London, Liverpool, Manchester, Birmingham and Sheffield, picked up the punk and new wave sensibility and attitude and deployed it in a range of musical genres that mixed in a whole array of other musical influences. Duran Duran, for instance, formed in Birmingham in 1978, fashioned both a visual look and music style that blended glam and art rock influences – such as David Bowie and Roxy Music – from the 1970s, the commercialism of disco and a name from the 1968 sci-fi film *Barbarella*, and then passed them through the new wave filter to end up with a pop aesthetic that was more visually innovative, appealing, sexually provocative and tuneful than anything emerging in US pop until Madonna. Duran Duran were also at the forefront of a new electronic sound that again was taken up in Britain and Europe more quickly than in the US. Guitars were either replaced by, or subordinated to, synthesizers in much of the New Romantic genre of which Duran Duran were a part, along with Spandau Ballet, Adam & the Ants, Visage and Ultravox. Make-up and cross-dressing were a vital component of this New Romantic look and epitomized by Boy George in Culture Club, a band which fused soul and reggae into its style to produce a hybrid pop act. The new electronic sound produced artists like The Human League, Depeche Mode, The Eurythmics and Soft Cell, whose single 'Tainted Love' (1981) in many ways is symptomatic of the fusing of musical genres in an original and commercially successful manner. Originally a northern soul classic, it was first released by Gloria Jones in 1964. Jones then went on to sing backing vocals for British glam-rock star Marc Bolan, with whom she also had a relationship and son, and was also driving the car that crashed when Bolan was killed. The fusion of soul with electronic synthesizers produced a 1980s classic and took Jones' soul song back to the *Billboard* 100 chart in the US for forty-three consecutive weeks, a record at that point.

The other factor that ensured many of these acts went down so well in the US was a stagnating pop scene across the Atlantic. While disco was an earlier competitor around the turn of the decade, its popularity was waning. There was the odd new wave-influenced success, like Kim Carnes' 'Bette Davis Eyes' (1981), but performers like Barbara Streisand and Olivia Newton-John, along with pop and r 'n' b acts like the J. Geils Band, and Hall and Oates, did not exactly have either innovative sounds or looks. Into this vacuum stepped the second British invasion of the US charts. It wasn't until the emergence of Prince and Madonna in 1984–5, the runaway success of Michael Jackson's *Thriller* album and the impact of hip hop by the mid-decade that the balance began to shift back toward American performers. This shift was inspired by black music and it is noticeable that towards the end of the decade, the more successful British artists were no longer the young bands, but the older artists who were both well established and appealed to the important older demographic who had supported the staid and less innovative American acts of the early 1980s. In many ways, then, the 1980s are the high-water mark of British musical influence in the US. Since that time, no genre of music has emerged in Britain that has had an impact on US audiences. While this may be down to the fragmenting nature of the music scene in the 1990s and the ready availability of many different genres and subgenres, it is also true to say that the influence of dance music and hip hop have shifted the directional flow of musical influence from the US to Britain, as well as to Europe, which has it own transatlantic connections with the US.

Disneyland Resort Paris

One of the most famous books about the US written in the nineteenth century is French thinker and historian Alexis de Tocqueville's *Democracy in America*. Published in two volumes in 1835 and 1840, the book is about the failings of democracy in France and what de Tocqueville reads as its success in the US. Originally sent to inspect US prisons, de Tocqueville spent nine months travelling through the country and the book is the result of his findings. Its praise for the characteristics that he saw as distinguishing Americans from Europeans led *Democracy in America* to become a staple of the kind of exceptionalist understanding of the US popular in Europe during the nineteenth and twentieth centuries.

In the 1980s, the French philosopher and cultural critic Jean Baudrillard also produced an account of his travels in the US, calling the book, simply, *America*. Fascinated and repelled by a nation where the popularity of jogging signifies less a desire to kept fit than an apocalyptic prophesy ('Nothing evokes the end of the world more than a man running straight ahead on a beach, swathed in the sounds of his walkman, cocooned in the solitary sacrifice of his energy'),[27] elsewhere in his work Baudrillard has also written about the significance of Walt Disney and the Disneyland phenomenon, which for him epitomizes the simulation inherent in American and contemporary culture. All the values of American culture are represented in Disneyland, for Baudrillard, 'in miniature and comic-strip form'.[28] Furthermore:

> Disneyland is there to conceal the fact that it is the 'real' country, all of 'real' America, which is Disneyland (just as prisons are there to conceal the fact that it is the social in its entirety, in its banal omnipresence, which is carceral). Disneyland is presented as imaginary in order to make us believe that the rest is real, when in fact all of Los Angeles and the America surrounding it are no longer real, but of the order of the hyperreal and of simulation. It is no longer a question of a false representation of reality (ideology), but of concealing the fact that the real is no longer real, and thus of saving the reality principle.[29]

These words were written before the opening of Disneyland Resort Paris in 1992, although the plans to locate a Disney resort in Europe had been at the planning stage since the mid-1970s and Disney signed an agreement for the project with the French government in March 1987, following up Disney's first excursion into overseas theme parks, Tokyo Disneyland, which was opened in 1983. Clearly the opening of these resorts was part of Disney's global entrepreneurial strategy and fitted synergistically with the sale of its other products. Disneyland Resort Paris, made up of two theme parks – Disneyland Park and Walt Disney Studios Park – is modelled on a similar structure to the US park but crucially alters certain aspects to try to account for its European location.

Tomorrowland, for instance, became Discoveryland and was designed around French writer Jules Verne's visions of the future. Lake Nautilus has a recreation of the Nautilus vessel from *20,000 Leagues Under the Sea*, a book that Disney had adapted into a film in 1954 with Kirk Douglas as Captain Nemo. Space Mountain became Space Mountain: De la Terre à la Lune (From the Earth to the Moon), again picking up Jules Verne's less well known science-fiction novel of the same name that tells the story of three members of a post-American Civil War gun club who build and launch a rocket to get to the moon. The Haunted Mansion became Phantom Manor in Paris and rather than the glossy exterior of its American version, the house was constructed to simulate a real crumbling manor house and the action that one walks through follows an entirely different story to that of the Haunted Mansion.

> These changes suggest ways in which the transatlantic circulation of imagery and stories intersects with the forces of globalization in ways which modify the content and the experience of globalization. While Jean Baudrillard tries to achieve a universalizing position – all culture is simulation – he does so within a national paradigm by suggesting that the originating impetus comes from the US; from his version of America wherein Disneyland has become the 'real' America. He also raises the spectre of globalization as American hegemony when he argues that 'The New World Order is in a Disney mode'.[30] But it is harder to substantiate these claims when Disneyland moves beyond America and by necessity is forced to interact with local and regional expectations. France may have donated the Statue of Liberty to the US in the nineteenth century and de Tocqueville may have written what some have seen as a homage to 'American' values, but the spirit of much French–American relations has been less cordial and more in the mode of suspicion epitomized by Baudrillard. France withdrew from NATO's military command in 1966 and only rejoined in 1993, and the support the French government has given to the French film industry to try and reduce the influence of US films in France signals some of the ways in which France has attempted to resist US political and cultural pressures. There is, then, a certain irony in Disney's European theme park being located in France. Its location there can be seen as an example of economic motives outstripping cultural imperatives, but then, once it becomes a cultural outlet, it has to negotiate the demands of a European audience increasingly familiar, and often uncomfortable with, US culture but whose own cultural origins, despite the de-territorialization of globalization, are differently rooted. It is in the complex intersection of local, regional, transatlantic and globalizing culture that Disneyland Resort Paris operates.

Immigrant Culture

If the objective of Emerson, Melville and Randolph Bourne in the passages quoted above was to urge into being a national culture which broke ties with Britain and gave full attention to an American landscape and character, then that project was always likely to be compromised by a landscape and character which was unevenly – if at all – commensurate with the geographical footprint of the nation. Bourne's attempt to bring within the orbit of this national culture the cosmopolitanism he saw emerging during a period of intense immigration at the end of the nineteenth and the beginning of the twentieth century was reminiscent of his contemporary Israel Zangwill's conception of the 'melting pot', an idea which comes from the play of the same name, first staged in 1908. Around the same time, Theodore Roosevelt was calling for a national allegiance from immigrants and their descendents which subordinated their state of origin. 'There is no room in this country for hyphenated Americanism',[31] he declared, while also suggesting that 'a hyphenated American is not an American at all'.[32] Roosevelt continues in apocalyptic tones about the consequences of ignoring his appeals:

> The one absolutely certain way of bringing this nation to ruin, of preventing all possibility of its continuing to be a nation at all, would be to permit it to become a tangle of squabbling nationalities, an intricate knot of German-Americans, Irish-Americans, English-Americans, French-Americans, Scandinavian-Americans or Italian-Americans, each preserving its separate nationality, each at heart feeling more sympathy with Europeans of that nationality, than with the other citizens of the American Republic.[33]

It is notable, of course, that Roosevelt makes no reference to either blacks or Asians in this speech. As Lisa Lowe points out in respect of Asian immigration, 'All too often, the periodisation of immigration to the United States schematically presumes Anglo-European immigration as the nation's originary past, while racialized immigration is temporalized as if it is a recent event.'[34] In fact, the forced immigration of African slaves and Asian immigration into the US after 1850 mean that racialized immigration is part and parcel of US history from its very beginnings. The problem with Roosevelt's understanding of national identity, and with other conceptualizations that try to manage ethnic and racial diversity in a similar way, is that ultimately they rely upon a version of Americanism which is supposedly neutral, but which in fact maintains implicit ideological assumptions about what constitutes Americanism – such as whiteness, Christianity and economic liberalism, for example. Furthermore, it assumes that points of origin, be they in Europe, Asia, Africa or Latin America, can be somehow cast aside simply by geographical relocation.

The idea that globalization involves de-territorialization – or 'the loss of the "natural" relation of culture to geographical and social territories'[35] – offers a way of understanding how American culture, despite the partisan demands for a national culture, is constituted by a web of disparate and conflicting voices and positions. If studies of American culture in the post-Second World War period up to the 1960s emphasized a range of myths and symbols which purportedly connected culture with national identity – works like Henry Nash Smith's *Virgin Land* (1957) and Leo Marx's *The Machine in the Garden* (1964) – it did so by way of national narratives, according to

Donald Pease, 'wherein official national fantasies were transmitted to a "national" people'.[36] Because of the way in which globalization puts into question the parameters of the nation (through space/time compressions, de-territorialization and the flows of peoples and information across borders, increasingly difficult to police and control), Pease suggests that analyses of American culture might better utilize what he describes as postnational narratives, the purpose of which is to 'make visible the incoherence, contingency, and transitoriness of . . . national narratives and . . . reveal [a] paradoxical space'[37] that exists between the nation and the state which has traditionally corresponded with the nation.

In thinking about the culture of the 1980s, this approach gives even more impetus to a way of approaching the decade that avoids a top-down model of political and economic decision-making determining cultural production and consumption. De-territorialization impinges upon the most basic elements of cultural interaction and transforms them in ways beyond the control of official or state bodies. John Tomlinson writes about the way in which people's homes and their 'relative degree of "openness to the world", particularly as a consequence of the routine use of domestic communications technologies' transform 'mundane cultural experience'.[38] This openness shifted dramatically in the 1980s as video recorders, computer game consoles, cable television and portable audio technology all brought into the domestic sphere a cultural diet and, perhaps more importantly, a way of experiencing culture that was markedly different from what had existed before. A corollary of this openness was a changed relationship to local space – of the home, of the town, city or neighbourhood, of the nation – that might be understood as a de-localization of space as the availability of cultural brands, products and technologies evened out distinctions in cultural activity such that culture was no longer 'rooted' in its local context but 'routed' into a global cultural matrix.

Paradoxically, perhaps, one of the other consequences of de-territorialization is cultural hybridity. So on the one hand, while globalization creates an increasing familiarity with common cultural products and technologies, the flows and movements of information and people are 'accompanied by an intermingling of . . . disembedded cultural practices producing new complex hybrid forms of culture'.[39] If one thinks about American food and globalization, the fast-food legacy and the brands of McDonalds, KFC and Subway would be an immediate starting point, but one that raises the spectre of Americanization and cultural homogeneity. If one considers American food from a different perspective, however, then globalization can be seen to have produced a cuisine the principal characteristic of which is its hybridity, and in recent years the uprooting of localized hybridity to national and international diners. The Creole cuisine of Louisiana is a fusion of French, Spanish, French Caribbean, African, and American influences, while its distinct Cajun sibling derives more specifically from the French Acadians who settled in Louisiana. Tex-Mex is a development of northern Mexican cuisine in Texas, while Floribbean is a meeting of Caribbean and American South cooking. During the 1970s and 1980s, one of the most popular forms of culinary hybridity emerged in California's fusion cuisine where Asian, Mexican and Pacific-island influences mirrored the state's immigrant populations. This concept of fusion gave rise in the 1980s to what became known as the 'New American Cuisine', a detailed accumulation of regional and ethnic specialities put together initially for wealthy diners in expensive restaurants.

Thinking about American food in this way reverses the tendency to see American culture as something which radiates; rather, it is something which is itself internally constituted from the outside and continually metamorphosing as different elements interact. The result of this inter-action is not the refashioning of a national culture so much as a colloca-tion of disparate elements that do not work together towards a larger project, primarily because of the nature of their journeys towards one another. Another example, from the sport of baseball – the oft-described 'national game' that did not have a fully racially integrated major league until 1959 – indicates the way that so-called 'national' culture is con-stantly being reconstituted. Whereas black players made up 30 per cent of all those registered in the major leagues in the mid 1970s, in 2006 that figure had dropped to just 8 per cent. In the intervening period, the number of Hispanic players has risen to 25 per cent. In the 2006 All Star game, almost half of the starting line-ups were born outside the US. While one might argue that this situation denotes the assimilation of immigrants into a national sporting paradigm, this ignores the fact that baseball itself – and in this it is little different to other sports – no longer sees the connection between team, sport, and region or nation. Baseball is driven by an economic and talent model that means Japan or the Dominican Republic are just as likely to be sources for players as the US, and which has the added benefit of making it easier to export the major league back to those nations.

When thinking about immigration and American culture, then, it is not enough simply to identify examples of immigrant cultural production. While this production is clearly important, it is also important to consider the way that immigration, in the context of ideas about globalization, changes the nature of that which comes to be considered 'American'. David Palumbo-Liu has suggested that 'the persistent deferral of the status of "American" to "hyphenated" Americans ... begs the question of the precise constitution of the totality presumed to inhere beneath the signifier "American".'[40] Trying to answer this question becomes problematic because just as the nature of hyphenated Americanism changes, so the signifier 'American' changes with it. This suggests that rather than a settled national culture constantly trying to fend off incursions from immigrant 'others', national culture is a mirage held in place by ideological discourses whose vestigial power emanates from hierarchically dominant socio-economic groups. American culture cannot avoid being internally riven because, ever more so as globalization accelerates, exogenous forces pour through and erupt within its geographic footprint. The delivery of the global to the local by way of a media industry that bypasses the official or state level enhances this process.

At no point was this more evident than in the media coverage of the war with Vietnam in the late 1960s and early 1970s. It was with the legacy of this representation that official culture, in the form of the state, engaged in the 1980s as it endeavoured to overcome what Reagan called the 'Vietnam syndrome'.[41] But the engagement produced an unexpected end result and one which helps illustrate the disjuncture between residual national forces and irresistible global ones.

The National Vietnam Veterans Memorial, Washington

The Vietnam War (1963–73), while in itself clearly a crucial event in recent US history, was also the next in a line of US conflicts in Asia, from the war with Spain over the Philippines and the annexation of Hawaii at the end of the nineteenth century, through the Pacific war with Japan (1941–5) to the Korean War (1950–3). During the same period a succession of legislative acts was passed, restricting immigration from Asia into the US. The first Chinese Exclusion Act was passed in 1882 and subsequent acts followed. The Immigration Act of 1917 widened the restriction on Asian immigration to places other than China, and Japanese Americans were interned in camps during the Second World War. It was not until the Immigration and Naturalization Services Act of 1965 that heavily restrictive quotas were lifted. Migration from Asia increased significantly as a result. Asia, however, has held a paradoxical place in US history. Manifest Destiny, and the opening up of the continent, was a westward movement that required moving towards the East, and Walt Whitman's 'Passage to India' is a hymn to Asia. It was the Chinese labourers who arrived in the US before the first exclusion act who helped build the transcontinental railway that opened up the continent, while American modernization relied upon expansion in the Pacific.

If Asia has at the same time been that place which threatens the US and a place where the US has defined itself, through economic expansion, military conflict and imaginative engagement, then Asian Americans find themselves in a complex and paradoxical relation to American culture, and did so especially once the citizenship laws were relaxed in the 1960s. How, as an Asian American, does one situate oneself in American culture? Lisa Lowe, in her groundbreaking *Immigrant Acts*, begins her study of this experience from the position that 'Citizens inhabit the political space of the nation' and that 'through the terrain of national culture . . . the individual subject is politically formed as the American citizen.'[42] But if the construction of a national culture – and its monuments, dreams and stereotypes – is meant to be the site through which, Lowe argues, the 'subject becomes, acts, and speaks itself as "American" ', then 'Asian American cultural productions [are] countersites to U.S. national memory and national culture.'[43] The gap between the expectation of 'America' and the moments of experiencing 'America' are the location for Lowe's Asian American 'countersites'. Driving this contention for Lowe is the fact that a national model of 'American' citizenship has, since the middle of the nineteenth century, struggled to come to terms with the Asian immigrant. After 1965, this problem is not solved but restructured: 'the state legally transforms the Asian *alien* into the Asian American *citizen*, it institutionalizes the disavowal of the history of racialized exploitation and disenfranchisement through the promise of freedom in the political sphere' and in so doing only 'exacerbates the contradictions of the national project that promises the resolution of material inequalities through the political domain of equal representation.'[44] For second-generation and multiple-generation Asian Americans, the problems of immigration exclusion are replaced by the dilemmas of immigration inclusion.

What is interesting about the Vietnam Veterans War Memorial is that it emerges as a countersite when the 'national' – in the form of the US state government – refuses to memorialize the soldiers who lost their lives in the conflict. The memorial fills the space the state refuses to fill. The Vietnam Veterans Memorial Fund, set up by Jan Scruggs and other Vietnam War veterans, was established in 1979 to raise funds for a war memorial after the US government showed no signs of coming forward with either funds or ideas for a memorial. In 1980, an open competition was held for designs for the memorial. The winning design was by a twenty-one-year old Chinese American, Maya Ying Lin, whose concept was a V-shaped wall sunk into the ground, on which are engraved the names of all those killed or declared missing in action. The design is notable for its divergence from traditional war memorials. There is no patriotic or heroic epigraph, nor any place for a flag. Lin's own description of the memorial, submitted with the design, indicates that she was thinking in an entirely different way about what a memorial should suggest:

> These names, seemingly infinite in number, convey the sense of overwhelming numbers, while unifying these individuals into a whole. The Memorial is composed not as an unchanging monument, but as a moving composition to be understood as we move into and out of it. The passage itself is gradual; the descent to the origin slow, but it is at the origin that the Memorial is to be fully understood. At the intersection of these walls, on the right side, is carved the date of the first death. It is followed by the names of those who died in the war, in chronological order. These names continue on this wall appearing to recede into the earth at the wall's end. The names resume on the left wall as the wall emerges from the earth, continuing back to the origin where the date of the last death is carved.[45]

The memorial was officially dedicated on 13 November 1982 and at that point became classified as a national memorial and authorized by Congress. At the dedication ceremony Lin's name was not mentioned.

Located between the Lincoln Memorial and the Washington Monument, the Vietnam Veterans Memorial is a testament to the way in which immigrant culture offers an alternative vision of suffering than that provided by other monuments whose official nature is there from the very beginning. While it may pass into official hands after the dedication, this memorial's Chinese American point of origin – and the complex histories contained therein – is a residual force in its capacity to move visitors. At the end of Bobbie Ann Mason's novel *In Country* (1985), Sam, her grandmother and her uncle Emmett, a Vietnam veteran, visit Washington, and it is precisely the dissonance between the different monuments that strikes Sam:

> Sam stands in the center of the V, deep in the pit. The V is like the white wings of the shopping mall in Paducah. The Washington Monument is reflected at the center line. If she moves slightly to the left, she sees the monument, and if she moves the other way she sees a reflection of the flag opposite the memorial. Both the monument and the flag seem like arrogant gestures, like the country giving the finger to the dead boys, flung in this hole in the ground. Sam doesn't understand what she is feeling, but it is something so strong, it is like a tornado moving in her, something massive and overpowering. It feels like giving birth to this wall.[46]

Sam and Emmet's trip from the margins of Kentucky to the centre of Washington is also a way, then, of meeting other margins – in this instance specifically racial and ethnic margins – which emerge and erupt there too through supposedly 'national' cultural artefacts.

Multicultural America

The US did not become a multicultural nation in the 1980s since, like many other nations, it had long been home to many different cultures

Figure 5.1 The sunken, V-shaped design of the Vietnam Veterans Memorial marks a break from traditional designs for national memorials.

thanks to its indigenous peoples and its immigration history. Certain immigration trends did develop in the 1980s which altered the cultural makeup of the US – the doubling of Mexican-born people between the censuses of 1980 and 1990, increased immigration from Cuba, Korea, China and India and the Philippines, declining immigration from Canada, Italy and the UK – but again, these were adjustments to an already multicultural network. It is perhaps more useful to think about the way that the idea of, and attitudes towards, multiculturalism changes during the 1980s.

In Canada during the 1970s, multiculturalism became part of official government policy and was eventually enshrined in the Act for the Preservation and Enhancement of Multiculturalism in Canada which was passed into law in 1988. It declared that the policy of the Canadian government was to 'recognize and promote the understanding that multiculturalism reflects the cultural and racial diversity of Canadian society and acknowledges the freedom of all members of Canadian society to preserve, enhance and share their cultural heritage.' Such official multiculturalism has not been without its critics, both conservative – on the grounds that it dilutes national culture – and liberal, on the grounds that it ghettoizes people by ethnicity. No such official multicultural agenda was implemented in the US during the 1980s, but the idea of multiculturalism did become part of an official agenda by other means.

Critics like Frederick Buell are sceptical of the ways that multiculturalism as a phenomenon and discourse developed after its initial emergence in the 1970s. But Buell is sceptical in ways different to writers like Allan Bloom. For Bloom, the relativism that was part of multiculturalism marked a national decline and was part of a 'rhetoric of endangered national foundations' which amounted to 'in effect, a new kind of fundamentalism'.[47] What Buell is sceptical of is the way that relatively quickly the forces of multiculturalism and globalization are incorporated in official discourses: of the state and of capitalism, most forcibly. Forces that potentially threaten the power of the nation state, through the rise to power of transnational corporations, and the mythology of a 'national' culture – through an emphasis on cultural diversity in education and culture industries – become worryingly susceptible to appropriation. In the same way that Fredric Jameson writes about the institutionalization of a potentially radical modernism, so Buell sees the institutionalization of the potentially destabilising forces of multiculturalism and globalization. Buell reads William Gibson's *Neuromancer* less as a dystopic warning about the future dangers of information technology than a novel which provides the term cyberspace in order that 'the corporate restructuring of American identity'[48] might take place. The protagonist, Case, is:

A cowboy on the new frontier of cyberspace [bringing] a pre-Frederick Jackson Turner excitement into a postmodern, hyperdeveloped world; if the old frontier has been built out thoroughly and its excitements become guilty ones in the wake of contemporary multicultural/postcolonial rewritings of Western history, try, then, cyberspace in an apparently polycultural, globalized era. Not only can many of the old attitudes be recuperated, but a basic, underlying fear prompted by global reorganization can be countered: the fear that the national space – its culture, social relations, and even geography – is being undone by contemporary capitalism. . . .Cyberspace becomes the new U.S. frontier, accessible to the privileged insider who happens to be a reconfigured version of the American pulp hero.[49]

In the aftermath of the economic downturn of the 1970s, what US business required was a rationale and an opportunity for recovery.

Information technology provided this by being the future. Rather than the national space falling apart because of the threat of contemporary capitalism, especially capitalism overseas, capitalism in its high-tech, globalized incarnation would become the saviour of the US economy.

Similarly, the ease with which simplistic understandings of cultural difference become part of official discourses is also unsettling. So while organizations – business and academic – are happy to represent themselves as institutions which value and encourage difference and diversity, there is often little attention paid in the course of such rhetoric to the material conditions which create cultural difference in the first place: inequality, racism and homophobia, for instance. The corporations operating in a globalized economy make virtue out of their commitment to difference by way of equal opportunities policies, at the same time as relocating and expanding overseas where labour is cheap and plentiful and employment legislation much less rigorous. Nike, for example, whose popularity amongst African Americans during the 1980s was fuelled by the company's sponsorship of basketball star Michael Jordan and the production of the Air Jordan shoe, and who from 1996 sponsored multicultural golfing icon Tiger Woods, has come in for severe criticism for using sweatshop labour in China, Vietnam and Mexico.

So while the culture wars, those battles over race, abortion, education, sexuality and the arts between Left and Right discussed in the Introduction, may be resolved in favour of multiculturalism, what results in the 1990s, despite the conservative antagonists who remain a powerful political force, is the dilution of some of the intentions of multiculturalist activity that emerged in the 1970s and 1980s. Multiculturalism becomes commodified in its transition to a mainstream and in the process its nature changes. In seeking to understand the multicultural makeup of the US in the 1980s, then, it is important not just to acknowledge the presence of marginalized voices in the cultural field, or to happily hold up one's reading of these voices – such as the writers Toni Morrison, Gloria Anzaldúa and Amy Tan, or the filmmaker Spike Lee, the artist Jean-Michel Basquiat or the rappers Public Enemy – as signs of progress or personal absolution from the discourses of overt and exclusionary discrimination which have gone before. The cultural objects of a multicultural society like the US, and the cultural processes of production, transmission and consumption, are complex and varied. Not only, then, is it important to distinguish between multicultural activity – with its own aims, objectives, failures and contradictions – and an official multiculturalism which negates and dilutes the impact of this multicultural activity, but it is also important to understand the often abstract context of broader economic and political prerogatives adopting and adapting cultural phenomena for entirely other purposes.

The Cultural Legacy of the 1980s

While it is tautologic to say that a decade is a period of transition from one decade to another, the urge to define decades in the past – the problem with which this book started out – has sometimes meant that decades have become unjustifiably isolated units of time. What is neglected is the way in which a decade emerges out of its predecessor and rolls over into the decade which follows. In the case of the 1920s and 1930s, the decades are conveniently stitched together by the economic depression arising around the financial crash and panic at the end of the 1920s. But the convenience of this link appears suspect when one considers that what are being linked are entirely different orders of experience and activity. The discourse of the 'Jazz Age' is based on the idea of cultural flowering and of a sense of modernity, hedonism and decadence. While this discourse may also root itself in economic and industrial conditions of expansion, the idea of the 1930s as a decade of economic depression dominated by New Deal politics changes the angle of vision from culture to politics and economics. So, while *The Great Gatsby* is read in terms of conspicuous cultural consumption and its attitude towards the 'American dream', *The Grapes of Wrath* is read almost as social documentary. The impetus that drives this incoherent shifting of vision is the urge to find a way of pinning down and defining a decade.

The added problem here is one mentioned in the Introduction: the 'illusion of synchronicity' of which Paul Giles writes. Cultural products, in this instance two novels, are treated as transparent windows on a period on the basis of their date of publication. While there can be no argument that *The Great Gatsby* is a 'product' of the 1920s and *The Grapes of Wrath* a 'product' of the 1930s, it is the confusion of the two meanings of the word 'product' that lead to the 'illusion of synchronicity'. A 'product' may be both an artefact and an outcome.

To read an artefact produced in a decade as an outcome of that decade is to mistake cause and effect. The reason why certain texts repeatedly circulate as cultural referents may have more to do with their internal qualities as, in this instance, pieces of writing than with what they can reveal about a context of production which is often so generalized as to be meaningless. To subordinate texts to their context is as problematic as sublimating them out of that context. Neither have much time for the temporal interplay of factors in the many years and decades leading up to publication and the many years and decades following publication.

It may well be, then, that cultural products – by which, in this case, I mean cultural artefacts – are not the best avenue through which to approach the culture of a decade. One of the noticeable dimensions of US culture in the 1980s is the emergence of cultural forms that alter not only the range of cultural products available for consumption, but also the mode of experiencing those cultural products such that these cultural forms themselves become cultural products. The video recorder, for instance, moved Hollywood films into the domestic space in a way which freed viewers from television schedules. The spin-offs from this development are manifold: videos become new kinds of cultural products; watching videos becomes a new method of consuming cultural products with its own styles of practice – it can be a group event, a solitary event, a repetitive event; the technology enabling the form becomes a source of cultural distinction, technical competence and an object of consumer desire; the portability of the video tape means it can be shared and copied. And the list could go on. This book has tried to highlight the importance of new cultural forms and practices like this. But then to suggest that the decade might be defined by these means would be a step too far, since the new cultural forms and practices do not sit conveniently within the confines of the 1980s.

Returning to my earlier point about decades as, by their nature, transitional periods, it is clear that much of the technology and the structures of corporate organization necessary to facilitate these new cultural forms were being established in the 1970s, and not only in the US but also elsewhere in the world. Although in the development and implementation of computing hardware and software the US proved extremely important, the technology behind the video recorder and the video tape, the digital compact disc and portable music players like the Walkman, had very little US input and was developed in Japan and Europe. If it is impossible to proclaim that a particular video, *Top Gun* perhaps, epitomizes the 1980s like *The Great Gatsby* epitomizes the

1920s, it is equally difficult to claim that video as a cultural form defines the 1980s, so embedded is it in the 1970s. The point here is that cultural forms and the culture industries of which they are a part embarrass attempts to delimit decades in ways which a concentration on individual cultural products does not. One point made in the Introduction is that a decade in American culture is too long a period of time to allow a definition of the decade that can sustain narratives of uniformity and commonality. But a decade is also too short a period of time to provide a sense of how cultural forms emerge and develop. Cultural products may be produced in a decade; cultural forms go beyond a decade.

One other factor which might help suggest the transitional nature of the 1980s is the importance to that decade of the 1960s and the values, changes and events which are retrospectively associated with it and become the source of ideological conflict and debate in the culture wars – which lingered on well into the 1990s – and elsewhere. If, in terms of official politics, the rise of neo-conservatism with Ronald Reagan as its figurehead seemed to signal a victory over liberalism, the economic and cultural fallout which often fell outside of presidential or political influence suggests quite different outcomes. The 1980s are fascinating, not because of the way in which neo-conservatism dominated politics, but because of the failure of neo-conservatism to control the agenda which it set itself. The series of scandals which flared in the US particularly during the latter part of the decade – insider trading and fraud on Wall Street, the Iran–Contra affair, the televangelists – were indicative of a polity riven with doubt and mistrust. And while official politics tried to keep the plates spinning it is also possible to see that these efforts were being undermined by forces well beyond the control of the nation state, even one as powerful as the US. If recent critical approaches to the study of the US in the post-9/11 world have emphasized worrying signs of US imperial aims in its attempts at conflict resolution, there is a different position which might be taken in respect of these events:

> Rather than specifically indicting the Bush administration for the state of American empire, then, a longer perspective might suggest that this state of conflict is an inevitable product of the fraught political relationship between the declining hegemony of the United States and the emerging pressures of what [Immanuel] Wallerstein calls the 'world-system.' Over the past couple of years, Secretary of Defense Donald Rumsfeld has tried repeatedly to reassure the American public with

ritualistic mantras of certainty – 'the outcome is certain' – but this rhetoric has served barely to conceal how such certainties can no longer lie within the province or control of any U.S. government.[1]

It is worth reflecting that the 1970s and 1980s, as the forces of globalization gathered pace, might well be better interpreted in the light of these comments and that consequently the emphasis placed on Reaganite neo-conservatism as the shaping force of the decade might need to be reduced accordingly. If neo-conservatism seemed to be trying to put the 1960s behind it, then it was doing so only at the expense of being blind to other forces undermining its national project; forces which may have had far more to do with the collapse of communism in central and eastern Europe at the end of the 1980s than Reagan's ideological crusade which had been ongoing since the 1960s.

Which leads on to the question of just where the 1980s ends. There seems to be little point in arguing with the notion that, geo-politically, the world, and US relations with the world, changed irrevocably, whatever the causes, in 1989 with the fall of the Berlin Wall and political revolutions in Poland, Czechoslovakia, Hungary, Bulgaria and Romania and the break-up of the Soviet Union two years later. The cold war had ended. But it is difficult to transpose this date onto American culture. If, as I have been suggesting, it is cultural forms rather than individual cultural products with a unique access to the spirit of the times which distinguish cultural periods, then the end of the 1980s can be delayed until well into the 1990s when video was usurped by the Digital Versatile Disc, the compact disc had finally put paid to the musicassette and, perhaps most importantly of all, the draft version of Hypertext Markup Language (HTML) was produced and ratification was given to the Uniform Resource Locators (URL) protocol in December 1994 and the HyperText Transfer Protocol (HTTP) in May 1996. These latter changes, along with the launch of Windows 95 and the availability of web browsers like Mosaic and Netscape Navigator, heralded public access to the internet and the world wide web, fuelling the dotcom boom from 1997.

If the longevity of the 1980s, with its early start and late finish, seems to do damage to the very idea of decade study then it should be countered that studying a decade need not necessarily be a process of decade definition. It might also be a process of questioning implicit assumptions about decades that circulate culturally, often in the seemingly endless number of nostalgic television programmes dedicated to capturing the spirit of times past, but also in important ideological debates about the meaning of the past. While numbers always retain a deceptively attractive evenness and simplicity, culture, as Raymond Williams once pointed out, is one of the most complicated words in the language and noted for its capacity to evade the boxes that are supplied for it.

Notes

Introduction

1. Paul Giles, 'European American Studies and American American Studies', *European Journal of American Culture*, 19 (1) (1999), p. 14.
2. Stephen Paul Miller, *The Seventies Now: Culture as Surveillance* (Durham NC: Duke University Press, 1999), p. 1.
3. Gary Wills, *Reagan's America: Innocents at Home* (New York: Doubleday, 1987), p. 1.
4. Ibid., p. 5.
5. Ibid., p. 371.
6. Ibid., p. 1.
7. Richard H. King, 'The Eighties', in *Introduction to American Studies*, 3rd edn, eds Malcolm Bradbury and Howard Temperley (London: Longman, 1998), p. 304.
8. Michael Rogin, *Ronald Reagan, the Movie and Other Episodes in Political Demonology* (Berkeley CA: University of California Press, 1987), p. 3.
9. Ibid., p. 8.
10. Ibid., p. 9.
11. Ibid., p. 5.
12. King, 'The Eighties', p. 316
13. Haynes Johnson, *Sleepwalking Through History: America in the Reagan Years* (New York: W. W. Norton, [1991] 2003), p. 99.
14. The Federal Reserve is an independent agency of the US and the country's central bank. As such, it is one of the most important directors of US economic policy.
15. Johnson, *Sleepwalking Through History*, p. 221.
16. Charles R. Geisst, *Wall Street* (Oxford: Oxford University Press, 1997), p. 339.

17. Johnson, *Sleepwalking Through History*, p. 194.
18. 'The Sentencing of Michael Milken', http://www.cortland.edu/polsci/ milken.html. Accessed 8 April 2005.
19. 'Manic Market: Is computer-driven stock trading good for America?', *Time*, 10 November 1986.
20. See William C. Berman, *America's Right Turn: From Nixon to Bush* (Baltimore MD and London: Johns Hopkins University Press, 1994).
21. Michael Lienesch, *Redeeming America: Piety and Politics in the New Christian Right* (Chapel Hill and London: University of North Carolina Press, 1993), pp. 4–6.
22. Ibid. p. 8.
23. Stephen Prince, *A New Pot of Gold: Hollywood under the Electronic Rainbow, 1980–1989* (Berkeley, Los Angeles and London: University of California Press, 2000), p. 363.
24. Lienesch, *Redeeming America*, p. 17.
25. Ibid., p. 17.
26. Dennis Altman, *AIDS and the New Puritanism* (London: Pluto Press, 1986), p. 14.
27. Quoted in Randy Shilts, *And the Band Played On: Politics, People and the AIDS Epidemic* (Harmondsworth: Penguin, [1987] 1988), p. 311.
28. Ibid., p. 347.
29. Ibid., p. 347.
30. Altman, *AIDS and the New Puritanism*, p. 11.
31. Ibid., p. 39.
32. Gil Troy, *Morning in America: How Ronald Reagan Invented the 1980s* (Princeton NJ: Princeton University Press, 2005), p. 200.
33. Ibid., p. 202.
34. Douglas Crimp, *AIDS: Cultural Analysis Cultural Activism* (Cambridge MA: MIT Press, 1988), p. 6.
35. Paul E. Ceruzzi, *A History of Modern Computing* (Cambridge MA: MIT Press, [1998] 2000), p. 9.
36. Po Bronson, *The Nudist on the Late Shift: And Other Tales from Silicon Valley* (London: Secker & Warburg, 1999), p. xvii.
37. Todd Gitlin, *The Twilight of Common Dreams: Why America is Wracked by Culture Wars* (New York: Metropolitan Books, 1995), p. 233.
38. Ibid., p. 233.
39. James Davison Hunter, *Culture Wars: The Struggle to Define America* (New York: Basic Books, 1991), p. 42.
40. Ibid., p. 54.
41. Ibid., p. 59. Original in italics.

42. http://www.operationrescue.org/?p=64. Accessed 9 August 2005.
43. Susan Faludi, *Backlash: The Undeclared War Against Women* (London: Vintage, [1991] 1992), p. 1.
44. Ibid., p. 3.
45. Ibid., pp. 290–1.
46. Ibid., p. 352.
47. Ibid., p. 352.
48. Ibid., p. 104.
49. Gitlin, *The Twilight of Common Dreams*, p. 114.
50. Ibid., p. 124.
51. Allan Bloom, *The Closing of the American Mind* (New York: Simon & Schuster, 1987), p. 19.
52. Ibid., p. 26.
53. Ibid., p. 25.
54. Ibid., p. 34.
55. Ibid., p. 34.
56. Ibid., p. 141.
57. Ibid., p. 39.
58. Ibid., p. 314.
59. Ibid., p. 314.
60. Ibid., p. 346.

1. Fiction and Poetry

1. Linda Hutcheon, *The Poetics of Postmodernism: History, Theory, Fiction* (London: Routledge & Kegan Paul, 1988).
2. Ibid., p. 120.
3. Ibid., pp. 285–6.
4. Don DeLillo, *Libra* (London: Penguin, [1988] 1989), p. 14.
5. Ibid., p. 15.
6. Ibid., p. 441.
7. Ibid., p. 442.
8. Ibid., p. 445.
9. See Dan Moos, 'Lacking the Article Itself: Representation and History in Cormac McCarthy's *Blood Meridian*', *Cormac McCarthy Journal*, 2 (2002), pp. 23–39; John Sepich 'The Dance of History in Cormac McCarthy's *Blood Meridian*', *Southern Literary Journal*, 24 (1) (1991), pp. 16–31; John Sepich, *Notes on Blood Meridian*, (Louisville KY: Bellarmine College Press, 1993).
10. Cormac McCarthy, *Blood Meridian, or the Evening Redness in the West* (London: Picador, [1985] 1989), p. 54.

11. William Gibson, *Neuromancer* (London: Voyager Classics, [1984] 2001), p. 12.

12. David Brande, 'The Business of Cyberpunk: Symbolic Economy and Ideology in William Gibson', *Configurations*, 2 (3) (1994), pp. 530–1.

13. Gibson, *Neuromancer*, p. 11.

14. Ibid., p. 62

15. James Annesley, *Blank Fictions: Consumerism, Culture and the Contemporary American Novel* (London: Pluto Press, 1998), p. 6.

16. Bret Easton Ellis, *Less Than Zero* (London: Picador, [1985] 1986), p. 23.

17. Ibid., p. 25.

18. Peter Stallybrass, 'Worn Worlds: Clothes, Mourning and the Life of Things', *Yale Review*, 81 (2) (1993), p. 47.

19. Jayne Anne Phillips, '*White Noise*, by Don DeLillo', *New York Times*, 13 January 1985.

20. Don DeLillo, *White Noise* (New York: Viking, 1985), p. 169

21. Ibid., p. 168.

22. Ibid., p. 170.

23. Ibid., p 12.

24. Ibid., p. 13.

25. Ibid., p. 262.

26. Ibid., p. 157.

27. Bill Buford, 'Editorial', *Granta*, 8 (1983), p. 4.

28. Ibid., p. 4.

29. Ibid., p. 4.

30. Ibid., p. 5.

31. Raymond Carver, *Cathedral* (London: Harvill, [1983] 1999), p. 31.

32. Ibid., p. 42.

33. Ibid., p. 39.

34. Jean-François Lyotard, *The Postmodern Condition: A Report on Knowledge* (Minneapolis: University of Minnesota Press, 1984).

35. Phillip E. Simmons, *Deep Surfaces: Mass Culture and History in Postmodern American Fiction* (Athens GA: University of Georgia Press, 1997), p. 20.

36. *Granta*, p. 110.

37. Bobbie Ann Mason, *In Country* (New York: Harper Perennial, [1985] 2005), p. 23.

38. Ibid., p. 23.

39. Ibid., p. 42.

40. Ibid., p. 42.

41. Ibid., p. 208.

42. Ibid., p. 210.

43. Kenneth Millard, *Contemporary American Fiction* (Oxford: Oxford University Press, 2000), p. 52.
44. A. O. Scott, 'In Search of the Best', *New York Times*, 21 May 2006.
45. Toni Morrison, *Beloved* (London: Picador, [1988] 1987), p. 3.
46. Frank Chin, Jeffrey Paul Chan, Lawson Fusao Inada and Shawn Wong (eds), *The Big Aiiieeeee!* (New York: Plume, 1991).
47. Helena Grice, Candid Hepworth, Maria Lauret and Martin Padget, *Beginning Ethnic American Literatures* (Manchester: Manchester University Press, 2001), p. 196.
48. Gloria Anzaldúa, *Borderlands/La Frontera: The New Mestiza* (San Francisco: Aunt Lute, 1987), p. 2.
49. Ibid., p. 3.
50. Ibid., p. 4.
51. Ibid., Preface.
52. Ibid., p. 59.
53. Christopher Beach, *The Cambridge Introduction to Twentieth-Century American Poetry* (Cambridge: Cambridge University Press, 2003), p. 204.
54. Ibid., p. 204.

2. Art and Photography

1. Phoebe Hoban, *Basquiat: A Quick Killing in Art* (London: Penguin, [1998] 2004), p. 186.
2. Ibid., p. 10.
3. Tom Wolfe, 'The Worship of Art', in *The Eighties: A Reader*, ed. Gilbert T. Sewall (Reading MA: Addison-Wesley, 1997), p. 326.
4. Ibid. p. 329.
5. Grace Glueck, 'What Big Business Sees in Fine Art', *New York Times*, 26 May 1985.
6. Ibid.
7. Ibid.
8. Wolfe, 'The Worship of Art', p. 329.
9. Quoted in Hoban, *Basquiat*, p. 187.
10. Ibid. p. 191.
11. Marylin Bender, 'High Finance Makes a Bid for Art', *New York Times*, 3 February 1985.
12. Quoted in Hoban, *Basquiat*, p. 192.
13. Michael Brenson, 'Artists Grapple with New Realities', *New York Times*, 15 May 1983.
14. Ibid.

15. Robert Hughes, 'Careerism and Hype Amidst the Image Haze: American Painters of the '80s are Buffeted by Cultural Inflation', *Time*, 17 June 1985.

16. Hoban, *Basquiat*, p. 11.

17. Ibid., p. 9.

18. Ibid., p. 11.

19. Fredric Jameson, 'Postmodernism and Consumer Culture', in Hal Foster (ed.) *Postmodern Culture* (London: Pluto Press, [1983] 1985), p. 111.

20. Ibid., pp. 111–12.

21. Douglas Coupland, http://www.eyestorm.com/feature/ED2n_article. asp?article_id=202. Accessed 19 April 2006.

22. Ibid.

23. David Bjelajac, *American Art: A Cultural History* (London: Laurence King, 2000), p. 385.

24. Robert Hughes, *The Culture of Complaint: The Fraying of America* (Oxford: Oxford University Press), p. 195. While the English Romantic writer Thomas Chatterton, like Basquiat, died at a young age, Hughes associates Basquiat with Chatterton because of Chatterton's skill as a forger of medieval poetry.

25. Lisa Phillips, *The American Century: Art and Culture 1950–2000* (New York: Whitney Museum of American Art in association with W. W. Norton, 1999), p. 287.

26. Jameson, 'Postmodernism and Consumer Culture', p. 114.

27. Ibid., p. 114.

28. See Vincent B. Leitch, *Postmodernism: Local Effects, Global Flows* (New York: State University of New York Press, 1996), pp. 95–107.

29. Jameson, 'Postmodernism and Consumer Culture', pp. 115–16.

30. Ibid., p. 123.

31. Phillips, *The American Century*, p. 287.

32. Douglas Crimp, 'The Art of Exhibition', *October*, 30 (Autumn, 1984), p. 50.

33. Lucy Lippard, 'Real Estate and Real Art', *Seven Days* (April, 1980), pp. 32–4. Reprinted at http://www.lehman.cuny.edu/gallery/talk-back/fmlippard.html. Accessed 29 May 2006.

34. Ibid.

35. Quoted at http://www.lehman.cuny.edu/gallery/talkback/fmwebster. html. Accessed 29 May 2006.

36. Phillips, *The American Century*, p. 290.

37. Claire F. Fox, 'The Portable Border: Site-Specificity, Art, and the U.S.–Mexico Frontier', *Social Text*, 41 (Winter, 1994), p. 61.

38. Phillips, *The American Century*, p. 270.
39. David Hopkins, *After Modern Art 1945–2000* (Oxford: Oxford University Press, 2000), p. 212.
40. See Patricia Morrisoe, *Mapplethorpe: A Biography* (London: Macmillan, 1995), p. 249.
41. Dennis Altman, *AIDS and the New Puritanism* (London: Pluto Press, 1986), p. 28.
42. Ibid., p. 3.
43. Quoted in Douglas Crimp, *AIDS: Cultural Analysis Cultural Activism* (Cambridge MA: MIT Press, 1988), p. 5.
44. Ibid., p. 6.
45. http://thomas.loc.gov/cgi-bin/bdquery/z?d101:HR02788:@@@D& summ2=3&. Accessed 26 July 2006.
46. George Chauncey, *Gay New York: The Making of the Gay Male World, 1890–1940* (London: Flamingo, [1994] 1995), p. 9.
47. The American Library Association tracks challenges to the stocking of book in libraries by various groups and organizations. See http://www.ala.org/ala/oif/ifissues

3. Film and Televsion

1. Stephen Prince, *A New Pot of Gold: Hollywood Under the Electronic Rainbow, 1980–1989* (Berkeley CA: University of California Press, [2000] 2002), p. xi.
2. Ibid., p. 12.
3. Ibid., p. 19.
4. Quoted in Prince, *A New Pot of Gold*, p. 51.
5. For a flavour of some of these debates, see: Robert McChesney with Edward S. Herman, *The Global Media: The New Missionaries of Corporate Capitalism* (London: Cassell, 1997); Robert McChesney, *Rich Media, Poor Democracy: Communication Politics in Dubious Times* (New York: New Press, 2000); Ben H. Bagdikian, *The Media Monopoly*, Sixth Edition (Boston MA: Beacon Press, 2000).
6. http://www.bfi.org.uk/sightandsound/feature/122/. Accessed 26 July 2006.
7. Prince, *A New Pot of Gold*, p. 99.
8. http://laws.findlaw.com/us/464/417.html. Accessed 17 February 2006.
9. Prince, *A New Pot of Gold*, p. 2.
10. Ibid., p. 79.
11. Ibid., p. 106.
12. Ibid., p. xii.

13. See Justin Wyatt, *High Concept* (Austin TX: University of Texas Press, 1994).
14. http://www.the-numbers.com/movies/1984/0MDS.html. Accessed 22 February 2006.
15. Andrew Britton, 'Blissing Out: The Politics of Reaganite Entertainment', *Movie*, 31 (2) (1986), p. 2.
16. Ibid., p. 4.
17. Ibid., p. 12.
18. Alan Nadel, *Flatlining on the Field of Dreams: Cultural Narratives in the Films of President Reagan's America* (New Brunswick NJ: Rutgers University Press, 1997), p. 3.
19. Ibid., p. 13.
20. http://industrycentral.net/director_interviews/JOCA01.HTM. Accessed 3 March 2006.
21. Mark Jancovich, *American Horror from 1951* (Keele: Keele University Press, 1994), p. 30.
22. Henry James, *The Bostonians* (London: Macmillan, 1886), pp. 333–4.
23. For more on this genre of films and their relationship with Reaganite politics, see Susan Jeffords, *Hard Bodies: Hollywood Masculinity in the Reagan Era* (New Jersey: Rutgers University Press, 1994).
24. 'Address Before a Joint Session of Congress on the State of the Union February 4, 1986', http://www.reagan.utexas.edu/archives/speeches/1986/20486a.htm, *The Public Papers of President Ronald W. Reagan*, Ronald Reagan Presidential Library. Accessed 26 July 2006.
25. Nadel, *Flatlining on the Field of Dreams*, p. 28.
26. Emily Stipes Watt, *The Businessman in American Literature* (Athens GA: University of Georgia Press, 1982), p. 150.
27. Prince, *A New Pot of Gold*, p. 25.
28. Prince, *A New Pot of Gold*, p. 27.
29. Ibid. p. 26.

4. Music and Performance

1. Larry Starr, *American Popular Music: The Rock Years* (New York: Oxford University Press, 2005), p. 231.
2. Ibid., p. 231.
3. Robert Burnett, *The Global Jukebox: The International Music Industry* (London: Routledge, 1996), p. 108.
4. Ibid., p. 107.
5. Ibid., p. 108.
6. Ibid., p. 110.

7. Ibid., p. 110.

8. John Covach, 'Pangs of History in Late 1970s New-Wave Rock', in *Analyzing Popular Music*, ed. Allan F. Moore (Cambridge: Cambridge University Press, 2003), pp. 178–9.

9. Ibid. ,p. 194.

10. Starr, *American Popular Music*, p. 243.

11. Ibid., p. 243.

12. Nelson George, *Post-Soul Nation: The Explosive, Contradictory, Triumphant, and Tragic 1980s, as Experienced by African American (Previously Known as Black and Before That Negroes)* (New York: Viking, 2004), p. 209.

13. Ibid., p. 24.

14. Ibid., p. 188.

15. Elizabeth L. Wollman, 'The Economic Development of the "New" Times Square and Its Impact on the Broadway Musical', *American Music*, 20 (4) (2002), pp. 453–4.

16. Steve Nelson, 'Broadway and the Beast: Disney Comes to Times Square', *The Drama Review*, 39 (2) (1995), p. 72.

17. Ibid., p. 454.

18. C. W. E. Bigsby, *Modern American Drama, 1945–2000* (Cambridge: Cambridge University Press, 2000), p. 363.

19. Ibid., p. 363.

20. Kate Davy, 'Constructing the Spectator: Reception, Context, and Address in Lesbian Performance', *Performing Arts Journal*, 10 (2) (1986), p. 46.

21. Ibid., 47.

22. Jill Dolan, 'Desire Cloaked in a Trenchcoat', *The Drama Review*, 33 (1) (1989), p. 64.

23. Jill Dolan, 'The Dynamics of Desire: Sexuality and Gender in Pornography and Performance', *Theatre Journal*, 39 (2) (1987), p. 170.

5. American Culture and Globalization

1. John Tomlinson, *Globalization and Culture* (Cambridge: Polity Press, 1999), p. 2.

2. See Benedict Anderson, *Imagined Communities: Reflections on the Origin and Spread of Nationalism* (London: Verso, 1983).

3. John Carlos Rowe, *Literary Culture and U.S. Imperialism: From The Revolution to World War II* (Oxford: Oxford University Press, 2000), p. 3.

4. See Graham Thompson, *The Business of America: The Cultural Construction of a Post-War Nation* (London: Pluto Press, 2004), pp. 11–17.
5. Tomlinson, *Globalization*, p. 79.
6. Ibid., p. 82.
7. Ibid., p. 83.
8. Shelley Streeby, *American Sensations: Class, Empire, and the Production of Popular Culture* (Berkeley CA: University of California Press, 2002), p. 28.
9. Tomlinson, *Globalization*, p. 85.
10. Ien Ang, *Watching Dallas: Soap Opera and the Melodramatic Imagination* (London: Methuen, 1985), p. 45.
11. William Gibson, *Neuromancer* (London: Voyager Classics, [1984] 2001), p. 18.
12. Ibid., p. 242.
13. Ibid., p. 18.
14. Ibid., p. 69.
15. See George Ritzer, *The McDonaldization of Society* (Newbury Park CA: Pine Forge Press, 1993) and Alan E. Bryman, *The Disneyization of Society* (London: SAGE, 2004).
16. Quoted in Tomlinson, *Globalization*, p. 78.
17. Edward Said, *Al-Ahram Weekly*, Cairo, 18–24, Issue No. 417, February 1999. Available at http://www.islamfortoday.com/powerofcnn.htm. Accessed 22 July 2006.
18. Ibid.
19. Ralph Waldo Emerson, 'The Poet', in *The Heath Anthology of American Literature Volume 1*, 4th edn, ed. Paul Lauter (Boston MA: Houghton Mifflin, 2002), p. 1585.
20. Herman Melville, 'Hawthorne and His Mosses', in *The Heath Anthology of American Literature Volume 1*, 4th edn, ed. Paul Lauter (Boston: Houghton Mifflin, 2002), p. 2721.
21. Randolph Bourne, 'Trans-National America', in *The American Studies Anthology*, ed. Richard P. Horwitz (Wilmington DE: Scholarly Resources, 2001), p. 150.
22. Martin Amis, *The Moronic Inferno and Other Visits to America* (Harmondsworth: Penguin, [1986] 1987), p. 1.
23. Paul Giles, *Virtual Americas: Transnational Fictions and the Transatlantic Imaginary* (Durham NC: Duke University Press, 2002), p. 5.
24. Ibid., p. 2.
25. Martin Amis, *London Fields* (London: Jonathan Cape, 1989), p. 3.
26. Ibid. p. 3.

27. Jean Baudrillard, *America* (London: Verso, [1988] 1989), p. 38.
28. Jean Baudrillard, *Selected Writings* (Cambridge: Polity Press, [1988] 1992), p. 171.
29. Ibid., p. 172.
30. Jean Baudrillard, 'Disneyworld Company', translated by Francois Debrix, *Liberation*, 4 March 1996.
31. *The Theodore Roosevelt Web Book*, http://www.theodoreroosevelt. org/TR%20Web%20Book/TR_CD_to_HTML53.html. Accessed 26 July 2006.
32. Ibid.
33. Ibid.
34. Lisa Lowe, 'The International within the National: American Studies and Asian American Critique', in *The Futures of American Studies*, ed. Donald Pease and Robyn Wiegman (Durham NC: Duke University Press, 2002), p. 76.
35. García Canclini, quoted in Tomlinson, *Globalization*, p. 107.
36. Donald Pease, 'National Narratives, Postnational Narration', *Modern Fiction Studies*, 43 (1) (1997), p. 4.
37. Donald Pease, 'National Narratives', p. 7.
38. Tomlinson, *Globalization*, p. 108.
39. Ibid., p. 141.
40. David Palumbo-Liu, *Asian/American: Historical Crossings of a Racial Frontier* (Stanford CA: Stanford University Press, 1999), p. 1.
41. Ronald Reagan used this phrase on a number of occasions. See: 'Remarks During a White House Briefing on the Program for Economic Recovery February 24, 1981', http://www.reagan.utexas.edu/archives/ speeches/1981/22481a.htm, *The Public Papers of President Ronald W. Reagan*, Ronald Reagan Presidential Library; 'Remarks at a White House Briefing for Supporters of United States Assistance for the Nicaraguan Democratic Resistance March 10, 1986', http://www. reagan.utexas.edu/archives/speeches/1986/31086a.htm, *The Public Papers of President Ronald W. Reagan*, Ronald Reagan Presidential Library; 'Remarks at a White House Briefing for Supporters of United States Assistance for the Nicaraguan Democratic Resistance June 16, 1986', http://www.reagan.utexas.edu/archives/speeches/1986/61686a. htm, *The Public Papers of President Ronald W. Reagan*, Ronald Reagan Presidential Library. All accessed 26 July 2006.
42. Lisa Lowe, *Immigrant Acts: On Asian American Cultural Politics* (Durham NC: Duke University Press, 1996), p. 2.
43. Ibid., pp. 3–4.

44. Ibid., p. 10.
45. Quoted at the official Vietnam Veterans Memorial Fund website: http://www.vvmf.org/index.cfm?SectionID=85. Accessed 23 July 2006.
46. Bobbie Ann Mason, *In Country* (New York: Harper Perennial, [1985] 2005), p. 240.
47. Frederick Buell, 'Nationalist Postnationalism: Globalist Discourse in Contemporary American Culture', *American Quarterly*, 50 (3) (1998), p. 555.
48. Ibid., p. 566.
49. Ibid., p. 566.

Conclusion

1. Paul Giles, 'Response to the Presidential Address to the American Studies Association, Hartford, Connecticut, October 17, 2003', *American Quarterly* 56 (1) (2004), p. 19.

Bibliography

'Manic Market: Is computer-driven stock trading good for America?', *Time*, 10 November 1986.

Dennis Altman, *AIDS and the New Puritanism* (London: Pluto Press, 1986).

Richard Armstrong, *The Next Hurrah: The Communications Revolution in American Politics* (New York: Beech Tree Books, 1988).

Kenneth S. Baer, *Reinventing Democrats: the Politics of Liberalism from Reagan to Clinton* (Lawrence KS: University Press of Kansas, 2000).

Fenton Bailey, *The Junk Bond Revolution: Michael Milken, Wall Street and the 'Roaring Eighties'* (London: Fourth Estate, 1991).

Ryan J. Barilleaux, *The Post-Modern Presidency: The Office after Ronald Reagan* (New York: Praeger, 1988).

Keith Beattie, *The Scar That Binds: American Culture and the Vietnam War* (New York: New York University Press, 1998).

William C. Berman, *America's Right Turn: From Nixon to Bush* (Baltimore MD and London: Johns Hopkins University Press, 1994).

Michael Bibby, *The Vietnam War and Postmodernity* (Amherst MA: University of Massachusetts Press, 2000).

Allan Bloom, *The Closing of the American Mind* (New York: Simon & Schuster, 1987).

David Bollier, *Brand-Name Bullies: And their Quest to Own and Control Culture* (Hoboken NJ: John Wiley, 2005).

Robert Boyer and Bob Jessop, *The Eighties: The Search for Alternatives to Fordism* (Aldershot: Edward Elgar, 1991).

Po Bronson, *The Nudist on the Late Shift: And Other Tales from Silicon Valley* (London: Secker & Warburg, 1999).

Steve Bruce, *The Rise and Fall of the New Christian Right: Conservative Protestant Politics in America 1978–1988* (Oxford: Clarendon Press, 1988).

Steve Bruce, *Pray TV: Televangelism in America* (London: Routledge, 1990).

Robert Busby, *Reagan and the Iran–Contra Affair: The Politics of Presidential Recovery* (Basingstoke: Macmillan, 1999).

Colin Campbell, *Managing the Presidency: Carter, Reagan, and the Search for Executive Harmony* (Pittsburgh PA: University of Pittsburgh Press, 1986).

Neil Campbell, *The Cultures of the American New West* (Edinburgh: Edinburgh University Press, 2000).

Paul E. Ceruzzi, *A History of Modern Computing* (Cambridge MA: MIT Press, [1998] 2000).

David Chidester, *Authentic Fakes: Religion and American Popular Culture* (Berkeley CA: University of California Press, 2005).

Alexander Cockburn, *The Golden Age is in Us: Journeys & Encounters, 1987–1994* (London: Verso, 1995).

Douglas Crimp, *AIDS: Cultural Analysis Cultural Activism* (Cambridge, MA: MIT Press, 1988).

Philip John Davies (ed.), *An American Quarter Century: US Politics from Vietnam to Clinton* (Manchester: Manchester University Press, 1995).

Mike Davis and Michael Sprinker (ed.), *Reshaping the US Left: Popular Struggles in the 1980s* (London: Verso, 1988).

Dinesh D'Souza, *Ronald Reagan: How an Ordinary Man became an Extraordinary Leader* (New York: Free Press, 1997).

Russell Duncan and Joseph Goddard, *Contemporary America* (Basingstoke: Palgrave Macmillan, 2003).

Barbara Ehrenreich, *The Worst Years of Our Lives: Irreverent Notes from a Decade of Greed* (New York: Pantheon Books, 1990).

John Ehrman, *The Eighties: America in the Age of Reagan* (New Haven CT: Yale University Press, 2005).

Marc Allen Eisner, *Antitrust and the Triumph of Economics: Institutions, Expertise and Policy Change* (Chapel Hill NC: University of North Carolina Press, 1991).

Susan Faludi, *Backlash: The Undeclared War Against Women* (London: Vintage, [1991] 1992).

Frances FitzGerald, *Way Out there in the Blue: Reagan, Star Wars, and the End of the Cold War* (New York: Simon & Schuster, 2000).

Charles R. Geisst, *Wall Street* (Oxford: Oxford University Press, 1997).

Nelson George, *Post-Soul Nation: The Explosive, Contradictory, Triumphant, and Tragic 1980s, as Experienced by African American (Previously Known as Black and Before That Negroes)* (New York: Viking, 2004).

Todd Gitlin, *The Twilight of Common Dreams: Why America is Wracked by Culture Wars* (New York: Metropolitan Books, 1995).

Paul Grainge, *Monochrome Memories: Nostalgia and Style in Retro America* (Westport CT: Praeger, 2002).

Lawrence Grossberg, *We Gotta Get out of This Place: Popular Conservatism and Postmodern Culture* (New York, London: Routledge, 1992).

Lawrence Grossberg, *Bringing It All Back Home: Essays on Cultural Studies* (Durham NC and London: Duke University Press, 1997).

Walter Grünzweig, Roberta Maierhofer and Adi Wimmer (eds), *Constructing the Eighties: Versions of an American Decade* (Tübingen: G. Narr, 1992).

Jeffrey K. Hadden and Anson Shupe, *Televangelism, Power, and Politics on God's Frontier* (New York: H. Holt, 1988).

Charles P. Henry, *Culture and African American Politics* (Bloomington IN: Indiana University Press, 1990).

Paul Hollander, *Anti-Americanism: Critiques at Home and Abroad, 1965–1990* (Oxford: Oxford University Press, 1992).

Allen D. Hertzke, *Echoes of Discontent: Jesse Jackson, Pat Robertson, and the Resurgence of Populism* (Washington DC: CQ Press, 1993).

Robert Hughes, *The Culture of Complaint: The Fraying of America* (Oxford: Oxford University Press).

James Davison Hunter, *Culture Wars: The Struggle to Define America* (New York: Basic Books, 1991).

Fredric Jameson, 'Postmodernism and Consumer Culture,' in Hal Foster (ed.), *Postmodern Culture* (London: Pluto Press, [1983] 1985).

Fredric Jameson, *Postmodernism or The Cultural Logic of Late Capitalism* (Durham NC: Duke University Press, 1991).

Brian Jarvis, *Postmodern Catographies: The Geographical Imagination in Contemporary American Culture* (London: Pluto, 1998).

Ted G. Jelen, *The Political Mobilization of Religious Beliefs* (New York: Praeger, 1991).

Robert S. Kahn, *Other People's Blood: U.S. Immigration Prisons in the Reagan Decade* (Boulder CO: Westview Press, 1996).

Douglas Kellner, *Media Spectacle* (London: Routledge, 2003).

Richard H. King, 'The Eighties,' in *Introduction to American Studies*, 3rd edn, eds. Malcolm Bradbury and Howard Temperley (London: Longman, 1998).

Naomi Klein, *No Logo: No Space, No Choice, No Jobs* (London: Flamingo, 2000).

Naomi Klein, *Fences and Windows: Dispatches from the Front Lines of the Globalization Debate* (London: Flamingo, 2002).

Joel Krieger, *Reagan, Thatcher, and the Politics of Decline* (Cambridge: Polity Press, 1986).

Haynes Johnson, *Sleepwalking Through History: America in the Reagan Years* (New York: W. W. Norton, [1991] 2003).

Michael Kazin and Joseph A. McCartin (eds), *Americanism: New Perspectives on the History of an Ideal* (Chapel Hill NC: University of North Carolina Press, 2006).

Alison Landsberg, *Prosthetic Memory: The Transformation of American Remembrance in the Age of Mass Culture* (New York: Columbia University Press, 2004).

Michael Lienesch, *Redeeming America: Piety and Politics in the New Christian Right* (Chapel Hill NC: University of North Carolina Press, 1993).

Edward Tabor Linenthal, *Symbolic Defense: The Cultural Significance of the Strategic Defense Initiative* (Urbana IL: University of Illinois Press, 1989).

Jean-François Lyotard, *The Postmodern Condition: A Report on Knowledge* (Minneapolis MN: University of Minnesota Press, 1984).

Trevor B. McCrisken, *American Exceptionalism and the Legacy of Vietnam: US Foreign Policy since 1974* (Basingstoke: Palgrave, 2003).

John Harmon McElroy, *Divided We Stand: The Rejection of American Culture since the 1960s* (Lanham MD: Rowman & Littlefield, 2006).

Nicolaus Mills, *Culture in the Age of Money: The Legacy of the 1980s in America* (Chicago: Ivan R. Dee, 1990).

Richard Nelson, *A Culture of Confidence: Politics, Performance and the Idea of America* (Jackson MS: University Press of Mississippi, 1996).

James T. Patterson, *Restless Giant: The United States from Watergate to Bush v. Gore* (New York: Oxford University Press, 2005).

James Petras and Morris Morley, *Empire or Republic?: American Global Power and Domestic Decay* (New York: Routledge, 1995).

Ronald Reagan, *An American Life* (New York: Simon and Schuster, 1990).

Richard Reeves, *President Reagan: The Triumph of Imagination* (New York: Simon and Schuster, 2005).

Michael Rogin, *Ronald Reagan, the Movie and Other Episodes in Political Demonology* (Berkeley CA: University of California Press, 1987).

Andrew Ross, *No Respect: Intellectuals & Popular Culture* (New York, London: Routledge, 1989).

Andrew Ross, *Strange Weather: Culture, Science, and Technology in the Age of Limits* (London: Verso, 1991).

Malise Ruthven, *The Divine Supermarket: Shopping for God in America* (London: Vintage, 1991).

Michael Schaller, *Reckoning with Reagan: America and its President in the 1980s* (New York: Oxford University Press, 1994).

Michael Schaller, *Right Turn: American Life in the Reagan-Bush Era, 1980-1992* (New York: Oxford University Press, 2006).

Larry M. Schwab, *The Illusion of a Conservative Reagan Revolution* (New Brunswick NJ: Transaction Books, 1991).

Gilbert T. Sewall (ed.), *The Eighties: A Reader* (Reading MA: Addison-Wesley, 1997).

Randy Shilts, *And the Band Played On: Politics, People and the AIDS Epidemic* (Harmondsworth: Penguin, [1987] 1988).

Werner Sollors, *Beyond Ethnicity: Consent and Descent in American Culture* (New York: Oxford University Press, 1986).

Mary E. Stuckey, *Playing the Game: The Presidential Rhetoric of Ronald Reagan* (New York: Praeger, 1990).

Gil Troy, *Morning in America: How Ronald Reagan Invented the 1980s* (Princeton NJ: Princeton University Press, 2005).

Fred Turner, *Echoes of Combat: Trauma, Memory, and the Vietnam War* (Minneapolis MN: University of Minnesota Press, 2001).

Jules Tygiel, *Ronald Reagan and the Triumph of American Conservatism* (New York: Longman, 2005).

Gore Vidal, *Armageddon?: Essays 1983–1987* (London: Grafton, [1987] 1989).

Vincent Virga, *The Eighties: Images of America* (New York: Edward Burlingame Books, 1992).

David C. Wills, *The First War on Terrorism: Counter-Terrorism Policy during the Reagan Administration* (Lanham MD: Rowman & Littlefield 2003).

Gary Wills, *Reagan's America: Innocents at Home* (New York: Doubleday, 1987).

Gary Wills, *Under God: Religion and American politics* (New York: Simon and Schuster, 1990).

Randall Bennett Woods, *Quest for Identity: America since 1945* (Cambridge: Cambridge University Press, 2005).

Fiction and Poetry

Martin Amis, *The Moronic Inferno and Other Visits to America* (Harmondsworth: Penguin, [1986] 1987).

James Annesley, *Blank Fictions: Consumerism, Culture and the Contemporary American Novel* (London: Pluto Press, 1998).

Christopher Beach, *The Cambridge Introduction to Twentieth-Century American Poetry* (Cambridge: Cambridge University Press, 2003).

Bernard W. Bell, *The Contemporary African American novel: Its Folk Roots and Modern Literary Branches* (Amherst MA: University of Massachusetts Press, 2004).

Alan Bilton, *An Introduction to Contemporary American Fiction* (Edinburgh: Edinburgh University Press, 2002).

Patrick B. Bjork, *The Novels of Toni Morrison: The Search for Self and Place Within the Community* (New York: Peter Lang, 1996).

Martyn Bone, *The Postsouthern Sense of Place in Contemporary Fiction* (Baton Rouge LA: Louisiana State University Press, 2005).

David Brande, 'The Business of Cyberpunk: Symbolic Economy and Ideology in William Gibson,' *Configurations*, 2 (3) (1994), pp. 509–36.

David Brauner, *Post-War Jewish Fiction: Ambivalence, Self-Explanation and Transatlantic Connections* (Basingstoke: Palgrave, 2001).

Robert H. Brinkmeyer Jr, *Remapping Southern Literature: Contemporary Southern Writers and the West* (Athens GA: University of Georgia Press, 2000).

Janet Burstein, *Telling The Little Secrets: American Jewish Writing since the 1980s* (Madison WI: University of Wisconsin Press, 2006).

Elliot Butler-Evans, *Race, Gender, and Desire: Narrative Strategies in the Fiction of Toni Cade Bambara, Toni Morrison and Alice Walker* (Philadelphia PA: Temple University Press, 1989).

Hector Calderon and José David Saldivar (eds), *Criticism in the Borderlands: Studies in Chicano Literature, Culture and Ideology* (Durham NC: Duke University Press, 1991).

Ewing Campbell, *Raymond Carver: A Study of the Short Fiction* (New York: Twayne, 1992).

Karen Carmean, *Toni Morrison's World of Fiction* (Troy NY: Whitston, 1993).

Dani Cavallaro, *Cyberpunk and Cyberculture: Science Fiction and the Work of William Gibson* (London: Athlone Press, 2000).

King-Kok Cheung, *Articulate Silences: Hisaye Yamamoto, Maxine Hong Kingston* (Ithaca NY: Cornell University Press, 1993).

King-Kok Cheung, *An Interethnic Companion to Asian American Literature* (Cambridge: Cambridge University Press, 1997).

Rey Chow, *Modern Chinese Literary and Cultural Studies in the Age of Theory: Reimagining a Field* (Durham NC: Duke University Press, 2000).

Keith Clark (ed.), *Contemporary Black Men's Fiction and Drama* (Urbana IL: University of Illinois Press, 2001).

Jay Clayton, *The Pleasures of Babel: Contemporary American Literature* (Oxford: Oxford University Press, 1993).

Josh Cohen, *Spectacular Allegories: Postmodern Writing and the Politics of Seeing* (London: Pluto, 1998).

David Cowart, *History and the Contemporary Novel* (Carbondale IL: Southern Illinois University Press, 1989).

David Cowart, *Don DeLillo: The Physics of Language* (Athens GA: University of Georgia Press, 2002).

Annie O. Eysturoy, *Daughters of Self-Creation: The Contemporary Chicana Novel* (Albuquerque NM: University of New Mexico Press, 1996).

Jan Furman, *Toni Morrison's Fiction* (Columbia SC: University of South Carolina Press, 1996).

Marâia Gonzâalez, *Contemporary Mexican-American Women Novelists: Toward a Feminist Identity* (New York: Peter Lang, 1996).

Helena Grice, Candid Hepworth, Maria Lauret and Martin Padget, *Beginning Ethnic American Literatures* (Manchester: Manchester University Press, 2001).

Matthew Guinn, *After Southern Modernism: Fiction of the Contemporary South* (Jackson MS: University Press of Mississippi, 2000).

Steffen Hantke, *Conspiracy and Paranoia in Contemporary American Fiction: The Works of Don DeLillo and Joseph McElroy* (Frankfurt: Peter Lang, 1994).

George Hartley, *Textual Politics and the Language Poets* (Bloomington IN: Indiana University Press, 1989).

David Holloway, *The Late Modernism of Cormac McCarthy* (Westport CT: Greenwood, 2002).

Linda Hutcheon, *The Poetics of Postmodernism: History, Theory, Fiction* (London: Routledge and Kegan Paul, 1988).

Earl G. Ingersoll, Judith Kitchen and Stan Sanvel Rubin, *The Post-Confessionals: Conversations with American Poets of the Eighties* (Rutherford: Fairleigh Dickinson University Press, 1989).

Robert L. Jarrett, *Cormac McCarthy* (New York: Twayne, 1997).

Elaine H. Kim, *Asian American Literature: An Introduction to the Writings and their Social Contexts* (Philadelphia: Temple University Press, 1982).

Arnold Krupat, *The Voice in the Margins: Native American Literature and the Canon* (Berkley CA: University of California Press, 1989).

Arnold Krupat, *New Voices in Native American Literary Criticism* (Washington DC: Smithsonian Institution Press, 1993).

Tom LeClair, *In the Loop: Don DeLillo and the Systems Novel* (Urbana IL: University of Illinois Press, 1987).

David Leiwei Li, *Imagining the Nation: Asian American Literature and Cultural Consent* (Stanford CA: Stanford University Press, 1998).

Frank Lentricchia (ed.), *Introducing Don DeLillo* (Durham NC: Duke University Press, 1991).

Frank Lentricchia (ed.), *New Essays on White Noise* (Cambridge: Cambridge University Press, 1991).

James D. Lilley (ed.), *Cormac McCarthy: New Directions* (Albuquerque NM: University of New Mexico Press, 2002).

Amy Ling, *Between Worlds: Women Writers of Chinese Ancestry* (New York: Pergamon, 1990).

Jinqi Ling, *Narrating Nationalisms: Ideology and Form in Asian American Literature* (New York: Oxford University Press, 1998).

Heidi Slettedahl Macpherson, *Women's Movement: Escape as Transgression in North American Feminist Fiction* (Amsterdam: Rodopi, 2000).

Brian McHale, *Postmodernist Fiction* (London: Methuen, 1987).

Brian McHale, *Constructing Postmodernism* (London: Routledge, 1992).

Nellie Y. McKay, *Critical Essays on Toni Morrison* (Boston MA: G. K. Hall, 1988).

Timothy Melley, *Empire of Conspiracy: The Culture of Paranoia in Postwar America* (Ithaca NY: Cornell University Press, 2000).

Kenneth Millard, *Contemporary American Fiction* (Oxford: Oxford University Press, 2000).

Angelyn Mitchell, *The Freedom to Remember: Narrative, Slavery, and Gender in Contemporary Black Women's Fiction* (New Brunswick NJ: Rutgers University Press, 2002).

Sharon Monteith, *Advancing Sisterhood?: Interracial Friendships in Contemporary Southern Fiction* (Athens GA: University of Georgia Press, 2000).

Dan Moos, 'Lacking the Article Itself: Representation and History in Cormac McCarthy's *Blood Meridian*', *Cormac McCarthy Journal*, 2 (2002), pp. 23–39.

'Toni Morrison Special Double Issue', *Modern Fiction Studies*, 39 (3, 4) (1993).

'Toni Morrison Special Issue', *Modern Fiction Studies*, 52 (2) (2006).

Kirk Nesset, *The Stories of Raymond Carver: A Critical Study* (Athens OH: Ohio University Press, 1995).

Patrick O'Donnell, *Latent Destinies: Cultural Paranoia and Contemporary U.S. Narrative* (Durham NC: Duke University Press, 2000).

Andrea O'Reilly, *Toni Morrison and Motherhood: a Politics of the Heart* (New York: State University of New York Press, 2004).

Mark Osteen, *American Magic and Dread: Don DeLillo's Dialogue with Culture* (Philadelphia: University of Pennsylvania Press, 2000).

Barcley Owens, *Cormac McCarthy's Western Novels* (Tucson AZ: University of Arizona Press, 2000).

Philip Page, *Reclaiming Community in Contemporary African-American Fiction* (Jackson MS: University Press of Mississippi , 1999).

Linden Peach, *Toni Morrison* (Basingstoke: Macmillan, 1995).

Jayne Anne Phillips, '*White Noise*, by Don DeLillo', *New York Times*, 13 January 1985.

Catherine Rainwater, *Dreams of Fiery Stars: the Transformations of Native American Fiction* (Philadelphia PA: University of Pennsylvania Press, 1999).

Tatiani G. Rapatzikou, *Gothic Motifs in the Fiction of William Gibson* (Amsterdam: Rodopi, 2004).

Robert Rebein, *Hicks, Tribes, And Dirty Realists: American Fiction after Postmodernism* (Lexington KY: University of Kentucky Press, 2001).

Linda Reinfeld, *Language Poetry: Writing as Rescue* (Baton Rouge LA: Louisiana State University Press, 1992).

Guy Reynolds, *Twentieth-Century American Women's Fiction* (London: Macmillan, 1999).

Cecil Robinson, *No Short Journeys: The Interplay of Cultures in the History and Literature of the Borderlands* (Tucson AZ: University of Arizona Press, 1992).

Hugh Ruppersburg and Tim Engles (eds), *Critical Essays on Don DeLillo* (New York: G. K. Hall, 2000).

Ramón Saldivar, *Chicano Narrative: The Dialectics of Difference* (Madison WI: University of Wisconsin Press, 1990).

Richard B. Schwartz, *Nice and Noir: Contemporary American Crime Fiction* (Columbia MO: University of Missouri Press, 2002).

John Sepich, 'The Dance of History in Cormac McCarthy's *Blood Meridian*', *Southern Literary Journal*, 24 (1) (1991), pp. 16–31.

John Sepich, *Notes on Blood Meridian* (Louisville KY: Bellarmine College Press, 1993).

Ron Silliman, *The New Sentence* (New York: Roof, 1987).

Ronald Silliman, *In the American Tree: Language, Realism, Poetry* (Orono ME: National Poetry Foundation, 2002).

Phillip E. Simmons, *Deep Surfaces: Mass Culture and History in Postmodern American Fiction* (Athens GA: University of Georgia Press, 1997).

Carlton Smith, *Coyote Kills John Wayne: Postmodernism and Contemporary Fictions of the Transcultural Frontier* (Hanover NH: University Press of New England, 2000).

Graham Thompson, *The Business of America: The Cultural Construction of a Post-War Nation* (London: Pluto Press, 2004).

Eric Sundquist, *The Hammers of Creation: Folk Culture in Modern African-American Fiction* (Athens GA: University of Georgia Press, 1992).

Laurie Vickroy, *Trauma and Survival in Contemporary Fiction* (Charlottesville VA: University of Virginia Press, 2002).

Rick Wallach (ed.), *Myth, Legend, Dust: Critical Responses to Cormac McCarthy* (Manchester: Manchester University Press, 2000).

Emily Stipes Watt, *The Businessman in American Literature* (Athens GA: University of Georgia Press, 1982).

Melissa Walker, *Down from the Mountaintop: Black Women's Novels in the Wake of the Civil Rights Movement, 1966–1989* (New Haven CT: Yale University Press, 1991).

Geoffrey Ward, *Language Poetry and the American Avant-Garde* (Keele: Keele University Press, 1993).

Alan Wilde, *Middle Grounds: Studies in Contemporary American Fiction* (Philadelphia PA: University of Pennsylvania Press, 1987).

Elizabeth Young and Graham Caveney, *Shopping in Space: Essays on American 'Blank Generation' Fiction* (London: Serpent's Tail, 1992).

Art and Photography

Romare Bearden and Harry Henderson, *A History of African-American Artists: From 1792 to the Present* (New York: Pantheon, 1993).

Romare Bearden, Sharon F. Patton et al., *Memory and Metaphor: The Art of Romare Bearden, 1940–1987* (New York: Oxford University Press, 1991).

David Bjelajac, *American Art: A Cultural History* (London: Laurence King, 2000).

Michael Brenson, 'Artists Grapple with New Realities', *New York Times*, 15 May 1983.

Ralph T. Coe, Irene Gordon and Bobby Hansson, *Lost and Found Traditions: Native American Art 1965–1985* (Seattle WA: University of Washington Press, 1986).

Douglas Crimp, 'The Art of Exhibition,' *October*, 30 (Autumn, 1984), pp. 49–81.

Jeffrey Deitch, *Young Americans: New American Art in the Saatchi Collection* (London: Saatchi Gallery, 1996).

Erika Lee Doss, *Twentieth-Century American Art* (Oxford: Oxford University Press, 2002).

Leonhard Emmerling, *Jean-Michel Basquiat: 1960–1988* (Kèoln: Taschen, 2003).

Russell Ferguson, Marcia Tucker and John Baldessari, *Discourses: Conversations in Postmodern Art and Culture* (Cambridge MA: MIT Press, 1990).

Claire F. Fox, 'The Portable Border: Site-Specificity, Art, and the U.S.–Mexico Frontier', *Social Text*, 41 (Winter, 1994), pp. 61–82.

Gretchen Garner, *Disappearing Witness: Change in Twentieth-Century American Photography* (Baltimore MD and London: Johns Hopkins University Press, 2003).

Grace Glueck, 'What Big Business Sees in Fine Art', *New York Times*, 26 May 1985.

Phoebe Hoban, *Basquiat: A Quick Killing in Art* (London: Penguin, [1998] 2004).

David Hopkins, *After Modern Art 1945–2000* (Oxford: Oxford University Press, 2000).

Robert Hughes, 'Careerism and Hype Amidst the Image Haze: American Painters of the '80s are Buffeted by Cultural Inflation', *Time*, 17 June 1985.

Robert Hughes, *American Visions: The Epic History of Art in America* (London: Harvill, 1997).

David Joselit, *American Art since 1945* (London: Thames & Hudson, 2003).

Miguel Juarez Jr, *Colors on Desert Walls: The Murals of El Paso* (El Paso TX: Texas Western Press, 1997).

Jeff Koons, *Pictures* (Verlag der Buchhandlung: Walther Konig, 2002).

Rosalind E. Krauss and Norman Bryson, *Cindy Sherman, 1975–1993* (New York: Rizzoli, 1993).

Donald B. Kuspit, *Signs of Psyche in Modern and Postmodern Art* (Cambridge: Cambridge University Press, 1993).

Samella S. Lewis, *African American Art and Artists* (Berkeley, London: University of California Press, 1994).

Lucy Lippard, 'Real Estate and Real Art', *Seven Days* (April, 1980), pp. 32–4. Reprinted at http://www.lehman.cuny.edu/gallery/talkback/fmlippard. html. Accessed 29 May 2006.

Margot Lovejoy, *Postmodern Currents: Art and Artists in the Age of Electronic Media* (Ann Arbor MI and London: UMI Research Press, 1989).

Edward Lucie-Smith, *Latin American Art of the 20th Century* (London: Thames and Hudson, 2004).

Richard Marshall, *Jean-Michel Basquiat* (New York: Harry N. Abrams, 1995).

Rosanne Martorella, *Corporate Art* (New Brunswick NJ: Rutgers University Press, 1990).

Patricia Morrisoe, *Mapplethorpe: A Biography* (London: Macmillan, 1995).

Francis M. Naumann, Thomas Girst, *Aftershock: The Legacy of the Readymade in Post-War and Contemporary American Art* (New York: Dickinson Roundell, 2003).

Miles Orvell, *American Photography* (Oxford: Oxford University Press, 2003).

Sharon F. Patton, *African-American Art* (Oxford: Oxford University Press, 1998).

Lisa Phillips, *The American Century: Art and Culture 1950–2000* (New York: Whitney Museum of American Art in association with W. W. Norton, 1999).

Phoenix Art Museum, *American Art of the 1980s: Phoenix Art Museum, January 5–May, 1986* (Phoenix AZ: Phoenix Art Museum, 1986).

Frances K. Pohl, *Framing America: A Social History of American Art* (New York: Thames & Hudson, 2002).

Shelley Rice, *Inverted Odysseys: Claude Cahun, Maya Deren, and Cindy Sherman* (Cambridge MA: MIT Press, 1999).

Irving Sandler, *Art of the Postmodern Era: From the Late 1960s to the Early 1990s* (New York: Icon Editions, 1996).

A. O. Scott, 'In Search of the Best', *New York Times*, 21 May 2006.

Marvin J. Taylor, *The Downtown Book: The New York Art Scene, 1974–1984* (Princeton NJ: Princeton University Press, 2006).

Chin-Tao Wu, *Privatising Culture: Corporate Art Intervention since the 1980s* (London: Verso, 2002).

Film and Television

Ien Ang, *Watching Dallas: Soap Opera and the Melodramatic Imagination* (London: Methuen, 1985).

Tino Balio, *United Artists: The Company That Changed the Film Industry* (Madison: University of Wisconsin Press, 1987).

Tino Balio, *Hollywood in the Age of Television* (Boston MA: Unwin Hyman, 1990).

Martin Barker and Thomas Austin, *Contemporary Hollywood Stardom* (London: Arnold, 2003).

Erik Barnouw, *Tube of Plenty: The Evolution of American Television* (New York, Oxford: Oxford University Press, 1990).

Peter Biskind, *Easy Riders, Raging Bulls: How the Sex Drugs and Rock 'N' Roll Generation Saved Hollywood* (London: Bloomsbury, 1998).

Peter Biskind, *Down and Dirty Pictures: Miramax, Sundance and the Rise of Independent Film* (New York: Simon & Schuster, 2004).

Andrew Britton, 'Blissing Out: The Politics of Reaganite Entertainment', *Movie*, 31 (2) (1986), pp. 1–42.

Douglas Brode, *The Films of the Eighties* (New York: Carol Publishing Group, 1990).

Richard Butsch, *The Making of American Audiences: From Stage to Television, 1750–1990* (Cambridge: Cambridge University Press, 2000).

Jim Collins, *Architectures of Excess: Cultural Life in the Information Age* (New York: Routledge, 1995).

Timothy Corrigan, *A Cinema without Walls: Movies and Culture after Vietnam* (London: Routledge, 1992).

C. Critcher, *Moral Panics and the Media* (Buckingham: Open University Press, 2003).

Jude Davies and Carol R. Smith, *Gender, Ethnicity and Sexuality in*

Contemporary American Film (Edinburgh: Edinburgh University Press, 1997).

Philip John Davies and Paul Wells (eds), *American Film and Politics from Reagan to Bush Jnr* (Manchester: Manchester University Press, 2002).

Manthia Diawara, *African Cinema: Politics & Culture* (Bloomington IN: Indiana University Press, 1992).

Manthia Diawara, *Black American Cinema* (New York, London: Routledge, 1993).

Robert J. Donovan and Ray Scherer, *Unsilent Revolution: Television News and American Public Life, 1948–1991* (Cambridge: Cambridge University Press, 1992).

Jane Feuer, *Seeing through the Eighties: Television and Reaganism* (London: British Film Institute, 1996).

Paul Grainge, *Memory and Popular Film* (Manchester: Manchester University Press, 2003).

Margaret J. Heide, *Television Culture and Women's Lives: thirtysomething and the Contradictions of Gender* (Philadelphia PA: University of Pennsylvania Press, 1995).

David Hesmondhalgh, *The Cultural Industries* (London: SAGE, 2002).

Jim Hillier, *The New Hollywood* (London: Studio Vista, 1993).

Joanne Hollows, Peter Hutchings and Mark Jancovich, *The Film Studies Reader* (London: Arnold, 2000).

Joanne Hollows and Mark Jancovich, *Approaches to Popular Film* (Manchester: Manchester University Press, 1995).

Mark Jancovich, *American Horror from 1951* (Keele: Keele University Press, 1994).

Mark Jancovich, *Defining Cult Movies: The Cultural Politics of Oppositional Taste* (Manchester: Manchester University Press, 2003).

Mark Jancovich and James Lyons, *Quality Popular Television: Cult TV, the Industry and Fans* (London: British Film Institute, 2003).

Susan Jeffords, *Hard Bodies: Hollywood Masculinity in the Reagan Era* (New Brunswick NJ: Rutgers University Press, 1994).

Geoff King, *Spectacular Narratives: Hollywood in the Age of the Blockbuster* (London: I. B. Tauris, 2000).

Geoff King, *New Hollywood Cinema: An Introduction* (London: I. B. Tauris, 2002).

Michael Medved, *Hollywood Vs. America: Popular Culture and the War on Traditional Values* (New York: HarperCollins, 1992).

Mullen, Megan, *The Rise of Cable Programming in the United States* (Austin TX: University of Texas Press, 2003).

Jeffrey S. Miller, *Something Completely Different: British Television and*

American Culture (Minneapolis MN, London: University of Minnesota Press, 2000).

Toby Miller, *Global Hollywood* (London: British Film Institute Publishing, 2001).

John Kenneth Muir, *Terror Television: American Series, 1970–1999* (Jefferson NC: McFarland, 2001).

Alan Nadel, *Flatlining on the Field of Dreams: Cultural Narratives in the Films of President Reagan's America* (New Brunswick NJ and London: Rutgers University Press, 1997).

Stephen Neale, *Genre and Contemporary Hollywood* (London: British Film Institute, 2002).

Stephen Neale and Frank Krutnik, *Popular Film and Television Comedy* (London: Routledge, 1990).

Stephen Neale and Murray Smith, *Contemporary Hollywood Cinema* (London: Routledge, 1998).

Robert A. Nowlan and Gwendolyn Wright Nowlan, *The Films of the Eighties: A Complete, Qualitative Filmography to over 3400 Feature-Length English Language Films, Theatrical and Video-Only, Released between January 1, 1980, and December 31, 1989* (Jefferson NC and London: McFarland, 1991).

William J. Palmer, *The Films of the Eighties: A Social History* (Carbondale IL: Southern Illinois University Press, 1995).

Fred Pfeil, *White Guys: Studies in Postmodern Domination and Difference* (London: Verso, 1995).

Stephen Prince, *A New Pot of Gold: Hollywood under the Electronic Rainbow, 1980–1989* (Berkeley CA: University of California Press, 2000).

Paul Rixon, *American Television on British Screens: A Story of Cultural Interaction* (Basingstoke: Palgrave Macmillan, 2006).

Michael Ryan and Douglas Kellner, *Camera Politica: The Politics and Ideology of Contemporary Hollywood Film* (Bloomington IN: Indiana University Press, 1988).

Jeffrey Scheuer, *The Sound Bite Society: How Television Helps the Right and Hurts the Left* (New York: Routledge, 2001).

Kerry Segrave, *American Television Abroad: Hollywood's Attempt to Dominate World Television* (Jefferson NC and London: McFarland, 1998).

Carol A. Stabile and Mark Harrison, *Prime-Time Animation: Television Animation and American Culture* (London: Routledge, 2003).

Julian Stringer, *Movie Blockbusters* (London: Routledge, 2003).

David Thelen, *Becoming Citizens in the Age of Television: How Americans Challenged the Media and Seized Political Initiative during the Ira–Contra Debate* (Chicago: University of Chicago Press, 1996).

Janet Wasko, *Hollywood in the Information Age: Beyond the Silver Screen* (Cambridge: Polity Press, 1994).

Janet Wasko, *Understanding Disney: The Manufacture of Fantasy* (Cambridge: Polity Press, 2001).

Janet Wasko, *How Hollywood Works* (London: SAGE, 2003).

Michael J. Wolf, *The Entertainment Economy: How Mega-Media Forces Are Transforming Our Lives* (London: Penguin, 1999).

Robin Wood, *Hollywood from Vietnam to Reagan* (New York: Columbia University Press, 1986).

Robin Wood, *Sexual Politics and Narrative Film: Hollywood and Beyond* (New York: Columbia University Press, 1998).

Justin Wyatt, *High Concept* (Austin TX: University of Texas Press, 1994).

Music and Performance

Houston A. Baker, *Black Studies, Rap, and the Academy* (Chicago: University of Chicago Press, 1993).

C. W. E. Bigsby, *David Mamet* (London: Methuen, 1985).

C. W. E. Bigsby, *Contemporary American Playwrights* (Cambridge: Cambridge University Press, 1999).

C. W. E. Bigsby, *Modern American Drama, 1945–2000* (Cambridge: Cambridge University Press, 2000).

C. W. E. Bigsby, *The Cambridge Companion to David Mamet* (Cambridge: Cambridge University Press, 2004).

Vladamir Bogdanov, *All Music Guide to Hip Hop: The Definitive Guide to Rap & Hip Hop* (San Francisco: Backbeat Books, 2003).

Mary L. Bogumil, *Understanding August Wilson* (Columbia SC: University of South Carolina Press, 1999).

Margaret Booker, *Lillian Hellman and August Wilson: Dramatizing a New American Identity* (New York: Peter Lang, 2003).

Herb Boyd, *Race and Resistance: African Americans in the 21st Century* (Cambridge MA: South End Press, 2002).

Todd Boyd, *The New H.N.I.C. (Head Niggas in Charge): The Death of Civil Rights and the Reign of Hip Hop* (New York: New York University Press, 2002).

Janet Brown, *Taking Center Stage: Feminism in Contemporary U.S. Drama* (Metuchen NJ: Scarecrow, 1991).

Michael Bull, *Sounding Out the City: Personal Stereos and the Management of Everyday Life* (Oxford: Berg, 2000).

Robert Burnett, *The Global Jukebox: The International Music Industry* (London: Routledge, 1996).

Dennis Carroll, *David Mamet* (Basingstoke: Macmillan, 1987).

Sue-Ellen Case, *Split Britches: Lesbian Practice/Feminist Performance* (London: Routledge, 1996).

Stephen Citron, *Sondheim and Lloyd-Webber: The New Musical* (London: Chatto & Windus, 2001).

Keith Clark, *Black Manhood in James Baldwin, Ernest J. Gaines, and August Wilson* (Urbana IL: University of Illinois Press, 2002).

Michael Coveney, *Cats on a Chandelier: The Andrew Lloyd Webber Story* (London: Hutchinson, 1999).

Jefferson Cowie and Lauren Boehm, 'Dead Man's Town: "Born in the U.S.A.", Social History, and Working-Class Identity', *American Quarterly*, 58 (2) (2006), pp. 353–78.

James L. Conyers, *African American Jazz and Rap: Social and Philosophical Examinations of Black Expressive Behavior* (Jefferson NC: McFarland, 2001).

Jim Cullen, *Born in the USA: Bruce Springsteen and the American Tradition* (London: Helter Skelter, 1998).

Chuck D. *Fight the Power: Rap, Race, and Reality* (New York: Delacorte Press, 1997).

Kate Davy, 'Constructing the Spectator: Reception, Context, and Address in Lesbian Performance', *Performing Arts Journal*, 10 (2) (1986), pp. 43–52.

Anne Dean, *David Mamet: Language as Dramatic Action* (Rutherford NJ: Fairleigh Dickinson University Press, 1990).

Gilbert Debusscher, Henry I. Schvey and Marc Maufort, *New Essays on American Drama* (Amsterdam: Rodopi, 1989).

Jill Dolan, 'Desire Cloaked in a Trenchcoat', *The Drama Review*, 33 (1) (1989), pp. 59–67.

Jill Dolan, 'The Dynamics of Desire: Sexuality and Gender in Pornography and Performance', *Theatre Journal*, 39 (2) (1987), pp. 156–74.

Paul du Gay, Stuart Hall et al., *Doing Cultural Studies; the Story of the Sony Walkman* (London: SAGE & The Open University, 1997).

Michael Dyson, *Between God and Gangsta Rap: Bearing Witness to Black Culture* (New York: Oxford University Press, 1996).

Harry Justin Elam, *The Past as Present in the Drama of August Wilson* (Ann Arbor MI: University of Michigan Press, 2004).

Joseph D. Eure, *Nation Conscious Rap* (New York: PC International Press, 1991).

Peter Evans, *Sounds of the Eighties: Like a Virgin* (London: Wise, 1993).

S. H. Fernando, *The New Beats: Exploring the Music, Culture, and Attitudes of Hip Hop* (New York: Anchor Books Doubleday, 1994).

Julian Flanders, *From Rock and Pop to Hip Hop* (London: Brown Partworks, 2001).

Murray Forman, *The 'Hood Comes First: Race, Space, and Place in Rap and Hip Hop* (Middletown CT: Wesleyan University Press, 2002).

Deborah R. Geis, *Postmodern Theatric(K)S: Monologue in Contemporary American Drama* (Ann Arbor MI: University of Michigan Press, 1993).

Nelson George, *Hip Hop America* (New York: Viking, 1998).

Sandor Goodhart, *Reading Stephen Sondheim: A Collection of Critical Essays* (New York: Garland, 2000).

Joanne Lesley Gordon, *Art Isn't Easy: The Achievement of Stephen Sondheim* (Carbondale IL: Southern Illinois University Press, 1990).

Georges-Claude Guilbert, *Madonna As Postmodern Myth: How One Star's Self-Construction Rewrites Sex, Gender, Hollywood and the American* (Jefferson NC: McFarland, 2002).

John Bush Jones, *Our Musicals, Ourselves: A Social History of the American Musical Theater* (Hanover NH: Brandeis University Press, 2003).

Leslie Kane, *David Mamet's* Glengarry Glen Ross*: Text and Performance* (New York: Garland, 1996).

Leslie Kane, *Weasels and Wisemen: Ethics and Ethnicity in the Work of David Mamet* (Basingstoke: Macmillan, 1999).

Norman Kelley, *R & B, Rhythm and Business: the Political Economy of Black Music* (New York: Akashic, 2002).

Bakari Kitwana, *The Rap on Gangsta Rap: Who Run It?: Gangsta Rap and Visions of Black Violence* (Chicago: Third World Press, 1994).

Bakari Kitwana, *The Hip Hop Generation: Young Blacks and the Crisis in African American Culture* (New York: Basic Civitas Books, 2002).

Raymond Knapp, *The American Musical and the Formation of National Identity* (Princeton NJ: Princeton University Press, 2005).

Josephine D. Lee, *Performing Asian America: Race and Ethnicity on the Contemporary Stage* (Philadelphia PA: Temple University Press, 1997).

David H. Lewis, *Broadway Musicals: A Hundred Year History* (Jefferson NC: McFarland, 2002).

Jonathan Mantle, *Fanfare: The Unauthorised Biography of Andrew Lloyd Webber* (Michael Joseph: London, 1989).

Dave Marsh, *Glory Days: Bruce Springsteen in the 1980s* (London: Sidgwick & Jackson, 1987).

Dave Marsh, *Bruce Springsteen: Two Hearts – The Definitive Biography, 1972–2003* (New York, London: Routledge, 2004).

Tony Mitchell, *Global Noise: Rap and Hip Hop Outside the USA* (Middletown CT: Wesleyan University Press, 2001).

Allan F. Moore (ed.), *Analyzing Popular Music* (Cambridge: Cambridge University Press, 2003).

Sheridan Morley and Ruth Leon, *Hey, Mr Producer: The Musical World of Cameron Mackintosh* (London: Weidenfeld & Nicolson, 1998).

Michael Moynihan and Didrik Soderlind, *Lords of Chaos: The Bloody Rise of the Satanic Metal Underground* (Los Angeles: Feral House, 2003).

Albert Mudrian, *Choosing Death: The Improbable History of Death Metal and Grindcore* (Los Angeles: Feral House, 2004).

Alan Nadel, *May All Your Fences Have Gates: Essays on the Drama of August Wilson* (Iowa City: University of Iowa Press, 1994).

Mark Anthony Neal, *What the Music Said: Black Popular Music and Black Public Culture* (New York: Routledge, 1999).

Steve Nelson, 'Broadway and the Beast: Disney Comes to Times Square', *The Drama Review*, 39 (2) (1995), pp. 71–85.

Nilgun Anadolu-Okur, *Contemporary African American Theater: Afrocentricity in the Works of Larry Neal, Amiri Baraka, and Charles Fuller* (New York: Garland, 1997).

Kim Pereira, *August Wilson and the African-American Odyssey* (Urbana IL: University of Illinois Press, 1995).

William Eric Perkins, *Droppin' Science: Critical Essays on Rap Music and Hip Hop Culture* (Philadelphia PA: Temple University Press, 1996).

Anthony B. Pinn, *Noise and Spirit: The Religious and Spiritual Sensibilities of Rap Music* (New York: New York University Press, 2003).

Russell A. Potter, *Spectacular Vernaculars: Hip Hop and the Politics of Postmodernism* (Albany NY: State University of New York Press, 1995).

Natalie J. Purcell, *Death Metal Music: The Passion and Politics of a Subculture* (Jefferson NC: McFarland, 2003).

Eithne Quinn, *Nuthin' but a 'G' thang: The Culture and Commerce of Gangsta Rap* (New York: Columbia University Press, 2005).

Ronin Ro, *Gangsta: Merchandizing the Rhymes of Violence* (New York: St. Martin's Press, 1996).

Jeffrey Pepper Rodgers, *Classic Rock of the '80s: Progressive, Glam and the Video Generation* (Miami FL: Warner Brothers, 2002).

Jeffrey Pepper Rodgers, *Classic Rock of the '80s: Punk to Heavy Metal* (Miami FL: Warner Brothers, 2002).

David Româan, *Acts of Intervention: Performance, Gay Culture, and Aids* (Bloomington IN: Indiana University Press, 1998).

Tricia Rose, *Black Noise: Rap Music and Black Culture in Contemporary America* (Hanover NH: University Press of New England, 1994).

Bernard Rosenberg and Ernest Harburg, *The Broadway Musical: Collaboration in Commerce and Art* (New York: New York University Press, 1993).

Andrew Ross, *Microphone Fiends: Youth Music & Youth Culture* (New York: Routledge, 1994).

Matthew Charles Roudanâe, *Public Issues, Private Tensions: Contemporary American Drama* (New York: AMS Press, 1993).

June Schlueter, *Modern American Drama: The Female Canon* (Rutherford NJ: Fairleigh Dickinson University Press, 1990).

Arnold Shaw, *Black Popular Music in America: From the Spirituals, Minstrels, and Ragtime to Soul, Disco, and Hip-Hop* (New York: Schirmer Books, 1986).

William Shaw, *Westside: the Coast to Coast Explosion in Hip Hop* (New York: Cooper Square Press, 2000).

John Snelson and Geoffrey Holden Block, *Andrew Lloyd Webber* (New Haven CT and London: Yale University Press, 2004).

Jon Michael Spencer, *The Emergency of Black and the Emergence of Rap* (Durham NC: Duke University Press, 1991).

Larry Starr, *American Popular Music: The Rock Years* (New York: Oxford University Press, 2005).

Robert Walser, *Running with the Devil: Power, Gender, and Madness in Heavy Metal Music* (Hanover NH: University Press of New England, 1993).

David F. Walsh and Len Platt, *Musical Theater and American Culture* (Westport CT: Praeger, 2003).

Brian Ward, *Just my Soul Responding: Rhythm and Blues, Black Consciousness and Race Relations* (London: UCL Press, 1998).

Deena Weinstein, *Heavy Metal: A Cultural Sociology* (New York: Lexington Books, 1991).

Sheila Whiteley, *Women and Popular Music: Sexuality, Identity and Subjectivity* (London: Routledge, 2000).

Stacy Ellen Wolf, *A Problem Like Maria: Gender and Sexuality in the American Musical* (Ann Arbor MI: University of Michigan Press, 2002).

Elizabeth L. Wollman, 'The Economic Development of the "New" Times Square and Its Impact on the Broadway Musical', *American Music*, 20 (4) (2002), pp. 445–65.

American Culture and Globalization

Arjun Appadurai, *Modernity at Large: Cultural Dimensions of Globalization* (Minneapolis MN: University of Minnesota Press, 1996).

Stanley Aronowitz, Barbara Martinsons, Michael Menser and Jennifer Rich, *Technoscience and Cyberculture* (New York, London: Routledge, 1996).

Ben H. Bagdikian, *The Media Monopoly*, Sixth Edition (Boston MA: Beacon Press, 2000).

Ashok Deo Bardhan, Dwight M. Jaffee and Cynthia A. Kroll, *Globalization and a High-Tech Economy: California, the United States, and Beyond* (Boston MA: Kluwer, 2004).

Andrew L. Barlow, *Between Fear and Hope: Globalization and Race in the United States* (Lanham MD: Rowman & Littlefield, 2003).

Chris Barker, *Television, Globalization and Cultural Identities* (Buckingham: Open University Press, 1999).

Jean Baudrillard, 'Disneyworld Company', translated by Francois Debrix, *Libération*, 4 March 1996.

Ulrich Beck, Natan Sznaider and Rainer Winter, *Global America?: The Cultural Consequences of Globalization* (Liverpool: Liverpool University Press, 2003).

Shane K. Bernard, *The Cajuns: Americanization of a People* (Jackson MS: University Press of Mississippi, 2003).

Philip Bell and Roger J. Bell, *Americanization and Australia* (Sydney: University of New South Wales Press, 1998).

Peter Beyer, *Religion and Globalization* (London: SAGE, 1994).

Jan Herman Brinks, Stella Rock and Edward Timms, *Nationalist Myths and Modern Media: Cultural Identities in the Age of Globalization* (London: I. B. Tauris, 2006).

Frederick Buell, *National Culture and the New Global System* (Baltimore MD: Johns Hopkins University Press, 1994).

Frederick Buell, 'Nationalist Postnationalism: Globalist Discourse in Contemporary American Culture', *American Quarterly*, 50 (3) (1998), pp. 548–91.

Alan E. Bryman, *The Disneyization of Society* (London: SAGE, 2004).

Neil Campbell, Jude Davies and George McKay, *Issues in Americanisation and Culture* (Edinburgh: Edinburgh University Press, 2004).

Robert S. Chang, *Disoriented: Asian Americans, Law, and the Nation-State* (New York, London: New York University Press, 1999).

Rey Chow, *The Protestant Ethnic and the Spirit of Capitalism* (New York: Columbia University Press, 2002).

Edward S. Cohen, *The Politics of Globalization in the United States* (Washington DC: Georgetown University Press, 2001).

Robin Cohen, *Global Diasporas: An Introduction* (Seattle: University of Washington Press, 1997).

Ian Condry, *Japanese Rap Music: An Ethnography of Globalization in Popular Culture* (Ann Arbor MI: UMI, 1999).

Diana Crane, Nobuko Kawashima and Ken'ichi Kawasaki, *Global Culture: Media, Arts, Policy, and Globalization* (New York: Routledge, 2002).

Ann Cvetkovich and Douglas Kellner, *Articulating the Global and the Local: Globalization and Cultural Studies* (Boulder CO: Westview Press, 1997).

Mark Dery, *Escape Velocity: Cyberculture at the End of the Century* (London: Hodder & Stoughton, 1996).

Mike Featherstone, *Global Culture: Nationalism, Globalization and Modernity: A Theory, Culture & Society Special Issue* (London: SAGE, 1990).

Mike Featherstone, *Undoing Culture: Globalization, Postmodernism and Identity* (London: SAGE, 1995).

Hilene Flanzbaum, *The Americanization of the Holocaust* (Baltimore MD: Johns Hopkins University Press, 1999).

Gerd Gemèunden, *Framed Visions: Popular Culture, Americanization, and the Contemporary German and Austrian Imagination* (Ann Arbor MI: University of Michigan Press, 1998).

Paul Giles, 'European American Studies and American American Studies', *European Journal of American Culture*, 19 (1) (1999), pp. 12–16.

Paul Giles, *Virtual Americas: Transnational Fictions and the Transatlantic Imaginary* (Durham NC: Duke University Press, 2002).

Paul Giles, 'Response to the Presidential Address to the American Studies Association, Hartford, Connecticut, October 17, 2003', *American Quarterly* 56 (1) (2004), pp. 19–24.

Paul Gilroy, *The Black Atlantic: Modernity and Double Consciousness* (Cambridge MA: Harvard University Press, 1993).

Tom Hanahoe, *America Rules: US Foreign Policy, Globalization and Corporate USA* (Dingle: Brandon, 2003).

Ulf Hannerz, *Transnational Connections: Culture, People, Places* (London: Routledge, 1996).

David Harvey, *The Condition of Postmodernity: An Enquiry into the Origins of Cultural Change* (Oxford: Basil Blackwell, 1989).

Lane Ryo Hirabayashi, Akemi Kikumura-Yano and James A. Hirabayashi, *New Worlds, New Lives: Globalization and People of Japanese Descent in the Americas and from Latin America in Japan* (Stanford CA: Stanford University Press, 2002).

Frederic Jameson and Masao Miyoshi (eds), *The Cultures of Globalization* (Durham NC: Duke University Press, 1998).

Amy Kaplan and Donald Pease (eds), *Cultures of United States Imperialism* (Durham NC: Duke University Press, 1993).

Anthony D. King (ed.), *Culture, Globalization and the World-System: Contemporary Conditions for the Representation of Identity* (Minneapolis MN: University of Minnesota Press, 1997).

Richard F. Kuisel, *Seducing the French: The Dilemma of Americanization* (Berkeley CA: University of California Press, 1993).

Rachel C. Lee and Sau-ling Cynthia Wong, *Asian America.Net: Ethnicity, Nationalism, and Cyberspace* (New York, London: Routledge, 2003).

Vincent B. Leitch, *Postmodernism: Local Effects, Global Flows* (New York: State University of New York Press, 1996).

Lisa Lowe, *Immigrant Acts: On Asian American Cultural Politics* (Durham NC: Duke University Press, 1996).

Lisa Lowe, 'The International within the National: American Studies and Asian American Critique', in *The Futures of American Studies*, eds Donald Pease and Robyn Wiegman (Durham NC: Duke University Press, 2002), pp. 76–92.

Sidney Eve Matrix, *Cyber Pop: Digital Lifestyles and Commodity Culture* (London: Routledge, 2006).

Robert McChesney with Edward S. Herman, *The Global Media: The New Missionaries of Corporate Capitalism* (London: Cassell, 1997).

Robert McChesney, *Rich Media, Poor Democracy: Communication Politics in Dubious Times* (New York: New Press, 2000).

George McKay, *Yankee Go Home: (and Take Me with U): Americanization and Popular Culture* (Sheffield: Sheffield Academic Press, 1997).

David Morley and Kevin Robins, *Spaces of Identity: Global Media, Electronic, Landscapes, and Cultural Boundaries* (London: Routledge, 1995).

Tom O'Dell, *Culture Unbound: Americanization and Everyday Life in Sweden* (Lund: Nordic Academic Press, 1997).

Daniel T. O'Hara, *Empire Burlesque: The Fate of Critical Culture in Global America* (Durham NC: Duke University Press, 2003).

David Palumbo-Liu, *Asian/American: Historical Crossings of a Racial Frontier* (Stanford CA: Stanford University Press, 1999).

Donald Pease, 'National Narratives, Postnational Narration', *Modern Fiction Studies*, 43 (1) (1997), pp. 1–23.

Constance Penley and Andrew Ross, *Technoculture* (Minneapolis MN: University of Minnesota Press, 1991).

Janice Radway, 'What's in a Name? Presidential Address to the American Studies Association, 20 November, 1998', *American Quarterly*, 51 (1) (1999), pp. 1–32.

Terhi Rantanen, *The Media and Globalization* (London: SAGE, 2005).

Harry Redner, *Conserving Cultures: Technology, Globalization, and the Future of Local Cultures* (Lanham MD: Rowman & Littlefield Publishers, 2004).

George Ritzer, *The McDonaldization of Society* (Newbury Park CA: Pine Forge Press, 1993).

Roland Robertson, *Globalization: Social Theory and Global Culture* (London: SAGE, 1992).

Kevin Robins and Frank Webster, *Times of the Technoculture: From the Information Society to the Virtual Life* (London: Routledge, 1999).

Andrew Ross and Kristin Ross, *Anti-Americanism* (New York: New York University Press, 2004).

Claudia Sadowski-Smith, *Globalization on the Line: Culture, Capital and Citizenship at US Borders* (New York and Basingstoke: Palgrave Macmillan, 2002).

Edward Said, *Culture and Imperialism* (New York: Vintage, 1994).

Anthony Smith, *The Age of Behemoths: The Globalization of Mass Media Firms* (New York: Priority Press, 1991).

David Steigerwald, *Culture's Vanities: The Paradox of Cultural Diversity in a Globalized World* (Lanham MD: Rowman & Littlefield, 2004).

John Tomlinson, *Globalization and Culture* (Cambridge: Polity Press, 1999).

John Carlos Rowe, *Literary Culture and U.S. Imperialism: From The Revolution to World War II* (Oxford: Oxford University Press, 2000).

John Storey, *Inventing Popular Culture: From Folklore to Globalization* (Malden MA: Blackwell, 2003).

Shelley Streeby, *American Sensations: Class, Empire, and the Production of Popular Culture* (Berkeley CA: University of California Press, 2002).

John Tomlinson, *Globalization and Culture* (Cambridge: Polity Press, 1999).

Michael Valdez Moses, *The Novel and the Globalization of Culture* (New York: Oxford University Press, 1995).

Victor M. Valle and Rodolfo D. Torres, *Latino Metropolis* (Minneapolis MN: University of Minnesota Press, 2000).

Georgette Wang, Anura Goonasekera and Jan Servaes, *The New Communications Landscape: Demystifying Media Globalization* (London: Routledge, 2000).

Min Zhou and James V. Gatewood, *Contemporary Asian America: A Multidisciplinary Reader* (New York: New York University Press, 2000).

Index

A&E Networks, 112
Abba, 133
Abbott, Jack, 38
ABC, 110, 114, 115
AC/DC, 133
Accidental Empires (Cringeley), 28
Acker, Kathy, 38
Adam & the Ants, 164
Adams, Ansel, 78
Adelphi University, 144
'Addicted to Love' (Robert Palmer), 163
Adobe, 28
Adorno, Theodor, 79
Adult Industry Medical Health Care
    Foundation, 96
'Adventures of Grandmaster Flash on
    the Wheels of Steel' (Grandmaster
    Flash & the Furious Five), 141
Aerosmith, 136, 142
Afrika Bambaataa, 141
After Walker Evans (Levine), 83
Aguilera, Christina, 130
AIDS, 6, 16, 20–5, 131, 146
AIDS Coalition to Unleash Power, 23
'AIDS Timeline', 77
Air Jordan, 176
Airplane (Abrahams, Zucker and
    Zucker), 99
Alba Madonna (Raphael), 63
Ali, Muhammad, 68, 110
Alien (Scott), 98
Aliens (Cameron), 100
'Altar of Sacrifice' (Slayer), 136
Althusser, Louis, 80

Altman, Dennis, 21–2
Altman, Dennis, 86
Amadeus (Forman), 97
America (Baudrillard), 166
American Family Association, 87
American Foundation for AIDS
    Research, 24
American Life League, 15
American Psycho (Ellis), 149, 158
American Werewolf in London, An
    (Landis), 127
Americans, The (Frank), 78
Amis, Martin, 161, 162
Amtrak, 20
Anatomy Lesson, The (Roth), 38
Ancient Evenings (Mailer), 38
Anderson, Benedict, 154
Andrews, Bruce, 62
Ang, Ien, 156
'Angel' (Madonna), 131
'Angel of Death' (Slayer), 136
Animals, The, 162
Annesley, James, 44–5
Annual Predator's Ball, 11
Anthrax, 135
Anzaldúa, Gloria, 38, 59–60, 176
AOL, 28
Apple Computers, 27, 28
    Apple I Computer, 27
Arbus, Dianne, 79
Armies of the Night (Mailer), 38
Arquette, Rosanna, 131
As I Lay Dying (Faulkner), 75
Aspen, 90

Atari 2600, 157
Atlanta, 158
Atlantic Records, 133
Auchincloss, Louis, 13
Auster, Paul, 48
Avalos, David, 78

Back to the Future (Zemeckis), 98, 104–5
Backlash (Faludi), 32
'Bad' (Jackson), 129
Bad Moon Rising (Sonic Youth), 138
Baker, Nicholson, 45
Bakker, Jim, 16–17
Bakker, Tammy Faye, 16–17
Baldwin, James, 54
Bambara, Toni Cade, 55
Banister, Guy, 40
Barnum (Coleman and Stewart), 147
Barrie, Dennis, 88
Barth, John, 38, 39, 48
Barthelme, Donald, 39, 48
Barthes, Roland, 62, 79
Basquiat (Schnabel), 69
Basquiat, Jean-Michel, 67–9, 73, 74, 76, 77, 140, 176
Batman (Burton), 97
Baudrillard, Jean, 166, 167
Bay City, 129
Beach, Christopher, 61
Beastie Boys, The, 142
Beatles, The, 129, 162
Beauty and the Beast (Menken, Ashman and Rice), 149
Beckett, Samuel, 39
Beijing, 160
Bel Geddes, Barbara, 115
Bel of Prairie Eden: A Romance of Mexico (Lippard), 154
Bellarosa Connection, The (Bellow), 37
Bellow, Saul, 37–8, 43, 48
Belly of the Beast (Abbott), 38
Beloved (Morrison), 54, 55–6
Benjamin, Walter, 79
Bennett, Tony, 106
Benton, Thomas Hart, 65
Berlin Wall, 182
Berlin, 94
Berman, William, 15

Bernstein, Charles, 62
Bertelsmann, 91
'Bette Davis Eyes' (Carnes), 165
Beverly Hills Cop (Brest), 91
Big Aiiieeeee!, The (Chin), 58
Big Chill, The (Kasdan), 12, 119
Bigsby, Chris, 149
Billboard, 94, 131, 163, 165
Billiards (Estes), 78
Biography Channel, The, 112
Birmingham, 164
Black Entertainment Television, 112
Black Hair (Soto), 61
Black Monday, 13, 65, 107
Black Periodical Literature Project, 55
Black Sabbath, 134, 135, 164
Blade Runner (Scott), 26
Blelajac, David, 73
Blondie, 68, 141, 164
Blood Meridian, or the Evening Redness in the West (McCarthy), 41–3, 54, 59
Blood Simple (Coen and Coen), 96
Bloom, Allan, 34–55, 74, 175
Blue Velvet (Lynch), 106–7
Blues Brothers, The (Landis), 127
Bluest Eye, The (Morrison), 54
Bluhdorn, Charles, 90
BMG, 132
Bochco, Steve, 118
Boesky, Ivan, 13–14
Bolan, Marc, 164
Bomb Squad, The, 144
Bond, Alan, 64
Bonfire of the Vanities, The (Wolfe), 13
Border Art Workshop, The, 77–8
Borderlands/La Frontera (Anzaldúa), 59–60
Borges, Jorge Luis, 39
Born in the U.S.A. (Springsteen), 53, 139–40
Boston, 135
Bostonians, The (James), 103
Boulton, Jack, 65
Bourne, Randolph, 160–1, 167
Bowie, David, 136, 163, 164
Boy George, 164
Boyle, T. Coraghessan, 49

Brande, David, 43
Breakfast Club, 130
Bright Lights, Big City (McInerney), 44
Bright, Bill, 19
Britton, Andrew, 98–9, 100, 101
Broadway, 147–50, 152
Bronson, Po, 27
Brooks, Garth, 129
Brooks, Gwendolyn, 54
Bruckheimer, Jerry, 93
Buchanan, Pat, 9, 15, 21–2
Buck, Peter, 137
Buell, Frederick, 175
Buford, Bill, 47–9, 52
Buggles, The, 127
Burnett, Robert, 132–3
'Burning Chrome' (Gibson), 26
Bush, George H. W., 7, 20
Butler, Judith, 152
Buzzcocks, The, 134
Byrds, The, 137
Byrne, David, 136, 137

Cable Franchise Policy and
    Communications Act, 113
Cadigan, Pat, 43
Cagney and Lacey, 117
California Childhood (Soto), 61
Cambridge University, 47
Campus Crusade for Christ, 19
Carmike Cinemas, 19
Carousel (Rogers and Hammerstein),
    147
Carpenter, Jon, 100–1, 102
Cars, The, 133, 134
Carter, Jimmy, 9, 10, 11, 23, 111
Carver, Raymond, 38, 49–51, 52
Cathedral (Carver), 49
Cato Institute, 15
Cats (Lloyd Webber), 148
CBS Records, 91, 157, 157
CBS, 110, 114, 117, 157
Center for Disease Control and
    Prevention, 21, 23
Centerfolds (Sherman), 82
Central Intelligence Agency, 22
Cerruzzi, Michael, 27
Cézanne, Paul, 64

Chagall, Marc, 81
Challenger Space Shuttle, 159
Chamberlain, Samuel, 41
Chan, Jeffrey Paul, 58
Chandler, Raymond, 44, 49
Chaplin, Charlie, 108
Chapman, Tracy, 133
Chase Manhattan Bank, 65
Chauncey Jr, George, 88
Cheers, 121
Chic, 141
Chin, Frank, 58–9
China Men (Kingston), 57
Christian Broadcasting Network, 16
Christian Crusade, 16
Chuck D, 144
Cinecom, 96
Cisco Systems, 28
Cisneros, Sandra, 60–1
Citibank, 66
Clapton, Eric, 164
Clash, The, 134
Cleveland, 5
Clinton, Bill, 32
Close Encounters of the Third Kind
    (Spielberg), 98
Close, Chuck, 78
Close, Glenn, 33, 35
Closing of the American Mind, The
    (Bloom), 34–5
CNN, 111, 158–160
Coal Miner's Daughter (Apted), 99
Coca-Cola, 91, 154, 157
Coen, Joel and Ethan, 96
Coffee and Cigarettes (Jarmusch), 96
Colab, 68, 77
Colbys, The, 115
Collins, Phil, 131, 133, 163, 164
Color Purple, The (Spielberg), 100
Color Purple, The (Walker), 57
Columbia Pictures, 91, 109
Columbia Records, 157
Columbia TriStar, 157
Columbo, 118
Commando (Lester), 103
Commission on Pornography, 96
Committee for the Survival of a Free
    Congress, 17

Commodore, 27
  Commodore 64, 94
Complete Book of Running (Fixx), 124
Comstock, Anthony, 85
Conan the Barbarian (Milius), 103
Conan the Destroyer (Fleischer), 103
Concerned Women for America, 15
Concorde, 164
Condé Nast, 79
Conrad, Michael, 118
Conservative Caucus, 17
Consumer Video Sales/Rental
  Amendment, 93
Contemporary Arts Center, Cincinnati,
  65, 88
Coolidge, Clark, 62
Corcoran Gallery of Art, 87
Cornell University, 34, 55
Cosby, Bill, 121
Cosby Show, The, 121
Coughlin, Charles, 16
Counterlife, The (Roth), 38
Coupland, Douglas, 71, 72
Covach, John, 134–5
Crash, 76
Crimp, Douglas, 24, 76, 87
Cringeley, Robert, 28
Cronenberg, David, 26
Crossing The Peninsula (Lim), 61
Cruise, Tom, 93, 94
Culture Club, 163
Cupertino, 27

D'Souza, Dinesh, 35
da Vinci, Leonardo, 63
Dallas, 108, 114–15, 116, 156
Daly, Tyne, 117
Dangling Man (Bellow), 38
Darkness on the Edge of Town
  (Springsteen), 138
Dave Clark Five, The, 162
Davidson, Michael, 62
Davis, Martin S., 90
Davy, Kate, 151
Day, Doris, 24
Daydream Nation (Sonic Youth), 138
De La Soul, 143, 144
de Tocqueville, Alexis, 165, 167

Dean's December, The (Bellow), 37
'Death of the Author' (Barthes), 62
Deep Purple, 134
Def Jam Records, 142
Def Leppard, 18, 163
Degas, Edgar, 64
Deitch, Jeffrey, 66
DeLillo, Don, 38, 40–1, 42, 45–7, 51, 54,
  56
DeLorean, John, 104
DeLorean Motor Company, 104
Democracy in America (de Tocqueville),
  165
Depeche Mode, 133, 164
Depository Institutions Deregulation
  and Monetary Control Act 1980,
  10
Dern, Laura, 106
Desperately Seeking Susan (Seidelman),
  131
Detroit, 5, 66, 129
Diary of a Yuppie (Auchincloss), 13
Diaz, Al, 68
Digital Versatile Disc, 182
Dirty Dancing (Ardolino), 127
Discovery Channel, The, 112
Disney, 112, 149, 154
  Disney World, 17
  Disneyland, 17, 166
  Disneyland Resort Paris, 165–7
  Walt Disney, 166
  Walt Disney Company, 91, 92
Divan (Schnabel), 73
Do the Right Thing (Lee), 96, 124, 146
Documenta 7, 77
Dokken, 135
Dolan, Jill, 151
Donovan, Casey, 96
'Don't Believe the Hype' (Public
  Enemy), 145
Doobie Brothers, The, 134
Douglas, Kirk, 166
Douglas, Michael, 32, 108
Douglass, Frederick, 54
Down By Law (Jarmusch), 96
Dr. Dre, 143
Drexel Burnham, 11–12
Driving Miss Daisy (Beresford), 98

Duffy, Patrick, 115
Dune (Lynch), 107
Duran Duran, 163, 164
Dürer, Albrecht, 81
Dustheads (Basquiat), 68
Dutton Books, 48
Dworkin, Andrea, 19
Dynasty, 24, 115, 116
Dyson, Michael, 33

E.T. (Spielberg), 93, 97, 98, 100
Eagle Forum, 15
Eagles, The, 129
Easton, Sheena, 18
eBay, 28
Economic Policy Advisory Board, 7–8
Economy Recovery Tax Act 1981, 10
Edinburgh Review, 160
Eins, Stefan, 76
Eisenstadt, Jill, 12
Electronic Arts, 28
Elektra, 133
Elephant (Carver), 49
Elephant Man (Lynch), 107
Eliminator (ZZ Top), 136
Eliot, T. S., 148
Ellis, Bret Easton, 12, 44–5, 47, 51, 149, 158
Ellison, Ralph, 54
Emerson, Ralph Waldo, 160, 167
EMI, 132
Emmy, 130
Empire Strikes Back, The (Lucas), 97, 98, 99
Encore, 112
Eno, Brian, 136
Equal Rights Amendment, 18
Equiano, Olaudah, 54
Equitable Life Assurance Society, 65
ER, 119
Eraserhead (Lynch), 107
Erving, Julius, 144
ESPN, 111
Estes, Richard, 78–9
Eurythmics, The, 164
Evans, Walker, 78
Everett, Win, 40

Evita (Lloyd Webber and Rice), 147, 149
EVOL (Sonic Youth), 138
Executioner's Song, The (Mailer), 38
'Eye of the Tiger' (Survivor), 136

'Factory, The', 71
Fairchild Semiconductor, 27
Fairchild, Morgan, 24
Fallwell, Jerry, 16–17, 19, 22
False Start (Johns), 64
Faludi, Susan, 32, 103
Fame (Parker), 127
Family Research Council, 15
Fashion Moda, 76–7
Fast Lanes (Phillips), 52
Fatal Attraction (Lyne), 32–3, 35
Faulkner, William, 75
Fear of Music (Talking Heads), 136
Federal Communications Commission, 111, 112
Federal Reserve, 10–11, 110
Fekner, John, 76, 77
Feminine Mystique, The (Friedan), 32
Feminists for the Life of America, 15
Fences (Wilson), 150
Ferris, Charles, 110
'Fight the Power' (Public Enemy), 146
Figures in Black (Gates Jr), 55
Finney, Albert, 101
First Blood (Kotcheff), 103
Fitzgerald, F. Scott, 44
560 (Estes), 78
Fixx, Jim, 124
Flack, Audrey, 78
Flashdance (Lyne), 91, 94, 127
Flavor Flav, 144
Flexible (Basquiat), 68
Fly, The (Cronenberg), 26
Focus of the Family, 15
Fonda, Jane, 124
Ford Foundation, 85
Ford, Harrison, 98
Ford, Richard, 49, 51, 52
Foreigner, 133, 134
42nd Street (Warren and Dubin), 147
Foucault, Michel, 62
Fox Enterprises, 90

Fox Entertainment, 90
Fox, Michael J., 104
Frank, Robert, 78
Frantz, Chris, 136
Frazier, Joe, 110
Freddie & the Dreamers, 162
Friday Night Videos, 129
Friday the 13th (Cunningham), 102
Friedan, Betty, 32
Friedman, Milton, 7, 8
'Fuck tha Police' (N.W.A.), 143

Gabriel, Peter, 86, 163
Gaddis, William, 38, 39, 48, 108
Galaxian, 158
Garner, Margaret, 55
Gass, William, 48
Gates Jr, Henry Louis, 33, 55
Gay Men's Health Crisis, 23
Gay Related Immune Deficiency, 21
Gender Trouble (Butler), 152
Genentech, 28, 157
General Cinema, 19
General Electric, 91
General Felt Industries, 66
Genesis, 134
Gentlemen Prefer Blondes (Hawks), 131
George, Nelson, 143, 144, 145
Gere, Richard, 86
Ghandi (Attenborough), 98
Ghostbusters (Reitman), 97, 98
Gibson, William, 26, 38, 43–4, 157, 175
Giles, Paul, 1, 5, 161, 179
Ginevra dei Benci (da Vinci), 63
Gitlin, Todd, 30, 35
Glanton, John Joel, 41
Glengarry Glen Ross (Foley), 108
Glengarry Glen Ross (Mamet), 150
Gless, Sharon, 117
Godspell (Schwartz), 147
'Gold Griot' (Basquiat), 140
Goldman Sachs, 14
Goldstein, Richard, 86–7
Goldwater, Barry, 7, 15
Good Times, 121
'Good Times' (Chic), 141
Google, 28
Gorbachev, Mikhail, 160

Grace High Tower (Schnabel), 73
Grandmaster Flash & the Furious Five, 141
Grandmaster Flash, 140, 141
Granta, 47, 49, 52
Grapes of Wrath, The (Steinbeck), 179
Gravity's Rainbow (Pynchon), 38, 39
Great Gatsby, The (Fitzgerald), 179, 180
'Greedom' (Grandmaster Flash & the Furious Five), 141
Gremlins (Dante), 98
'Grillo' (Basquiat), 140
Group Material, 77
Gulf and Western Industries Inc., 89–90
Gutenberg Galaxy, The (McLuhan), 158

Hahn, Jessica, 17
Hair (MacDermot, Rado and Ragni), 147
Hall and Oates, 165
Halloween (Carpenter), 102
Hamel, Victoria, 118
Hamish Hamilton, 48
Hammerstein, Oscar, 149
Hammett, Dashiell, 44
Hanks, Tom, 25
Haraway, Donna, 26
Hargis, Billy James, 16–17
Haring, Keith, 67, 69, 76, 77, 86
Harjo, Joy, 61
Harrison, George, 163
Harry, Debbie, 86
Hawkes, John, 48
'Hawthorne and His Mosses' (Melville), 160
Hawthorne, Nathaniel, 55
Heidegger, Martin, 35
Hejinian, Lyn, 38
Hello, Dolly! (Herman), 147
Helms, Jesse, 15, 17, 87
Hemingway, Ernest, 49
Hendrix, Jimi, 162
Heritage Foundation, 15
Herman's Hermits, 162
Hewlett, Bill, 27
Hewlett-Packard, 28

Hill Street Blues, 117–19
Him With his Foot in his Mouth (Bellow), 38
Hinckley, John, 4
Hirsch, E. D., 35
Hirshhorn, Joseph H., 65
History Channel, The, 112
History Portraits (Sherman), 82
Hoban, Phoebe, 68, 69
Hoefler, Don C., 27
Holden, Judge, 41
'Holiday' (Madonna), 130
Hollywood, 89–92, 97, 98, 99, 109–10, 154
Holmes, John, 96
Holzer, Jenny, 76
Home Box Office, 110, 113, 158
Home Shopping Network, The, 111–12
Honey, I Shrunk the Kids (Johnston), 98
hooks, bell, 33
Hopkins, David, 84
Hopper, Dennis, 106
House on Mango Street, The (Cisneros), 61
Houston, Whitney, 131
Howard University, 55
Howe, Susan, 62
HTML, 182
HTTP, 182
Hucksters, The (Conway), 108
Hudson, Rock, 22, 24
Hughes, Robert, 66, 67, 68, 71, 73
Hugo, Victor, 149
Human Genome Project, 25
Human League, The, 163, 164
Human Touch (Springsteen), 112
Humboldt's Gift (Bellow), 38
Hunger, The (Scott), 93
'Hungry Heart' (Springsteen), 138–9
Hunter, James Davison, 31, 35
Hüsker Dü, 137–8
Hutcheon, Linda, 39–40

I Spit on Your Grave (Zarchi), 103
IBM, 27
Ice Cube, 143
Ice T, 143
Iggy and the Stooges, 134

Immigrant Acts (Lowe), 172
Immigration Act, The, 171
Immigration and Naturalization Services Act, 171
In Country (Mason), 52–3, 173
In Italian (Basquiat), 68
In the American Tree (Silliman), 62
Inada, Lawson Fusao, 58
Independence Day (Ford), 51
Indiana Jones and the Last Crusade (Spielberg), 98
Indiana Jones and the Temple of Doom (Spielberg), 98
Insider Trading, 13
Institute of Contemporary Art, Philadelphia, 87
Intel, 27, 28
Internal Revenue Service, 23
International Art Alliance, 65
International Directory of Corporate Art Collections, 65
'Into the Groove' (Madonna), 131, 138
'Into the Groove(y)' (Sonic Youth), 138
Into The Woods (Sondheim), 149
iPod, 124
Iran–Contra, 181
Irises (Van Gogh), 64
Ironside, 118
IRS Records, 137
Island, 96
It Takes a Nation of Millions to Hold Us Back (Public Enemy), 145–6

J. Geils Band, 165
J. Paul Getty Museum, 64
Jackson, Michael, 52, 72–3, 127, 131, 165
Jacobs, Harriet, 54
Jagger, Mick, 164
James, Henry, 103, 160, 161
Jameson, Fredric, 70–1, 74–5, 175
Jancovich, Mark, 102–3
Janowitz, Tama, 12, 44
Jarmusch, Jim, 96
Jaws (Spielberg), 98
Jeffersons, The, 121
Jeffords, Susan, 103
Jen, Gish, 58

Jesus Christ Superstar (Lloyd Webber and Rice), 147
'Jesus Saves' (Slayer), 136
Jethro Tull, 134
JFK Stadium, 163
Jobs, Steve, 27
Joe Glassco (Schnabel), 73
Joe Turner's Come and Gone (Wilson), 150
John Lindsay, 76
John, Elton, 163
Johns, Jasper, 63–4
Johnson, Haynes, 8, 12
Johnson, Lyndon B., 9
Jones, Gayl, 55
Jones, Gloria, 164–5
Jordan, Michael, 176
Journey, 135
Joy Luck Club, The (Tan), 58
Joyce, James, 85
JR: A Novel, 39, 108
Judas Priest, 135, 136, 164
'Jump' (Van Halen), 136
Junk Bonds, 11–12
Justice Department, 110

Kaposi's Sarcoma, 20
Karlen, John, 117
Kasdan, Lawrence, 12, 119
Kennedy, John F., 9, 40, 41
Kennedy, Joseph, 16
KFC, 169
Kill 'Em All (Metallica), 135
Kimball, Roger, 35
King and I, The (Rogers and Hammerstein), 147
King, Richard H., 4, 5, 9
King, Stephen, 101
Kingston, Maxine Hong, 57, 60
Knack, The, 142
Knots Landing, 115
Kool DJ Herc, 140
Kooning, Willem de, 67
Koons, Jeff, 71–3
Kozoll, Michael, 118
Kraftwerk, 141
Kramer, Larry, 23
Kramer vs Kramer (Benton), 99

Kruger, Barbara, 79–81
Ku Klux Klan, 113
Kubrick, Stanley, 99
Kurtis Blow, 141

L.A. Law, 12, 119
$L=A=N=G=U=A=G=E$, 62
Laffer, Arthur, 7
Land Speed Record (Hüsker Dü), 137
Landis, John, 127
lang, k. d., 133
Last Temptation of Christ, The (Scorsese), 19, 88
Lauper, Cyndi, 18
Lawrence, D. H., 1
Led Zeppelin, 129, 134, 162–3, 164
Lee (Estes), 78
Lee, Chang-rae, 58
Lee, Spike, 96, 125, 146, 176
Legends of Mexico (Lippard), 154
Leo Castelli Gallery, 63
Leroux, Gaston, 149
Les Misérables (Schönberg and Boublil), 148, 149
Less Than Zero (Ellis), 44–5
Levine, Sherrie, 83
Levis, 154
Lewis, Wyndham, 158
LeWitt, Sol, 65
Libra (DeLillo), 40–1
Lichtenstein, Roy, 65
Lienesch, Michael, 15–16, 19–20
Life's Rich Pageant (R.E.M.), 137
Like a Prayer (Madonna), 131
Like a Virgin (Madonna), 130, 131
Lim, Shirley Geok-lin, 61
Lin, Maya Ying, 172–3
Lincoln Center (Estes), 78
Lincoln Memorial, 173
Linden Hills (Naylor), 57
Lindquist, Mark, 44
Lippard, George, 154, 155–6
Little Night Music, A (Sondheim), 149
Little Review, The, 85
Live Aid, 163
Liverpool, 164
Living Up the Street (Soto), 61
LL Cool J, 142

Lloyd Webber, Andrew, 147–8
Lockhart Commission, 84
Lois and Clark: The New Adventures of Superman, 98
London Fields (Amis), 162
London, 164
Longo, Robert, 67, 69
Los Altos, 27
Los Angeles, 21, 44, 47, 143, 166
Lovebug Starski, 141
Lowe, Lisa, 168, 172
'Lucky Star' (Madonna), 130
Lynch, David, 105–7
Lyne, Adrian, 32, 94
Lynn, Loretta, 99
Lynyrd Skynryd, 134
Lyotard, Jean-François, 51

M*A*S*H, 52, 121
Ma Rainey's Black Bottom (Wilson), 150
Macalaster College, 137
Machine Dreams (Phillips), 51–2
Machine in the Garden, The (Marx), 168
MacKinnon, Catherine, 19
Mackintosh, Cameron, 148
MacLachlan, Kyle, 106
Mademoiselle, 79
Madison Square Garden, 138
Madonna, 18, 24, 68, 129–31, 133, 138, 147, 165
Mailer, Norman, 38, 43, 48
Making of Thriller, The (Landis, Abel, Giraldi, Kramer), 129
Mama Day (Naylor), 57
Mamet, David, 38, 150
Man in a Polyester Suit (Mapplethorpe), 86
Manchester, 164
Manfred Mann, 162
'Manifesto for Cyborgs' (Haraway), 26
Mapplethorpe, Robert, 85–8
Margolin, 150
Marlboro, 83–4
Marr, Johnny, 137
Marx, Leo, 168
Mason, Bobbie Ann, 38, 49, 52–3, 173
'Material Girl' (Madonna), 130–1

MC5, 134
MCA, 19, 91, 109, 132
McAfee, 28
McCarthy, Cormac, 38, 41–3, 51, 54, 56
McDonalds, 154, 169
McGann, Jerome, 62
McGillis, Kelly, 93, 94
McInerney, Jay, 12, 44–5, 47
McLuhan, Marshall, 158
McMillan and Wife, 118
McNeil, George, 67
Me and My Girl (Gay, Furber and Rose), 149
Meese, Ed, 84, 96
Megadeth, 135
Mellon, Andrew, 63
Melville, Herman, 55, 160, 162, 167
Menlo Park, 27
Merill Lynch, 14
Merrick, David, 148
'Message, The' (Grandmaster Flash & the Furious Five), 141–2
Metallica, 135
Metropolitan Museum of Art, New York, 64
Mezzanine, The (Baker), 45
Miami Vice, 67
Michael Jackson and Bubbles (Koons), 72
Michael Joseph, 48
Michael, George, 163
Michigan Plating & Stamping, 90
Microsoft, 27, 155
  Windows 95, 182
Midway Games, 29
Milken, Michael, 11–14
Millard, Kenneth, 53
Miller, Arthur, 149–50
Miller, Stephen Paul, 2–3
Miramar Naval Air Station, 93
Miramax, 96
Mitchell, Sharon, 96
Mitsubishi, 157
'Miuzi Weighs a Ton' (Public Enemy), 144–5
Modern Medea, The (Noble), 55
Modern Times (Chaplin), 108

Moffet Field, 27
Momaday, N. Scott, 61
Monet, Claude, 64
Money (Amis), 161, 162
Monroe, Marilyn, 131
More Die of Heartbreak (Bellow), 37
More Songs about Buildings and Food
    (Talking Heads), 136
Morgan Stanley, 14
Moroder, Georgio, 94
Morrison, Toni, 38, 54–6, 176
Mosiac, 182
Motherwell, Robert, 67, 70
Motion Picture Association of America,
    102
Mötley Crüe, 133, 135
Motörhead, 135
Mould, Bob, 137
Mountain View, 27
Mozart, Wolfgang Amadeus, 97
MTV, 94, 111, 127, 129, 130, 135, 136,
    142
Mundell, Robert, 7
Murdoch, Rupert, 90
Murphy, Eddie, 144
Museum of Modern Art, New York, 137
Musicians United for Safe Energy, 138
Mustaine, Dave, 135
My Fair Lady (Lerner and Loewe), 147
'My Sharona' (The Knack), 142
My Wicked, Wicked Ways (Cisneros),
    61
Myers, Mike, 113
Mystery Train (Jarmusch), 96

N.W.A., 143
Nabokov, Vladimir, 52
Nadel, Alan, 98, 100, 101, 104
Namco, 158
National Education Association, 18
National Endowment for the Arts, 85,
    87
National Gallery, Washington, 63
National Gay Task Force, 22–3
National Obscenity Enforcement Unit,
    96
National Parents and Teachers
    Association, 18

National Vietnam Veterans Memorial,
    Washington, 171–3
NATO, 167
Naylor, Gloria, 57
NBC, 110, 114, 119, 129
Nebraska (Springsteen), 139
NEC, 158
Nelson, Steve, 148, 149
Netscape, 28
    Netscape Navigator, 182
Neuromancer (Gibson), 26, 43–4, 157,
    175
New American Library, 48
New Day Rising (Hüsker Dü), 138
*New Hoover Quik-Broom & New
    Hoover Celebrity IV* (Koons), 71
New Line, 96
New York City, 10, 21, 22, 47, 64, 112,
    130, 143, 144, 149, 163, 164
New York Dolls, 134, 163
New York School, 67
New York Society for the Suppression
    of Vice, 85
New York Times, 53, 65, 131
News Corporation, 90
Newton-John, Olivia, 165
Nicolson, Jack, 99
Nietzsche, Friedrich, 35
Nightmare on Elm Street, A (Craven),
    102
Nike, 154, 176
Nintendo, 29
Nintendo Entertainment System, 94
Nixon, Richard, 2
Noble, Thomas Satterwhite, 55
Nuremburg, 35
NVIDIA, 28
NYPD Blue, 119

O' Leary, Jean, 23
O'Connor, Flannery, 49
Ochoa, Victor, 78
Oklahoma! (Rogers and Hammerstein),
    147
'Once in a Lifetime' (Talking Heads),
    137
Old Possum's Book of Practical Cats
    (Eliot), 148

Operation Rescue, 31
Oracle, 28
Orchard Keeper, The (McCarthy), 41
Oswald, Lee Harvey, 40–1
Our Nig (Wilson), 55
Outer Dark (McCarthy), 41

Packard, Dave, 27
Pac-Man, 29, 123, 158
Palm, Inc., 28
Palmer, Michael, 62
Palmer, Robert, 163
Palo Alto, 27
Palumbo-Liu, David, 171
Paramount Communications, 90
Paramount Pictures, 89–90, 109
Parents Music Resource Center, 18
Parker, Charlie, 68
Parmenter, Lawrence, 40
Parsons School of Design, 79
'Passage to India' (Whitman), 172
PayPal, 28
Pearson, 48
Pease, Donald, 168–9
Pebble Beach, 14, 90
Peña, Guillermo Gómes, 78
Penguin Books, 48, 49
Penguin Putnam Inc., 48
'People's Choice', 77
Perelman, Bob, 62
'Perfect Moment, The' (Mapplethorpe),
     87
Peron, Eva, 147
Peron, Juan, 147
Pet Sematary (Lambert), 101
Pet Shop Boys, The, 163
Peterson, Denis, 78
Petty, Tom, 138
Peyton Place, 114
Philadelphia (Demme), 25
Phantom of the Opera, The (Lloyd
     Webber and Hart), 148, 149
Philadelphia, 164
Philips, 29, 125
Phillips, Howard, 15, 17
Phillips, Jayne Anne, 46, 49, 51–2
Phillips, Lisa, 74, 75, 77
Piano Lesson, The (Wilson), 150

Piece of My Heart, A (Ford), 51
Pink Floyd, 134, 163
Pink Panther (Koons), 72
Piss-Christ (Serrano), 85, 87
Pitcher (Salle), 73
Pittsburgh, 5
'Planet Rock' (Afrika Bambaataa), 141
'Poet, The' (Emerson), 160
Pollock, Jackson, 67, 73
Poltergeist (Hooper), 101
'Postmodernism, or, the Cultural
     Logic of Late Capitalism'
     (Jameson), 70
Prague Orgy, The (Roth), 38
Predator (McTiernan), 103
Premiere, 109–10
'Preservation' (Carver), 49–51
Presley, Elvis, 129, 146
Pretenders, The, 133
Price, Vincent, 127
Prince, 131, 165
Prince, Richard, 83–4
Prince, Stephen, 89, 94, 97, 110
Princeton University, 121
Principal, Victoria, 115
Proust, Marcel, 45
PTL–The Inspirational Network,
     16–17
Public Enemy, 144–6
Publishers Weekly, 62
Puppy (Koons), 73
Putnam Berkley Group, 48
Pynchon, Thomas, 38, 39, 43, 48

Quaker City Weekly, The, 154
Quiet Riot, 135
QVC, 112

R.E.M., 137
Raiders of the Lost Ark (Spielberg), 98
Raising Arizona (Coens), 96
Raising Hell (Run D.M.C.), 142
Rakim, 144
Rambo III (MacDonald), 103
Rambo: First Blood Part II (Cosmatos),
     103
Ramones, The, 133, 134, 163
Random House, 55

Raphael, 63
'Rapper's Delight' (The Sugarhill Gang), 141
'Rapture' (Blondie), 141
Rauschenberg, Robert, 63
Ray Ban, 94
Reagan Democrats, 10, 109
Reagan, Ronald, 3–6, 7, 8, 9, 10, 11, 16, 18, 22, 24, 30, 76–7, 84, 98–9, 104, 105, 109, 182
Reaganomics, 6–10, 15
'Real Estate Show, The', 77
Recording Industry Association, 19
'Red Notebook, The' (Auster), 48
Reed, Donna, 115
Reign of Blood (Slayer), 136, 142
Remain in Light (Talking Heads), 136
Rembrandt, 81
Renoir, Pierre-Auguste, 64
Return of the Jedi, The (Lucas), 98
Rhode Island School of Design, 136
Rice, Tim, 147–8
'Rightstarter (Message To A Black Man)' (Public Enemy), 145
River, The (Springsteen), 138
Roach, Max, 68
'Road to Nowhere' (Talking Heads), 137
Roberts, Oral, 16
Robertson, Pat, 16–17, 19–20
Robinson, Sugar Ray, 68
Rock Springs (Ford), 51
Rockefeller Center, 14
Rockefeller Foundation, 85
Rocky III (Stallone), 103, 136
Rocky IV (Stallone), 103
Roe v. Wade, 31
Rogers, Nile, 141
Rogin, Michael, 4–5
Rolex, 158
Rolling Stone, 18
Rolling Stones, The, 162
Roosevelt, Franklin, 16
Roosevelt, Theodore, 167–8
Rose, Billy, 148
Rossellini, Isabella, 106
Roth, Dave Lee, 135
Roth, Philip, 38

Rothko, Mark, 67
Rousseau, Jean-Jacques, 35
Rowe, John Carlos, 154
Roxy Music, 136–7, 164
Rubin, Rick, 142
Ruby, Jack, 40
Rucker, Rudy, 43
Rumsfeld, Donald, 181
Run D.M.C., 136, 142
Running Dog (DeLillo), 40
Running Man, The (Glaser), 103

SAAB, 93
Said, Edward, 159
St Elsewhere, 119
Salle, David, 67, 69, 73–4
Salt, Henry, 1
San Diego, 77, 93
San Fernando Valley, 96
San Francisco, 21–2, 27
Santa Clara Valley, 27
Saturday Night Live, 113
Schiller, Dan, 155
Schiller, Herbert, 155
Schjeldahl, Peter, 77
Schlafly, Phyllis, 15, 18, 32
Schlesinger, Arthur, 35
Schnabel, Julian, 67, 69, 73–4
Schoolly D, 143
Schwarzenegger, Arnold, 103
Scorsese, Martin, 19, 129
Scott, Tony, 93
Scuggs, Jan, 172
Seagram, 91
Search for Signs of Intelligent Life in the Universe, The (Wagner), 151
Second Stage, The (Friedan), 32
Secrets from the Center of the World (Harjo), 61
Securities and Exchange Commission, 13
Sega, 29
Self-Portrait (Basquiat), 68
Senate Subcommittee on Juvenile Delinquency, 85
Serrano, Andreas, 85, 87–8
Sex and the City, 113
Sex Pistols, The, 134, 163

sex, lies, and videotape (Soderbergh), 96

Shaw, Peggy, 150

She Had Some Horses (Harjo), 61

Sheen, Charlie, 108

Sheen, Martin, 108

Sheffield, 164

Sherman, Cindy, 81–2

She's Gotta Have It (Lee), 96

Shields, Brooke, 84

Shining, The (Kubrick), 99–100

Showtime, 112

Signifying Monkey, The (Gates Jr), 55

Silence = Death Project, 23

Silicon Valley, 27–8

Silko, Leslie Marmon, 61

Silliman, Ron, 38, 62

Simmons, Philip E., 51

Simmons, Russell, 142

Simple Minds, 164

Simpson, Don, 91, 93

Sire Records, 133

Sister (Sonic Youth), 138

Six Feet Under, 113

Slayer, 135

Sleepaway Camp (Hiltzik), 102

Slumber Party Massacre (Brown), 102

Smith, Henry Nash, 168

Smith, Patti, 86, 134

Smith, Sidney, 160

Smiths, The, 137

Snoop Doggy Dog, 143

Soderbergh, Steven, 96

Soft Cell, 164

Sondheim, Stephen, 149

Song of Solomon (Morrison), 54

Sonic Youth, 138

Sony, 14, 29, 91, 92, 94, 124, 125, 132, 157

   Sony Playstation Portable, 124

   Sony Walkman, 30, 124, 133, 166, 180

Sophie's Choice (Pakula), 110

Sopranos, The, 113

Sotheby's, 64, 66

Soto, Gary, 61

Sot-Weed Factor, The (Barth), 39

Sound of Music, The (Rogers and Hammerstein), 147

Soundabout, 124

South Pacific (Rogers and Hammerstein), 147

Southeastern Center for Contemporary Art, 85

Space Invaders, 29, 30, 123

Spandau Ballet, 164

Spears, Britney, 130

Spielberg, Steven, 57, 93, 100, 101

Spinal Tap (Reiner), 163

Spiritual America (Prince), 84

Split Britches (Split Britches Company), 151

Split Britches Company, 150–2

Sportswriter, The (Ford)

Springsteen, Bruce, 52, 112, 131, 138–9

SST Records, 137

Stained Class (Judas Priest), 136

Staller, Ilona, 73

Stallone, Sylvester, 136

Stallybrass, Peter, 45

Stanford University, 27, 34

Star Trek, 98

Star Trek: The Next Generation, 98

Starkweather, Charles, 139

Starr, Larry, 123

Steely Dan, 134

Steichen, Edward, 78

Stein, Chris, 68

Steinbeck, John, 49

Sterling, Bruce, 43

Stieglitz, Alfred, 78, 84

Stipe, Michael

Stone, Oliver, 13, 107–9

Storyteller (Silko), 61

Straight Outta Compton (N.W.A.), 143

Stranger Than Paradise (Jarmusch), 96

Streeby, Shelley, 155

Streisand, Barbara, 165

Stryker, Eric, 96

Stuyvesant, Peter, 10

Styx, 135

Subway, 169

Sugarhill Gang, The, 141

Sugarhill Records, 141

Sukenick, Ronald, 48

Sula (Morrison), 54

Sun Microsystems, 28
Sunday in the Park with George
    (Sondheim), 149
Sunflowers (Van Gogh), 64
Superman, 98
Survivor, 136
Sutree (McCarthy), 41
Swaggart, Jimmy, 16–17, 18, 19–20
Symantec, 28

'Tainted Love' (Soft Cell), 164
Taito Corporation, 29
Talking Heads, 133, 134, 136–7, 164
Tan, Amy, 58, 176
Tar Baby (Morrison), 54
Taubman, Alfred, 66–7
Taxi, 121
Taxi Driver (Scorsese), 4
Taylor, Elizabeth, 24
Televangelism, 16–17, 181
Television (band), 134
Terminator (Cameron), 26, 98, 103
Terminator X, 144
Terner, Andrew, 66
Terry, Randall, 31–2
Testoni, 158
Texas Southern University, 55
Thaw, Eugene E., 66
Theft, A (Bellow), 37
Their Greatest Hits 1971–1975 (The
    Eagles), 129
Thing from Another World, The
    (Nyby), 101
Thing, The (Carpenter), 98, 100–1
thirtysomething, 12, 119
Thompson, Jim, 49
Three Ball 50/50 Tank (Koons), 71
3 Feet High and Rising (De La Soul),
    143
Three Flags (Johns), 63, 67
Three Mile Island, Harrisburg, 138
Thriller (Jackson), 127–9, 165
'Thriller' (Jackson), 127–9
Tiananmen Square, 160
Tijuana, 77
Time, 66
Time Inc., 91
Time-Life, 83

Time Warner, 91
'Times Square Show', 68, 77
Titanic (Cameron), 149
Todd, Mike, 148
Tokyo Disneyland, 166
Tomlin, Lily, 151
Tomlinson, John, 153, 155–6
Top Gun (Scott), 91, 93–4, 100, 127, 180
Toshiba, 158
Trading Places (Landis), 127
'Trans-Europe Express' (Kraftwerk),
    141
Travanti, Daniel J., 118
Tremaine, Burton, 63
Trinity Broadcasting Network, 16
Tripmaster Monkey: His Fake Book
    (Kingston), 57–8
Troggs, The, 162
Troy, Gil, 23, 24
True Blue (Madonna), 131
Trump, Donald, 12
Tupac Shakur, 143
Turner, Ed, 159
Turner, Frederick Jackson, 175
Turner, Ted, 158, 159
TV Party, 68
Twentieth Century-Fox, 90, 109–10
20000 Leagues Under the Sea (Verne),
    166
Twisted Sister, 18, 135
Two Heads on Gold (Basquiat), 68

U2, 158
*Ugly George Hour of Truth, Sex and
    Violence, The*, 113
Ultimate Good Luck, The (Ford), 51
Ultravox, 164
Ulysses (Joyce), 85, 88
Underworld (DeLillo), 54
United Nations, 25
Universal, 19, 92
Universal Zulu Nation, 141
University of Georgia, 137
University of Michigan, 130
Untitled Film Stills (Sherman), 82
Updike, John, 38, 43
Upwardly Mobile Home (Split Britches
    Company), 151

US Civil Service Commission, 22
US–Mexico War, 41, 59, 153
US Supreme Court, 25, 29, 31, 92

Van Gogh, Vincent, 64, 81
Van Halen (Van Halen), 135
Van Halen, 135
Van Halen, Eddie, 135
Velvet Underground, The, 134
Venom, 18
Verisign, 28
Verne, Jules, 166
Vestron, 96
Video Cassette Recorder, 29, 92, 95, 96, 112
'Video Killed the Radio Star' (The Buggles), 127
Vietnam War, 9, 52–3, 171
Viguerie, Richard, 15
Viking Press, 48
Village Voice, 77
Vineland (Pynchon), 38
Vinton, Bobby, 106
Virgin Land (Smith), 168
Virgin Tour, The (Madonna), 131
Visage, 164
VisiCalc, 27
Vizenor, Gerald, 61
Volcker, Paul, 10, 110
Vollman, William, 49
Vonnegut, Kurt, 39

W.A.S.P, 18, 135
Wagner, Jane, 151
'Walk this Way' (Run D.M.C.), 136, 142–3
Walker, Alice, 57, 100
Wall Street, 10–15, 27, 28, 66, 72, 181
Wall Street (Stone), 13, 14, 107–9
Wallace, David Foster, 49
Wallerstein, Immanuel, 181
Wal-Mart, 18
Waltons, The, 115, 118
Wanniski, Jude, 7, 8
Warhol, Andy, 67, 68, 71, 86
Warner Brothers, 137
Warner Communications, 91, 127
Warner Music Group, 132, 133

Warren Commission, 40
Washington Monument, 173
Watching Dallas (Ang), 156
Watergate, 8
Watt, Emily Stipes, 108
Wayne, John, 67, 146
Wayne's World, 113
Weaver, Lois, 150
Wembley Stadium, 163–4
West Side Story (Bernstein and Sondheim), 149
West, Cornell, 33
Weymouth, Tina, 136
Weyrich, Paul, 15, 17
'What is an Author?' (Foucault), 62
What We Talk About When We Talk About Love (Carver), 49
Wheatley, Phillis, 54
Where Sparrows Work Hard (Soto), 61
'White Lines' (Grandmaster Flash & the Furious Five), 142
White Noise (DeLillo), 40, 46–7
White, Edmund, 86
Whitlock, Tom, 94
Whitman, Walt, 160, 172
Whitney Museum, New York, 63, 65, 67, 74
Williams, Raymond, 183
Williams, Tennessee, 149–50
Wills, Gary, 3–5
Wilson, August, 38, 150
Wilson, Harriet, 55
Winfrey, Oprah, 57
Winwood, Steve, 163
Wojnarowicz, David, 25, 86
Wolfe, Tom, 13, 64–6
Wolfen (Wadleigh), 101
Wolff, Tobias, 49
Wollman, Elizabeth, 148
Woman Warrior, The (Kingston), 57, 60
Women of Brewster Place, The (Naylor), 57
Wometco Theaters, 19
Wong, Shawn, 58
Woods, Tiger, 176
Woodstock, 35
World Health Organization, 25
WOW Café, 150

Wozniak, Steve, 27
Wright, Richard, 54

'X Portfolio' (Mapplethorpe), 86
Xerox Palo Alto Research Center, 28

Yahoo!, 28
Yale University, 55
Yes, 134

Yo! Bum Rush the Show (Public
    Enemy), 144–5
Yuppies, 12–14

Zangwill, Israel, 167
Zen Arcade (Hüsker Dü), 138
Zuckerman Unbound (Roth), 38
ZX Spectrum, 94
ZZ Top, 136